D0220256

Mill on Liberty

This Routledge Philosophy GuideBook introduces John Stuart Mill and one of his major works, *On Liberty*. We see that in *On Liberty* Mill insists on the importance of individuality and, to that end, defends a moral right to absolute liberty with respect to certain self-regarding concerns.

'In *Mill on Liberty* Jonathan Riley offers a vigorous, and at times, passionate, defence of Mill's theory of freedom and of Millian liberalism more generally. Riley has produced a guide which offers a lucid exposition of the arguments in *On Liberty*, and a powerful case for their coherence against critics who have persistently misinterpreted them.'

Chandran Kukathas, *Associate Professor of Politics,*
University of New South Wales.

'This is an excellent introduction to Mill's essay *On Liberty*. Riley is a sure-footed guide, who has thoroughly mastered the complex literature, and is able to steer his readers through it with an easy authority.'

Professor C.L. Ten, *Philosophy Department, Monash University*

'Jonathan Riley's GuideBook to Mill's *On Liberty* can be recommended without reservation both to beginning students and to professional philosophers. To the former he offers a thorough and coherent commentary on the text written in a straightforward and accessible style. To philosophers he offers both a critique of revisionist readings of these doctrines and a vigorous defence of them against many of the standard criticisms commonly accepted as decisive.'

Wayne Sumner, *University of Toronto*

Jonathan Riley is an Associate Professor of the Murphy Institute of Political Economy and the Department of Political Science, both at Tulane University. He is also the author of *Liberal Utilitarianism* and the World Classics edition of Mill's *Principles of Political Economy and Chapters on Socialism*.

Routledge Philosophy GuideBooks

Edited by Tim Crane and Jonathan Wolff
University College London

ROUTLEDGE

LONDON AND NEW YORK

Mill
on Liberty

■ Jonathan Riley

First published 1998
by Routledge
11 New Fetter Lane,
London EC4P 4EE

Simultaneously published in the
USA and Canada
by Routledge
29 West 35th Street,
New York, NY 10001

Typeset in Times and Frutiger by
Florencetype Ltd, Stoodleigh,
Devon

Printed and bound in Great Britain
by Clays Ltd, St Ives PLC

*British Library Cataloguing in
Publication Data*
A catalogue record for this book is
available from the British Library.

*Library of Congress Cataloguing in
Publication Data*
Riley, Jonathan.
  Mill on liberty/Jonathan Riley.
  (Routledge Philosophy
  GuideBooks)
  Includes bibliographical
  references and index.
  1. Mill, John Stuart, 1806–1873.
  On liberty 2. Liberty. I. Title.
  II. Series.
  JC585.M75R55   1998
  323.4–dc21   97–35429

ISBN 0–415–14188–5 (hbk)
ISBN 0–415–14189–3 (pbk)

In memory of
Patrick Sutherland Fallis (1948–1981)
'le feu follet'

Contents

Part three

Preface

Mill's classic essay on individual liberty is the focus of a large literature. Surely there is nothing new to say about it, some (perhaps most)
will think. Anyway, aside from his grand rhetoric, what is the interest
for students of philosophy? Isn't his argument pretty straightforward,
at least to the extent that we can make sense of it? Importance of moral
rights, respect for rule of law and all that. Who needs a GuideBook to
such ho-hum liberalism?

But a new guide to *On Liberty* is very much needed, I shall
insist. Mill's radical argument has largely been obscured by commentators, where it has not been dismissed as incoherent. His doctrine is
not now, and has never been, what most people understand by that
ambiguous term 'liberalism'. In its place, much more conventional liberalisms continue to predominate in the philosophical literature. Today,
students are likely to be misdirected toward one of these tamer alternatives, or worse, in the name of Millian liberalism.

It is my hope that this book might begin to remedy the misunderstandings surrounding Mill's radical argument. I depart very little
from his own arrangement of the argument. But I have subdivided it
into more sections, and have otherwise attempted to provide clarification where that seemed possible. At the same time, certain ambiguities

are highlighted as they arise in the text, and reference is made to how they are ultimately resolved, to facilitate the reader's understanding without unduly interrupting the flow of Mill's discussion. This exegesis comprises Part Two, the bulk of the GuideBook.

Part One of the guide generally introduces Mill's life and work, and relates the *Liberty* to his *Autobiography*. Since his defence of absolute liberty of thought and what he calls 'purely self-regarding' action is predicated in part on the great value of self-development or 'individuality', the story of his own process of development is of unusual interest. An indication of the *Liberty*'s early reception and current status in philosophy is also provided.

Part Three presents, and briefly discusses, some familiar criticisms which are often levelled against Mill's form of argument. The criticisms are framed as a series of eleven pointed questions. It is very much a matter of continuing debate whether compelling replies can be given. Given the current state of the literature, I see no reason to take a negative view, and I sketch my corresponding series of preferred answers accordingly.

My sketch of a defence in this GuideBook is intended to encourage students to make up their own minds about Mill's doctrine, by means of further thought and discussion of the relevant issues. But, as for myself, I am not neutral between his argument and alternatives: I think his doctrine has great appeal for anyone who values individual liberty and social improvement. A more complete defence of Millian liberalism is offered in my monograph, *Mill's Radical Liberalism: An Essay in Retrieval*, which is also to be published by Routledge. It presupposes some familiarity with this GuideBook, and, as a somewhat more advanced companion, concentrates on the logical structure of Mill's utilitarian liberalism, with a view to clarifying the ways in which it diverges sharply from more familiar liberalisms, such as those of John Rawls and Isaiah Berlin. Also, the practical implications of the doctrine are worked out in more detail for a couple of issues, namely, prostitution and pornography.

I wish to take this opportunity to express my gratitude to Jonathan Wolff, for inviting me to do the GuideBook, suggesting improvements to earlier drafts and encouraging me to elaborate my views in the forthcoming monograph. I am also grateful for the advice and support offered by referees, one of whom remains anonymous, two of whom kindly identified themselves as Chin Liew Ten and Wayne Sumner. Amartya Sen and John Gray also deserve my thanks for many stimulating discussions of related themes during the past fifteen years or so, ever since my days as a graduate student at Oxford. Obviously, none of these people can be held responsible for my stated opinions. Indeed, Gray has made clear in various publications that he takes a far less sympathetic view of Mill's doctrine. But one can always hope to repay at least some of the gifts of one's teachers and colleagues.

I am indebted to Tulane's Murphy Institute of Political Economy for research support provided during the time in which this GuideBook was completed.

The book is dedicated to the memory of my dear friend, who died so young at 33. Pat was the embodiment of a generous spontaneity, which it is the goal of the liberty principle to unleash and foster. He was a great joy to be around, as the many who knew and loved him will confirm. I will always miss him very much.

Last, but certainly not least, I thank Molly Rothenberg for her unfailing love and encouragement.

Part one

General introduction

Chapter 1

Mill and the *Liberty*

Mill's life and work

Mill lived for much of the nineteenth century, a period of remarkable social change in which, among much else, traditional religious beliefs continued to erode, without new faiths (whether religious or secular) taking their place as a general source of ideas and maxims of morality and politics. In his *Autobiography*, he describes the period as a 'critical' one, in the sense of the St Simonians and Comte, meaning a 'period ... of criticism and negation, in which mankind lose their old convictions without acquiring any new ones, of a general or authoritative character, except the conviction that the old are false'. Such transitional periods alternate throughout history with more settled 'organic' ones, in which, for the most part, 'mankind accept with firm conviction some positive creed, claiming jurisdiction over all their actions' (1873, p. 171). The critical period in which he lived 'began with the Reformation', he thought, 'has lasted ever since, still

3

lasts, and cannot altogether cease until a new organic period has been inaugurated by the triumph of a yet more advanced creed' (ibid.).

The more advanced creed, which he hoped might eventually replace fading Christian dogma, was what he called the 'Religion of Humanity' (1874), a comprehensive liberal utilitarian system of belief, in which extensive liberty of the individual is conjoined with a code of general rules designed to maximize the public good or happiness. As he recalls, by the time he was about 24, he 'looked forward, through the present age of loud disputes but generally weak convictions [surely reminiscent of our own age], to a future which shall unite the best qualities of the critical with the best qualities of the organic periods';

> unchecked liberty of thought, unbounded freedom of individual action in all modes not hurtful to others; but also, convictions as to what is right and wrong, useful and pernicious, deeply engraven on the feelings by early education and general unanimity of sentiment, and so firmly grounded in reason and in the true exigencies of life, that they shall not, like all former and present creeds, religious, ethical, and political, require to be periodically thrown off and replaced by others.
>
> (1873, p. 173)

His great essay, *On Liberty*, dedicated to his beloved wife, is an impassioned defence of that 'unchecked liberty of thought' and 'unbounded freedom of individual action in all modes not hurtful to others', which are the 'best qualities' of critical periods.

Although he had grand hopes for mankind amidst the 'loud disputes' and social upheaval of the age, his own life was 'uneventful' (ibid., p. 5). Born in London on 20 May 1806, he was the eldest of nine children of James and Harriet Mill. His father was a charismatic man, whose publications, wit and upstanding character made him a leader of the reform-minded intellectuals who banded together under Jeremy Bentham's standard of utility. James put his son through an extraordinary early education, and, in 1823, arranged for his employ at the East India Company. John worked there for thirty-five years (in the same office as his father until the latter's death in 1836), retiring only when the Company itself was terminated in 1858. As of 1856, he had risen to the same senior position that his father had achieved, namely, Examiner of India Correspondence, and thus was second in the chain of command, next to the Secretary.

He was married but once, in 1851, to Harriet Taylor (*née* Hardy), about two years after the death of her first husband, John Taylor. She died just over seven years later, only a few months after his retirement, while they were travelling to Montpellier. Their friendship, the 'most valuable' of his life, extended back to 1830, and had given rise to gossip for some time prior to their marriage. After she died, he bought a cottage near her gravesite in Avignon, and spent a good part of each of his remaining years there, usually accompanied by his stepdaughter, Helen Taylor.

During those fifteen remaining years, his writings were his main occupation. From 1865–8, he also served as a Liberal Member of Parliament for Westminster. His political career gives an indication of his character. He was elected despite giving public notice to the voters of his district that he would not run a campaign, or bear any of the costs of his election or be instructed by them. As an MP, he also refused to curry popular favour. Rather, he made parliamentary speeches proposing radical liberal reforms, which he knew lacked support yet believed might get a hearing, leading to a redirection of public opinion, during the ongoing critical period. His proposals included extension of the franchise to women, as well as the introduction of Hare's system of proportional representation, neither measure finding its way into the Reform Act of 1867. Perhaps his most controversial activity was his chairmanship of the extraparliamentary Jamaica Committee, which for two years sought in vain to persuade the government to prosecute Governor Eyre and his principal subordinates for unjustified military violence against Jamaican blacks.

He died, apparently of erysipelas, at Avignon on 7 May 1873, and is buried there with Harriet.

Evidently, his story is unlikely to be confused with the tales of Pericles or Napoleon. Even so, he expects that anyone capable of rational persuasion will be interested to learn more about his 'unusual and remarkable' education (ibid.). Although many have been interested, he might well have been surprised by the frequency with which the reaction is one of alarm and hostility. Typical is Carlyle's well-known jibe that the *Autobiography* reads like the story of a deeply troubled 'logical steam engine'. When he goes on to depict Mill's record of self-development as 'a mournful psychical curiosity', however, the latter-day Diogenes would be more persuasive if he were talking about himself.

By all accounts, Mill was a man of prodigious intellect and learning, whose moral and political opinions were not only far too progressive for the reactionary Carlyle but also far in advance of much contemporary liberal opinion. His various articles and treatises, emerging over a period of more than fifty years, span an incredibly broad range of topics in philosophy, politics and economics. Long regarded as a muddle-headed synthesizer of other people's ideas, he is seen in recent scholarship as a cogent and imaginative philosopher of liberal democracy, whose writings are of permanent importance.

To provide insight into his education process, he divides his life into three major periods. The first includes the period of his early education, lasting until he was about 14. During this time, his father was his 'schoolmaster' and directed his studies with a view to making him a fellow Benthamite reasoner. Then, after a year in France, he very gradually took control of his own education, by cultivating his intellectual and emotional capacities as *he* desired and thought best.

Initially, he merely carried on with the programme of his early education. During this first phase of his self-development or individuality, he threw himself into the path of intellectual enlightenment which his schoolmaster had laid out for him and accustomed him to pursue. After about five years, however, when he was still not yet 21, he lost interest in that path and, by the spring of 1827, found that he wanted to take a more varied journey, one that embraced the cultivation of his sympathetic capacities *as well as* his reasoning powers. He thereby moved into a second period (also his second phase of self-culture), in which he reacted strongly against the narrow way in which he had been brought up by his father.

His more diversified experience led quickly to a fundamental transformation in his opinions and character. By about 1830, he could envisage an enlarged utilitarian radicalism, one that went beyond narrow Benthamism without abandoning its insights. He apparently did not scotch all that was excessive in his reaction against Benthamism, however, until about 1840. Thereafter, he entered into his 'third period' of 'mental progress', as he calls it, 'which now went hand in hand with [Harriet's]' (ibid., p. 237). During this period, as lengthy as the other two combined, he, with assistance from her for nearly twenty years, tried to clarify his novel liberal utilitarian creed, through the writings that make up the bulk of his published work. The *Liberty*, composed over 1854–8 and published in 1859 (shortly after Harriet's death), was a product of this final phase of his individuality.

Given that his doctrine of liberty aims to encourage individuality as an element of general utility, his own process of education and self-development is of special interest for present purposes. His odyssey is a truly remarkable one, and further discussion of it provides an opportunity to dispel some common misconceptions and prejudices, which are afloat in the literature.

Early education

The main lesson of his early education, Mill suggests, is that young people are capable of far more development than is commonly thought possible. His own case illustrates 'how much more than is commonly supposed may be taught, and well taught, in those early years which, in the common modes of what is called instruction, are little better than wasted' (1873, p. 5; cf. p. 33). His father began teaching him Greek at about age 3 and Latin at 8. By 12, he had read an astonishing selection of texts in those languages, though he never composed at all in Greek and rarely in Latin. He particularly liked ancient history, he says, and was 'much addicted' to writing about it throughout his boyhood, in imitation of his father, whose *History of British India* was published in 1818 (ibid., p. 17).

When he was about 12, he began studying logic, and was required by his father to practise and master the Socratic dialectical method of dissecting the truth of an argument, as illustrated in Plato's dialogues (ibid., p. 25). He was also encouraged to pay special heed to the orations of Demosthenes, as being valuable for understanding the genius of Athenian political institutions and the art of the orator. During 1819–20, he completed an intensive course in political economy, reading and discussing with his father the well-known works of Adam Smith and David Ricardo. Indeed, he occasionally benefited from discussions with Ricardo himself, who was his father's 'loved and intimate friend' (ibid., p. 31).

Ricardo was not the only friend of his father's who took an interest in the son's education. Bentham himself, a lifelong bachelor who spent far more time writing than conversing with others about ideas, seems to have taken something of a paternal interest in John. He made clear that he could be counted on to provide for the son's upbringing in the event of something happening to James. The Mill family actually lived with him from time to time during 1810–17, renting accommodation for the first four or five years and then visiting in summers. But these arrangements ceased once James won permanent employment at the East India Company, shortly after the publication of his *History*.

John also met several rising liberal intellectuals who were attracted by his father's sharp mind and high moral character. Worthy of special note is George Grote, whom he apparently met about 1819. Grote and his wife Harriet saw a great deal of John, their junior by a dozen years or so, during the 1820s and 1830s. Despite some rifts, the friendship between the two men proved to be of enduring value for Mill's continuing intellectual growth. They apparently shared a great admiration for ancient Athenian culture and institutions, especially during the Periclean 'golden age'.[1] Indeed, Grote's magisterial *History of Greece*, on which he had been working for more than twenty-five years before it began to appear in 1846, seems to have supplied vital material for the argument of the *Liberty*, which gives prominence to a Greek ideal of self-development or education.

In May 1820, James Mill's role as schoolmaster came to an end. John was sent to France for more than a year, where he lived most of the time with the family of Samuel Bentham, Jeremy's brother. Among the advantages which he thereby gained were 'a familiar knowledge of the French language', continuing studies in higher mathematics and the sciences, and, perhaps most important, exposure to 'the free and genial atmosphere of Continental life', so different from the hidebound and aloof atmosphere of its English counterpart (ibid., pp. 59, 61).

Father and son

Contrary to a common view, Mill does not appear to think that his father's training method was wrongheaded or overly demanding. Though his father was severe and, at times, impatient beyond reason, the method itself was 'in the main . . . right, and it succeeded' (ibid., p. 31). 'Mine . . . was not an education of cram', he insists (ibid., p. 35). Rather, the 'mode of instruction was excellently calculated to form a thinker', and, focused as it was on logic and political economy, it 'made me a thinker on both' (ibid., pp. 31, 33). As already indicated, James was devoted to the Socratic method, so highly lauded by the son in the third chapter of the *Liberty*.[2] Thus, John's early education confirmed for him the power of Socratic dialogue to improve one's intellectual capacities.

He seems duly grateful to his father for this intellectual growth: 'the early training bestowed on me by my father [gave] . . . an advantage of a quarter of a century over my cotemporaries' (ibid., p. 33). By 15, in other words, he had learned with his father's help what most people at 40 are still struggling to learn for themselves. Moreover, he has no illusions that his headstart is the result of his own peculiar 'natural gifts', which he admits are 'rather below than above par'. His development is not the unfolding of some inherent personal excellence unique to himself. Rather, any young person of 'average capacity and healthy physical constitution' could accomplish the same, he emphasizes, if placed in his 'fortunate circumstances' (ibid.).

Nor does Mill ever betray resentment of his father for depriving him of his childhood. His early education, he says, 'was not such as to prevent me from having a happy childhood' (ibid., p. 53). True, his father had largely isolated him from children other than his own siblings, so that he apparently had few, if any, friends of his own age and had inadequate opportunities to develop physical skills or practical expertise in the conduct of daily life. But Mill confirms that this isolation prevented him from recognizing that he was mentally superior to other children, so that he never became arrogant or self-satisfied.[3] It also allowed him to 'escap[e] not only the ordinary corrupting influence which boys exercise over boys, but the contagion of vulgar modes of thought and feeling' (ibid., p. 39). Later in the

Autobiography, he makes clear that he agrees with his father that escape from the latter contagion is essential if the individual is to develop and maintain 'any mental superiority' (ibid., p. 235). The need for such escape explains why he chooses to limit his society to a 'very small' number of friends, beginning in the 1840s (ibid., pp. 235–7). More importantly, this implicit conflict between the cultivation of individuality and the 'despotism' of vulgar social customs is a central concern of the *Liberty*.

We must be wary, then, of any suggestion that Mill bore a grudge against his father, or that his love of individual liberty is rooted in his resentment of the training regimen which his father compelled him to follow. He was justifiably proud of James and 'was always loyally devoted to him', even if he 'cannot say' that he 'loved him tenderly' (ibid., p. 53). Moreover, there is no doubt that he agrees with his father that 'rigid discipline, and known liability to punishment, are indispensable as means' for the education of children (ibid.). The principle of liberty, he is careful to say, does not apply to children (I. 10, 1859c, p. 224; henceforth all references to *On Liberty* will take the shortened form of chapter reference followed by page number). Rather, young people are properly subject to coercion for their own good. Paternalism is a legitimate policy in their case, as when they are forced to undergo a demanding training programme designed to cultivate their capacities to think for themselves.[4]

Yet Mill does complain about his father's severity: 'I hesitate to pronounce whether I was more a loser or a gainer by his severity' (1873, p. 53). The problem was that James relied on fear of punishment *to the virtual exclusion of* love and praise. He was too quick to scorn and punish any failure to meet his (sometimes unreasonably) high standards, and he refused to praise his son's motivation and efforts to succeed (ibid., p. 51). By working his otherwise admirable teaching method in such a harsh spirit, he made it impossible for John to regard him with affection and trust, and perhaps even discouraged his son from 'frank and spontaneous' communication with others (ibid., p. 55). Thus, although fear is an 'indispensable' element in education, a wise paternalism will not use it indiscriminately, but will instead rely predominantly on more positive incentives to cultivate a desire to study and learn.

Mill's considered remarks convey sadness rather than anger at the absence of love between himself and his father. Whatever he may have felt as a child or young man, he seems to have recognized the obvious later in life, when drafting and redrafting the *Autobiography*, namely, that his father must have loved him very much to spend so much time and effort on his early education. Perhaps with Harriet Taylor's help, he came to appreciate the cultural constraints on his father's personality, and the extent to which prevailing English customs smothered any man's natural capacities of feeling:

> I believe [my father] to have had much more feeling than he habitually shewed [*sic*], and much greater capacities of feeling than were ever developed. He resembled most Englishmen in being ashamed of the signs of feeling, and, by the absence of demonstration, starving the feelings themselves.

(ibid., p. 53)

Under the circumstances, 'true pity' rather than resentment must be felt 'for a father who did, and strove to do, so much for his children, who would have so valued their affection, yet who must have been constantly feeling that fear of him was drying it up at its source' (ibid.).

The tension between existing social customs and the cultivation of spontaneity, already alluded to as a central theme of the *Liberty*, makes its appearance, then, within the very character of James Mill.[5] His son describes him as a 'leader' whose 'energetic' personality, impressive analytical skills and 'moral rectitude' combined to make a lasting impression on those he met (ibid., pp. 39, 105, 205). He evidently had strong feelings about education, for example, and, more generally, was an earnest advocate of social and political reforms which he thought were recommended by general utility. Yet, under the sway of prevailing custom, he depreciated spontaneity and the display of passionate emotion: 'For passionate emotions of all sorts, and for everything which has been said or written in exaltation of them, he professed the greatest contempt' (ibid., p. 51). For that reason, and because he seems to have mistakenly supposed that his son would acquire strong feelings like his 'without difficulty or special training', he neglected cultivation of the feelings in his conception of education (ibid., p. 39). Strong desires and sentiments *per se* were apparently of little value, until harnessed by reason and directed toward the public good. The serious business of social and political reform demanded abstract principles of logic, political economy and morality. To identify them, education must fiercely concentrate on cultivation of the powers of analysis and reasoning.

James' conventional contempt for passion had at least two important consequences for his son. First, John's early education was too narrow in scope. Since he was generally told what to do and given little encouragement to develop his own feelings, he seems to have been moulded into a 'mere reasoning machine', with no strong desires of his own (ibid., p. 111). This imbalance in his character, which erupted into a 'mental crisis' by the time he was 20, was exacerbated by his isolation. He never learned to fend for himself when his wants came into conflict with those of other children, for example. Thus: 'The education which my father gave me, was in itself much more fitted for training me to *know* than to *do*' (ibid., p. 39, emphasis added).

Second, and related, his father's (and, apparently, mother's) failure to express love and affection left him at 16 without much self-confidence, so that he became overly passive and withdrawn. His 'mental crisis' would soon force him to recognize that such self-abnegation and absence of desire can lead to severe depression. Evidently, a broader education than his, including development of the feelings, was needed to foster passionate emotion and aplomb. Ideally, the compulsory education of children ought to achieve this, by duly mixing affection and praise with discipline and fear. But it was too late for that in his own case. Rather, it would largely be up to *him* to remedy any imbalance in his development. Yet, remedying the problem would not be easy for a young man like himself, so socially awkward and starved for affection. Perhaps this may help to account for the immeasurable value which he was to place on the love and support he found in Harriet. But they did not meet until he was 25, nearly ten years down the road, and his path of self-development was rocky in the interval.

Young Benthamite radical

After returning from France in July 1821, Mill joined the circle of utilitarian radicals revolving loosely around his father and Bentham.

During the first year or two, he read Roman law with John Austin, became friendly with Austin's younger brother Charles and his Cambridge associates, and began studying Bentham's ideas as interpreted by Dumont in the *Traité de Législation*, the reading of which was 'an epoch in my life' (ibid., p. 67). He also read Condillac, Locke, Helvetius, Hartley, Hume and others, but says that Grote's attack on the utility of Deism in *Natural Religion* (privately circulated in 1822, under the pseudonym of Philip Beauchamp) 'produced the greatest effect upon me' next to the *Traité* (ibid., p. 73).

He began publishing in newspapers and journals as of 1822, and became the most frequent contributor to the radical *Westminster Review* (founded by Bentham in 1823) until he ceased writing for it in 1828 (after a dispute with Bowring, the editor). He also wrote frequently for the radical *Parliamentary History and Review* (edited by Bingham and Charles Austin) during its three years of existence, 1825–8.

He also formed the Utilitarian Society, a small study group which met fortnightly during 1822–6. The term 'utilitarian' thereby entered into public discourse, he says, although he did not invent the word (ibid., p. 81). As that group waned, another (the Society of Students of Mental Philosophy) was formed, which met twice-weekly in Grote's house until about 1830. In addition to studying German, its members critically discussed various sciences, including political economy (Mill's *Essays on Some Unsettled Questions of Political Economy*, though not published until 1844, dates from this period), logic and analytic psychology (James Mill's *Analysis of the Phenomena of the Human Mind*, published in 1829, was the final work discussed).

During 1825–30, he also took part in numerous public debates which pitted utilitarian radicals against competing sects, including Owenite socialists and (in the context of the London Debating Society, which he helped form) Tory lawyers and liberal disciples of Coleridge (notably Maurice and Sterling, the latter subsequently becoming a close friend of Mill and, through him, of Carlyle).

On top of these various activities, he had his duties at the East India Company as of May 1823, when he began as a clerk in his father's office. But even that was not all. Remarkably, he also agreed to devote much of his spare time during 1825–6 to condensing and constructing, from Bentham's 'three masses' of draft papers on evidence, a 'single treatise', eventually published in 1827 as the five-volume *Rationale of Judicial Evidence* (ibid., p. 117). Although he emphasizes that it was an invaluable spur to his powers of composition, that difficult task may have been the straw that broke the camel's back, so to speak. Perhaps because of overwork, he became disenchanted with Benthamite radicalism during the autumn of 1826. His disenchantment translated into a loss of a sense of purpose in his life, and grew into a severe depression for the next six months. Even so, his mental crisis did not interrupt his busy schedule as a utilitarian radical, and must have been quite invisible to observers.

The general direction of his life appears fairly predictable throughout the 1820s, even if appearances were deceptive after his depression, because his formidable intellectual skills continued to be displayed in the service of the 'official' utilitarian goals associated with his father and Bentham. That Benthamite type of radicalism glorified reason as an instrument of reform, to the neglect of cultivation of higher motives and noble character. Like the eighteenth-century Enlightenment *philosophes* (including Voltaire, Helvetius and Condorcet), the Benthamites tended to attack prevailing customs and institutions, including legal rules, as irrational emanations of aristocratic class prejudice and religious superstition. At the same time, they took for granted that most people are predominantly motivated by notions of self-interest. As a result, their reform efforts were focused on improving the intellectual capacities of the masses and establishing institutions compatible with competitive pursuit of enlightened self-interest. Little if any attention was paid to visionary institutions, such as market socialism or voluntary communal lifestyles beyond the traditional family, the feasibility of which depends on cultivation of higher moral and aesthetic sentiments (including the desire for equal justice): 'While fully recognising the superior excellence of unselfish benevolence and love of justice', Mill says of the Benthamites, among whose number he counted himself at this time, 'we did not expect the regeneration of mankind from any direct action on those sentiments, but from the effect of educated intellect, enlightening the selfish feelings' (ibid., p. 113).

Benthamite radicalism combined at least five leading elements (ibid., pp. 107–11). First, Bentham's version of utilitarianism provided the general philosophical underpinnings. According to Bentham, social institutions should be designed such that self-interested persons, strongly motivated to acquire wealth and power, have adequate 'external' incentives (rewards and punishments) to act so as to maximize the general welfare, understood as the sum of the personal welfares (enlightened self-interests), each to count for one and only one. He seems to have believed that the general welfare is in principle calculable in any situation because different personal welfares are quantifiable and comparable. But he offered no general mechanical procedure for measuring or comparing personal welfares. Rather, he claimed that the general welfare is comprised of certain permanent goods or interests (including security of expectations, subsistence, abundance and equality), the joint attainment of which should guide the design of institutions. Evidently, the radicals committed to the establishment of such institutions must be 'themselves impelled by nobler principles of action' than the principle of self-interest, which Bentham holds impels the majority (ibid., p. 113).[6]

A second element of the 'official' radical creed was a hedonistic psychology which, as developed by James Mill from a basis provided by Hartley's *Observations on Man* (1749), viewed any person's sole ultimate motivation as his own welfare or happiness, in the sense of pleasure (including absence of pain), and treated wealth and power as sources of pleasure inseparably associated with most persons' ideas of their welfare in observed civil societies. Again, radicals themselves must be motivated by uncommonly noble ideas of their own welfare, ideas that effectively merge personal welfare with attainment of the general happiness.

The remaining elements highlight major institutional implications of this hedonistic utilitarianism. 'In politics', the radicals displayed 'an almost unbounded confidence in the efficacy of two things: representative government, and complete freedom of discussion' (1873, p. 109). If aristocratic rule could be replaced by 'a democratic suffrage', it was thought, then, when most voters had been sufficiently enlightened through basic education and the free flow of opinions to make 'a good choice of persons to represent them', an elected legislature would impartially 'aim at the general interest' (ibid.).

In religion, the radicals were sceptics who rejected any established church as incompatible with liberty of thought and discussion. Like James Mill, they attacked 'the vulgar prejudice, that what is called, very improperly, unbelief, is connected with any bad qualities either of mind or heart' (ibid., p. 47). The belief systems commonly accepted as Christian struck them not only as corruptions of Christ's own teachings, but also as incoherent in that 'an Omnipotent Author of Hell' is 'nevertheless identified' with 'perfect goodness' (ibid., p. 43).

In economics, they favoured private ownership of productive resources, freely competitive markets and, as a means of raising the wages of the working classes in the long run, birth control (enforced by social stigma rather than legal penalties). They relied on Ricardo's theory as elaborated in his great treatise *On the Principles of Political Economy and Taxation* (1817), a simplified account of which was published by James Mill (with substantial drafting assistance from John) as *Elements of Political Economy* (1821).

It was against utilitarian radicalism of this 'official' sort, the radicalism to which he had been bred by his father, that he rebelled as a 20-year-old, even as he continued to pursue radical projects and to mingle with his radical associates.

Mental crisis and reaction

Mill's 'mental crisis' lasted for some six months, extending into the spring of 1827, when he feared that critics might be correct to denounce utilitarianism as 'cold calculation; political economy as hard-hearted; [and] anti-population doctrines as repulsive to the natural feelings of mankind' (1873, p. 113). He grew gloomy and suicidal as he became aware that he would not feel 'great joy and happiness' even if the reforms prescribed by the radicals were 'completely effected at this very instant' (ibid., p. 139). It was not that he ceased to understand that his 'greatest and surest sources of happiness' lay in working to bring about a liberal conception of the public good. He *knew* he ought to feel pleasure in promoting the good of mankind. But he did not actually *feel* that pleasure, or *expect* to feel it: 'to know that a feeling would make me happy if I had it, did not give me the feeling' (ibid., p. 143). The 'continual pursuit' of a Benthamite conception of the general happiness 'had ceased to charm' (ibid., p. 139). An 'egotistical' dejection choked his 'love of mankind', so that his life seemed to have no purpose and his 'fabric of happiness' was ruined (ibid., p. 149).

His mental crisis was tied up, he suggests, with an imbalance produced in his character by his early education, to wit, strong analytical powers combined with weak feelings and desires. His father's programme of study had left him 'irretrievably analytic', without encouraging him to develop passions and loves of his own. Moreover, he feared that there was no remedy for the imbalance. The 'habit of analysis' necessarily erodes such a complex passion as the desire for public good, he thought, by identifying it as a mere prejudice, whose force depends on 'artificial' associations – created by means of 'praise and blame, reward and punishment' – between feelings of pleasure and ideas of general welfare (ibid., p. 141). Only simple natural feelings could survive the 'analysing spirit' unscathed, namely, 'the purely physical and organic' desires and pleasures. But these were surely insufficient 'to make life desirable' (ibid., p. 143). Thus, because he had never really experienced strong complex passions and emotions of his own, he seems to have been unaware at this time that he still *could* cultivate such feelings, by immersing himself in the fine arts and giving free rein to his powers of imagination. The latter powers, he was shortly to discover, are 'natural complements and correctives' (ibid., p. 141) to the powers of analysis, so that there is no necessary incompatibility between complex moral and aesthetic feelings and analytic acumen.

The depression gradually lifted, Mill tells us, after he was 'moved to tears' by Marmontel's memoir of when, as 'a mere boy', he had acted to alleviate the distress of his beloved family at the time of his father's death (ibid., p. 145). By vividly imagining the scene and sympathizing with the feelings of the boy and his family, John realized that he too was capable of such feelings, and 'could again find enjoyment, not intense, but sufficient for cheerfulness', in life.

Similarly, he found that Wordsworth's poetry evoked his love of beautiful natural scenery, especially mountains, as a kind of perfect ideal, a 'perennial' source of happiness in which all humans might share, suggestive of what might be possible 'when all the greater evils of life shall have been removed' (ibid., p. 151). 'And the delight which these poems gave me, proved that with culture of this sort, there was nothing to dread from the most confirmed habit of analysis' (ibid., p. 153). Thus, 'there was, once more, excitement, though of a moderate kind, in exerting myself for my opinions, and for the public good' (ibid., p. 145). He now recognized that he could largely remedy any character defect produced by his early education by pursuing a suitable course of self-improvement. He would never again be so bothered by depression, despite 'several' recurrences of 'the same mental malady' (ibid., pp. 143–5).

The point to emphasize is that the mental crisis did pass. It did not reveal some irremediable flaw in Mill's personality, for which his father could endlessly and justifiably be blamed. Nor did it signal that the critics of utilitarian radicalism were right on the main points. Even so, the crisis is a turning point because it did have 'two very marked effects' on his philosophy and character. First, it led him to take an indirect approach to the goal of happiness. Direct pursuit of his own happiness and pleasure had involved him in counterproductive analysis of the extent to which any idea of public good could serve as a means to the end. But now he would aim at public good as 'itself an ideal end', finding personal happiness 'by the way' (ibid., p. 147). That indirect strategy would produce the most personal happiness for the vast majority, he claims, who (like himself) 'have but a moderate degree of sensibility and of capacity for enjoyment' (ibid.). Perhaps some highly sensitive artists and philanthropists might do better for themselves with a direct strategy. But most people will find more happiness for themselves by adopting and following a code of general rules designed to promote a conception of the general good. Remarkably, it is not clear that his father or Bentham would have any serious quarrel with this indirect strategy.

Second, his crisis led him to cultivate 'a due balance among the faculties', rather than focusing exclusively on his powers of analysis and reasoning. As he explains:

I, for the first time, gave its proper place, among the prime necessities of human well-being, to the internal culture of the individual. I ceased to attach almost exclusive importance to the ordering of outward circumstances, and the training of the human being for speculation and action. I had now learned by experience that the passive susceptibilities needed to be cultivated as well as the active capacities, and required to be nourished and enriched as well as guided. I did not, for an instant, lose sight of, or undervalue, that part of the truth which I had seen before; I never turned recreant to intellectual culture, or ceased to consider the power and practice of analysis as an essential condition both of individual and social improvement. But I thought that it had consequences which required to be corrected, by joining other kinds of cultivation with it. The maintenance of *a due balance among the faculties*, now seemed to me of primary importance. The cultivation of the feelings became one of the cardinal points in my ethical and philosophical creed.

(ibid., p. 147, emphasis added)

In short, he now saw that no fundamental incompatibility exists between intellectual enlightenment, the only form of culture pursued by the Benthamite school, and the cultivation of higher moral and aesthetic sentiments, generally ignored by that school as ineffectual for purposes of social reform. Henceforth, he would be more open to ideals of noble character and visions of social harmony, which were rejected by the 'official' utilitarians as useless if not antagonistic to their programme.

The real import of his crisis, on this interpretation, is that it stirred him to formulate a better version of liberal utilitarianism, a 'new' radicalism that retains what was valuable in the 'old' Benthamite doctrine but also makes more adequate provision for the cultivation of the higher feelings and for ideal social arrangements founded upon them. The crisis was 'the origin' of an 'important transformation in my opinions and character', he says, which preoccupied him 'for some years' (ibid., p. 137). He could imagine his new radicalism in outline by 1830, it seems, and was able to fill in most of the details before the summer of 1834, when he began to edit the

London Review (as of 1836, the *London and Westminster Review*) started by Molesworth. Even so, he was unable to 'give full scope to my own opinions and modes of thought', before his father died (ibid., p. 215). After that, a principal goal of his conduct of the *Review*, he emphasizes, was 'to shew [sic] that there was a radical philosophy, better and more complete than Bentham's, while recognising and incorporating all of Bentham's which is permanently valuable' (ibid., p. 221). Indeed, to achieve this goal of driving a wedge between philosophical radicalism and 'sectarian Benthamism', he went so far as to purchase the journal in 1837, operating it at a loss until 1840, when he sold it to Hickson.[7]

Mill insists that, despite his reaction against Benthamism, he never ceased to consider himself a kind of utilitarian radical, however peculiar his brand of radicalism might appear in relation to the 'official' brand. 'I never, indeed, wavered in the conviction that happiness is the test of all rules of conduct, and the end of life', he says (ibid., p. 145). 'Like me', he says of John Austin, who had also undergone a transformation in his Benthamite opinions and character after living and studying for some time in Germany, 'he never ceased to be an utilitarian' (ibid., p. 185). Similarly, despite his Romantic turn toward the cultivation of feelings, Mill 'never turned recreant to intellectual culture' and 'never joined in the reaction against [the Enlightenment]' of the 'great' eighteenth century (ibid., pp. 147, 169).

Rather than abandon utilitarian radicalism, he proposes to modify and enlarge it into an even 'more heretical' doctrine, in which alien materials are grafted onto a Benthamite stock to breathe new life into the whole. The foreign supplements, as he tells us, included insights into will, imagination and character offered by German Idealists, including Goethe, Kant and Schiller and their British followers, notably Coleridge, Maurice, Sterling, and Carlyle. He also made room for egalitarian social Utopias of the sort proposed by Owen and the French 'socialists' and 'communists', including Saint-Simon, Fourier, Cabet and Louis Blanc. Moreover, his interest in birth control and equal rights for women was heightened by his exposure to the feminist views of his future wife. She and her circle of Unitarian friends did not hold sacrosanct the prevailing social conventions relating to marriage and personal lifestyle.[8]

Harriet

Harriet enters Mill's story just when his new radicalism seems to have assumed a definite shape in his mind. He soon came under her spell: 'I very soon felt her to be the most admirable person I had known', he says, although about ten years went by 'before her mental progress and mine went forward in the complete companionship they at last attained' (ibid., pp. 193, 197). He was ripe from the first for the passionate love she inspired in him, the deep emotion that he had missed until she came along, and that he was never to find with another after she died. She was the light of his life and, if his own testimony is believed, a brilliant and original thinker in her own right (ibid., pp. 195–7, 251–61).

He praises her to a remarkable degree, making her into a paragon of moral and intellectual development. He apparently learned from her 'the constituent elements of the highest realizable ideal of human life' (ibid., p. 197), that is, an ideal conception of happiness, which he refers to in the *Liberty* as 'utility in the largest sense' (I.11, p. 224). She also seems to have taught him 'a wise scepticism' about his practical conclusions in moral and political science, saving him from a kind of dogmatism toward which his Benthamite training may have inclined him (1873, pp. 197–9). In short, she was the 'fiery' artist and wise practitioner all rolled into one, the originator of their 'most valuable ideas', whereas he was predominantly a methodical 'interpreter', a synthesizer and systematizer of other people's important thoughts, which the original thinkers themselves did not know how, or could not be bothered, to integrate and reconcile (ibid., pp. 251–3).

His high praise for her patently annoys some commentators, who do not take it seriously. But, even allowing for his tendencies to downplay his own originality and to exaggerate the brilliance of those whom he loved (he also lauds Helen, for example, as virtually another Harriet), it is not clear that third parties are in any position to second-guess his assessment of her abilities. Nor is it clear why anyone should *wish* to denigrate her contributions in any case. If he thinks enough of her critical advice and discussion to want to include her as the 'joint author' of some of his important texts, despite the absence of evidence that she wrote much of anything, why should that trouble anyone? He is certainly not disclaiming responsibility for the textual arguments, of which the clarity and power do not depend on such particulars of authorship.

What *is* clear is that Harriet's close friendship with Mill during her first marriage raised eyebrows. Her rather hasty remarriage may also have struck many of those who knew them (including members of his own family) as a breach of moral convention. Given his depiction of her proud personality, she would hardly have been intimidated by stigma of this sort.[9] Such a woman, deliberately forming unconventional relationships with other consenting adults as she likes, in defiance of prevailing norms of church and family, might well acquire a bad reputation, whatever her capacities of intellect and feeling. Defenders of traditional ideas and attitudes would surely deny all possibility that she might be a brilliant thinker, of impeccable moral character. Moreover, once acquired, her reputation, as a thoughtless and irresponsible eccentric, would tend to take on a life of its own. Perhaps Mill's emphatic praise of her good qualities ought to be considered in this context, as a calculated response to the predictable string of invective against her from the usual quarters.

In this one respect at least, the lives of Mill and Pericles do show some overlap, in the sense that Harriet is to Mill as Aspasia of Miletus is to the great Athenian.[10] According to the ancient sources, Pericles may have offended against traditional religious values and marriage customs, because he openly treated Aspasia – a free-thinking resident alien – as not merely his lover but his wife and confidante (a status customarily reserved for dutiful Athenian women). She was vilified at the time, no doubt at the urging of his political opponents, and has continued to be vilified through history, as a manipulator, a whore, a seducer of an otherwise brilliant man who somehow lost all common sense in her presence and attributed his brilliance to her (Henry, 1995). The doctrine of the *Liberty* signals that we should be cautious before accepting such assessments, since they may be nothing more than manifestations of more or less subtle forms of social coercion directed against extraordinary individuals for pursuing their personal affairs in their own ways, without hurt to others.

In any case, there seems little reason to deny Mill's claim that Harriet contributed valuable ideas to his new liberal utilitarian philosophy. He tells us that she encouraged him to take more seriously the possibility of a decentralized form of socialism, for example, in which co-operative associations of highly educated producers would compete on product and factor markets, men and women enjoying equal rights of participation within the enterprises (1873, pp. 237–45, 255–7). She may also have helped him to grasp that women, as they gained equality with men, would be more likely to demand more prudent family practices (including birth control measures) than had hitherto been observed or could otherwise be expected under the prevailing system of male domination. Even more importantly for our purposes, she may have impressed on him the truth of the 'one very simple principle' of the *Liberty*. Nothing like that principle is recognized in his earlier writings, where, indeed, he seems more dubious about freedom of expression than one would expect from the author of the essay.[11]

If she did contribute such insights, Harriet had a large hand in the central project of Mill's life, to wit, his clarification of a new utilitarian radicalism, more adequate and complete than Bentham's related doctrine.

New utilitarian radicalism

The essays and treatises published after 1840 are properly seen to elaborate that 'better and more complete' liberal utilitarianism. The *Liberty* is perhaps the crowning jewel of the new radical creed. But the jewel is surrounded by an unusually broad array of contributions on virtually every important aspect of a liberal democratic philosophy. Although his major texts on logic and political economy were both in print by 1848, most of his work on moral and political themes was published during 1859–69. In addition to the *Liberty*, it includes a statement of his utilitarianism, his thoughts on representative government, association psychology and the subjection of women, and his critiques of transcendental idealism and Comtean positivism. His unfinished essays on religion and socialism, as well as the *Autobiography*, were published posthumously, by Helen, by 1879.

This is not the place to attempt to detail all of the ways in which the new radicalism modifies and enlarges upon its Benthamite ancestor. The differences between them are rooted in the fact that Mill is more cognizant than the old radicals of human capacities of imagination (including sympathy for others) and mutual co-operation, more open to the possibility that individuals might form noble characters that reflect repeated acts of imagination and co-operation, and consequently less committed to social institutions that presuppose the predominantly selfish type of characters observed hitherto. At the same time, elements of the old are retained in his new outlook. Like Bentham, for example, he offers no general mechanical procedure for directly measuring and adding up personal happinesses. Rather, like Bentham again, he works with a conception of the public good, in which security, subsistence, abundance and equality figure as 'constituent elements', and holds that most will attain personal happiness indirectly, by complying with a code of rules designed to promote that conception of public good. (The code must also contain rules for utilitarian reformers to live by in situations where widespread compliance cannot be expected, though it should always be encouraged.) But Mill's conception of public good is 'more heretical' than that of any Benthamite.

As conceived by Benthamites, the public good apparently involves sustained economic growth under capitalist institutions, peaceful majoritarian government under democratic institutions, sufficient redistribution to assure the subsistence of those who need help, and more or less material equality depending on the progress of intellectual education and birth control among the masses. A Benthamite utilitarian code promotes abundance and reduces inequality, for example, by distributing private property rights and fostering free markets, such that the individual is guaranteed the fruits of his own labour and saving (net of fair taxation); primogeniture and entails are abolished; and aristocratic privileges regarding the natural fruits of the earth are curtailed. The code also minimizes the danger of political misrule, by distributing rights to vote that secure to each citizen an opportunity to make his voice heard by elected legislators. The individual must also be assigned rights to subsistence, personal safety, reputation and the like. The resulting system of equal rights and correlative duties facilitates each person's happiness, by allowing each to enjoy security of expectations with respect to certain vital elements or 'primary goods' in his plan of life.

This Benthamite approach retained appeal for Mill as far as it went. But he also looked beyond it, by imagining that certain 'higher' aesthetic and moral feelings might eventually come to trump self-interest (enlightened or otherwise). His account of these complex higher feelings did not entail for him a departure from hedonism. Rather, their status as higher pleasures, inherently more valuable than the pleasures of self-interested behaviour, could be explained, he thought, by a more sophisticated version of the psychology champ-ioned by his father. That more sophisticated hedonism was largely developed by Bain and himself, as outlined in their notes to the second edition of the *Analysis of the Phenomena of the Human Mind* (1869). This modified and enlarged account of human nature opened his eyes to possibilities of personal nobility and social organization not entertained (or insufficiently considered) by Benthamite radicals. It also made him less sanguine than they were about the advantages of democracy and market capitalism, in the absence of moral and aesthetic progress by the majority.

In politics, for example, Mill suggested that, unless the people have developed to a point of virtual moral unanimity, good govern-ment cannot be ensured merely by democratic elections:

> Identity of interest between the governing body and the commu-nity at large, is not, in any practical sense which can be attached to it, the only thing on which good government depends; neither can this identity of interest be secured by the mere conditions of election.
>
> (1873, p. 165)

His father was wrong on this point, whereas Macaulay was right. A prudent system of auxiliary checks and balances was also essential, to forestall majority oppression of minority interests. Unlike Tocqueville, however, John did not favour the US system, with its bicameral legislature elected from, respectively, districts and states by majority or plurality vote, its independent chief executive and its fixed dates of election. Rather, as he makes clear in *Considerations on Representative Government* (1861a), he favoured a unicameral parlia-mentary system, with Hare's method of elections to ensure propor-tional representation. In addition to providing minorities with voices in the legislature in proportion to their numbers, auxiliary safeguards against majority incompetence and/or tyranny included an independent commission of experts (appointed by the executive) with exclusive authority to draft or amend legislation as requested by the legislature (which retained the authority to enact or veto whole bills), and perhaps even plural voting based on education as opposed to one person, one vote – although he clearly had qualms about the latter innovation (1873, pp. 261–2).

In economics, given the possibility that a high degree of moral solidarity (as well as intelligence) might emerge among workers and investors, he speculated that competitive capitalism might eventually be transformed, by a series of voluntary exchanges among market participants, into an ideal sort of decentralized socialism, in which competition among small-scale self-managed worker co-operatives is constrained by some higher morality of distributive justice. Also in his *Principles of Political Economy* (1871), he hopes that highly developed producers might opt for a so-called 'stationary state' (i.e., stationary population and capital stock), rather than continued economic growth beyond a reasonable threshold of national wealth and population. By implication, economic rights associated with the interest in abundance – whether private property rights or rights to participate in socialist enterprises – come into conflict, in his view, with superior types of rights beyond that threshold. Those superior rights might include rights to breathe clean air and drink clean water, for example, as well as rights to contemplate unspoiled natural beauty in solitude, rights to engage freely and exclusively with other consensual adults in intimate activities of no legitimate concern to anyone else and so on. At some point, if growth of wealth and population continues unchecked and natural beauty is increasingly sacrificed to mankind's economic purposes, such rights will be endangered for many of us. His liberal utilitarianism at that point prescribes a halt to further economic growth (for further discussion of these points, see Riley, 1996, 1997b).

In purely personal matters, including opinions on all subjects as well as actions in all modes not hurtful to other people, Mill defends absolute liberty, so that the individual might develop his intellectual and moral capacities. He generalizes the argument, accepted by

Benthamites and others, for absolute liberty of religious opinion. But the old radicals do not seem to have anticipated his generalization, despite Kelly's suggestions to the contrary (1990, pp. 150–4). In short, Mill's conception of the public good includes a distinctive 'permanent interest' in 'individuality', which is not found among the 'constituent elements' of the Benthamite conception.

Mill's new utilitarian radicalism modifies and enlarges Benthamism, then, by adding to Bentham's list of 'constituent elements' of the good life, by imagining the possibility of a distinctive ideal mix of those permanent ingredients, and by identifying novel codes of rules, rights and duties associated with that ideal blend of security, subsistence, abundance, equality and individuality. But the reader must go elsewhere for further discussion of the apparent structure of this distinctive Millian creed (see Riley, 1988, forthcoming a, b, c).

'Text-book of a single truth'

Mill says that the *Liberty* is 'a kind of philosophic text-book of a single truth . . . the importance, to man and society, of a large variety in types of character, and of giving full freedom to human nature to expand itself in innumerable and conflicting directions' (1873, p. 259). Most people do not really appreciate that truth, he insists. Rather, the majority tends 'to fetter the development, and, if possible, prevent the formation, of any individuality not in harmony with its own ways' (I.5, p. 220). Obedience to prevailing customs and norms is typically regarded as important, not the freedom to explore diverse paths of self-development and to form one's opinions and character as one thinks best (so crucial in his own case).

The truth affirmed by the 'text-book' is not entirely original, he admits. Its 'leading thought . . . is one which, though in many ages confined to insulated thinkers, mankind have probably at no time since the beginning of civilisation been entirely without. To speak only of the last few generations', he goes on, its 'doctrine of the rights of individuality, and the claim of the moral nature to develope [*sic*] itself in its own way', has been asserted in one form or another by Pestalozzi, Wilhelm von Humboldt, Goethe and the German Romantics, William

Maccall and Josiah Warren (1873, p. 260). Recall also his observation that broad liberty of thought and freedom of action in all modes not harmful to others, are among the 'best qualities' of critical periods in general (ibid., pp. 173, 259–60).

Nevertheless, he also hints that his conception of this long-standing doctrine of liberty is more novel than he has been letting on: 'It is hardly necessary here to remark that there are abundant differences in detail, between the conception of the doctrine by any of the predecessors I have mentioned, and that set forth in the book' (ibid., p. 261). Moreover, we should not be fooled into thinking that the best qualities of transitional periods will automatically persist into subsequent organic periods, he insists, in the absence of any principled defence of those qualities. If we expect unbridled freedom of thought and of action in all modes harmless to others to be included as constituent elements of whatever new creed eventually 'rallies the majority around it', a *principle of liberty*, 'grounded in reason and in the true exigencies of life' and thus capable of persuading reasoning persons in all periods, is essential (ibid., pp. 260, 173). It is within later *organic* periods, which he assumes will inevitably replace the critical age in which he lived, that 'the teachings of the *Liberty* will have their greatest value' (ibid., p. 260). And he issues a warning, made to sound ominous in hindsight by the rise of fascist and totalitarian creeds, far removed from liberal reason, during the twentieth century: 'it is to be feared that [its teachings] will retain that value a long time' (ibid.).

The aim of the *Liberty* is to set forth 'one very simple principle' of liberty, of enduring value across critical and organic periods. That 'simple principle' is distinctive, I shall argue, in that it prescribes the individual's *absolute* freedom to choose as he pleases among certain 'purely self-regarding' acts said to be harmless to other people: 'In the part [of his conduct] which merely concerns himself, his independence is, of right, *absolute*' (I.9, p. 224, emphasis added). Whatever Harriet's influence in the matter, this prescription of a licence to think and do as one likes is not some offhand remark or a casual slip of the pen. As documented in Part Two of this GuideBook, similar statements can be found throughout the 'textbook'.

Mill emphasizes that the *Liberty* is a carefully constructed piece of work: 'None of my writings have either been so carefully composed, or so sedulously corrected as this' (1873, p. 249). He first prepared an abbreviated version of it in 1854, he says, and then decided, while travelling in Italy in early 1855, to convert it into a volume. Despite other pressing business relating to the East India Company, he and Harriet revised the entire manuscript numerous times in the interval before her death, 'reading, weighing and criticising every sentence' (ibid.). The volume 'was more directly and literally our joint production than anything else which bears my name' (ibid., p. 257). It never received its 'final revision'. But it remains a highly polished production: '[T]here was not a sentence of it that was not several times gone through by us together, turned over in many ways, and carefully weeded of any faults, either in thought or in expression, that we detected in it' (ibid., pp. 257–9).

He is also clearly proud of the arguments of the volume. In his view, 'the *Liberty* is likely to survive longer than anything else that I have written (with the possible exception of the *Logic*)' (ibid., p. 259). Indeed, he sees it as a fitting tribute to the love of his life: 'After my irreparable loss one of my earliest cares was to print and publish the treatise, so much of which was the work of her whom I had lost, and consecrate it to her memory' (ibid., p. 261). Its present form is apparently the best he can offer: 'Though it wants the last touch of her hand, no substitute for that touch shall ever be attempted by me' (ibid.). The first edition was published by Parker in February of 1859, only three months after Harriet's death. Aside from some minor typos, no revisions were ever made.

Under these circumstances, it seems incumbent on the reader to treat the arguments of the essay with due care and respect. Contrary to the suggestions of many critics, the doctrine of liberty is not some ill-considered musing or slapdash effort. It deserves, and repays, careful study.

Early reaction

The *Liberty* seems to have been something of an instant sensation among English readers. Rees (1956, pp. 1–2) cites some contemporary statements to that effect. Mill himself speaks of 'the great impression' made by the essay 'at a time [i.e, a critical period] which, to superficial observation, did not seem to stand much in need of such a lesson' (1873, p. 259). The first edition quickly sold out, and a second edition of 2,000 copies appeared in August 1859, followed by a third in 1864. Only one more Library Edition was published during Mill's lifetime, in 1869, largely because an inexpensive and oft-reprinted People's Edition appeared in 1865. Since his death, the essay has been reprinted numerous times, in various languages. It is still generally regarded as a classic statement of the case for individual liberty.

That is not to say that his argument has ever been widely accepted, or that it is now adequately reflected in the legal and moral systems of advanced societies such as Britain or the United States. But it remains influential to some extent and continues to be admired by many who are prepared to be critical of existing law and morality. H.L.A. Hart noted in 1963, for example, that 'Mill's principles [sic] are still very much alive in the criticism of law' (1963, p. 15). Joel Feinberg (1984–8) turns to 'Mill's principles' as he reconstructs them in his critical assessment of legal rules in an American context. Most recently, C.L. Ten has argued that Mill's doctrine contains important lessons for modern multicultural societies, and that '[i]t will be a long time before the message of *On Liberty* becomes redundant' (1995, p. 204).[12]

At the same time, the fame of the essay should not be taken to imply that its argument has been fully comprehended by most of its readers. From the start, most critical notices of the book have been infected by remarkable confusions and misunderstandings. As J.T. Mackenzie complained in 1880, in a cogent reply to the smug conservatism expressed by Max Muller during the previous year, 'scarcely anybody' seems to have understood the 'plain language' of the text (as reprinted in Pyle, 1994, p. 397). It is difficult to know whether such incomprehension generated the hostility among philosophers which rather quickly surrounded the book, and which has since hardened into a dogma, or whether a pre-existing climate of hostility predisposed most critics to make little effort to understand its form of reasoning in the first place, let alone to clarify that reasoning for a wider public.

As Mackenzie continues, however, Mill's 'words contain the germ of a social revolution; there is not a corner of life into which they do not pierce' (ibid., pp. 397–8). It is tempting to suggest that certain elements of society had a vested interest in blunting the revolutionary implications of the liberty doctrine. And, like Oscar Wilde, I can resist everything but temptation. In particular, I shall ask the reader to keep in mind the possibility that influential defenders of established social institutions may have deliberately misrepresented Mill's position, so as to obsure the radical liberal reforms that flow from his 'very simple principle'.[13] Influential defenders of the established order included many ministers and professors imbued with a faith in traditional religious and moral ideals.[14]

In any case, there is no doubt that the reviews published during his lifetime and shortly thereafter, are, for the most part, hostile.[15] There are occasional exceptions. I have already mentioned Mackenzie's review. Morley's (1873) reply to Fitzjames Stephen's crude utilitarian attack on Mill (1967; originally published 1873), is also cogent and devastating.[16] Walt Whitman (1871), despite his affinity for idealist metaphysics, refers to Mill in support of an argument that the rights of individuality must be protected to elevate the character of American democracy. But these are relatively rare. Many more, after expressing grudging admiration for the author, go on to charge him with fatal inconsistency, hopeless ambiguity, immoral subversion of family values and/or something akin to blasphemy. Indeed, as Rees (1956, pp. 1–38) and Pyle (1994, pp. vii–xx) document, the panoply of criticisms now largely taken for granted by philosophers can be found in these early reviews, including: liberalism is incompatible with utilitarianism; liberty is defined improperly by Mill, in purely negative terms; harm is not defined at all; self-regarding acts cannot be distinguished from others; the liberty principle is inapplicable; and on and on.

In this regard, many of the early reviewers are evidently offended by Mill's claims in the essay that Christianity has decayed into a 'dead dogma' for most members of advanced societies, such that what is now called Christian morality, and habitually practised as such, is something very different from the 'maxims and precepts contained in the New Testament', which no longer guide conduct and indeed are scarcely understood. Modern Christianity, he suggests, boils down for most to a doctrine of 'passive obedience' to prevailing social customs and conventions, and would be largely unrecognizable to Christ or even to Saint Paul. To put it mildly, this was unwelcome news to those who considered themselves Christians, and it may have led many to discount the value of his argument in support of the liberty principle. Even Bain was bothered. 'Such a line of observation is felt at once as challenging the pretensions of Christianity to be a divine revelation', he intoned, 'and this ought not to be done in a passing remark . . . The whole subject is extraneous to his treatise, and impedes rather than assists the effect that he desires to produce' (1882a, pp. 105–6).

The problem was exacerbated over time by the periodic outbursts of traditional religious sentiment which (in defiance of the long-term erosion) continued to sweep across America, Britain, France and elsewhere, revivals that tended to help identify freedom with the abolition of slavery, polygamy, intemperance and any other practices which the majority had learned to condemn. Indeed, the notion that Mill's 'text-book' is anti-Christian, or hostile to religious faith as such, still resonates today among some critics.

But Bain is quite incorrect to assert that 'the whole subject' of Christian morality is 'extraneous' to the argument of the *Liberty*. Moreover, Mill (1874) evidently admires the figure of Christ, apart from the question of divinity, and would certainly include the 'golden rule', maxims of good Samaritanship and other reasonable Christian precepts, within a liberal utilitarian 'Religion of Humanity'. Rather than anti-Christian, he is against hypocrisy and blind conformity to customary standards of conduct whose Christian pedigree is open to doubt.

Current status

As already suggested, the early hostility surrounding the *Liberty* hardened over time, leaving us today with an essay whose rhetoric is apparently much admired, at least by liberals, even while its form of reasoning is not taken seriously. Those few who might be considered disciples of Mill's utilitarian liberalism, including Morley, Helen

Taylor, perhaps Bain, Cairnes and Fawcett, and, through Morley, perhaps even Pater, were quickly swamped by a rejuvenated pan-Christian idealism among academics, which, though it was arguably more egalitarian and democratic than its ancestors, largely reflected the evolution of majoritarian customs and practices.[17] The majority's understanding of traditional religious and moral values continued – and continues yet – to be revised as a result of sustained economic growth and the extension of democratic institutions. But the 'one very simple principle' of liberty has never gained acceptance. Indeed, if, as seems doubtful, a new organic period has ever arrived in Western societies to supplant the critical period in which Mill lived, its creed has not been his liberal utilitarianism. At best, we now have some pallid imitation, a somewhat more liberal democratic version of Judeo-Christian ethics or American constitutionalism, which most accept more or less intuitively as providing justification for the general shape of social institutions as they have evolved.

And yet, the eloquence of the 'text-book' still inspires those who recognize the immense value of individual liberty. In our times, such influential scholars as Berlin (1969), Rawls (1971, 1993), Ten (1980, 1995), Hart (1982), Gray (1983, 1989), Berger (1984), Feinberg (1984–8) and Skorupski (1989), for example, have been inspired to propose alternative doctrines that attempt to preserve Mill's liberal spirit, while abandoning his form of reasoning as defective. Even these friendly critics charge him with incoherence, however, or revise the plain meaning of his text, in the course of elaborating whatever form of liberalism strikes them as an adequate substitute for his allegedly flawed utilitarian form.

But any hostility toward a Millian creed implicit in those revisionist accounts pales in comparison to the outright condemnation and disgust expressed by his unfriendly critics, of whom there continue to be many in the recent literature. Thus, Himmelfarb (1974, 1994) derides him as a weak and incoherent figure, pushed and pulled in contradictory directions by others. She seems to think that he was manipulated by Harriet into a deviant brand of radical liberalism, sharply at odds with the classical liberalism to which he otherwise seemed attracted. The radical Mill, spouting nonsense about individual licence, abrasive feminism and socialism, is seen mainly in *On Liberty* and perhaps *The Subjection of Women*. The classical Mill, voicing more or less reasonable support for conventional pieties, family values, private property and free markets, predominates in his other writings. But it is the radical Mill, let loose upon the world by the evil Harriet, who now 'sets the terms of debate' in advanced liberal cultures, with his perverse model of individual licence in matters that are properly of moral concern, and government interference in markets and family activities that are properly left alone by classical liberals.

Hamburger (1991a, 1991b, 1995) accuses him of deliberately misrepresenting his true convictions in the *Liberty*, apparently out of wild political ambition. To preserve the Radicals' electoral appeal during the 1830s, and, when that failed, to foster acceptance of a new utilitarian religion that, despite what he said, really involved subtle forms of coercion against the lower and middle classes, he was prepared to disguise his truly illiberal belief that some utilitarian vanguard of journalists, professors and public intellectuals ought to *impose* its notion of a morally superior type of character on the ignorant and passive majority. The majority, he supposedly thought, displayed a 'miserable individuality' that included, *inter alia*, a commitment to Christianity. But these miserable creatures could be fooled into accepting new forms of coercion, foisted upon them by their betters in the name of liberty. Once the new religion was accepted and utilitarian radicals like himself could gain electoral majorities, suitable laws could be enacted, if necessary, to compel any dissenters to refashion themselves in the preferred mould. Cowling (1990) takes this line to its logical extreme. He charges bluntly that Mill is a moral totalitarian, bent on destroying Christian civilization and replacing it with his barbaric all-encompassing 'Religion of Humanity'.

Contemptuous critiques of this sort are rather jolting, if taken seriously. They surely test any liberal's sense of humour. But they also reveal something about the critic. The critic is either deeply confused about what Mill is saying, or, assuming otherwise, intensely dislikes his liberal doctrine and is prepared to distort and caricature it for partisan purposes. The confusions, at least, can be remedied, by properly attending to the conceptual distinction between purely self-regarding and other conduct, or so I shall suggest. Absolute liberty of opinion and of action in all modes not hurtful to others *is* compatible with the enforcement of reasonable rules of other-regarding conduct, designed to prevent harm to others. Given a reasonable idea of 'harm', these two aspects of Mill's liberalism are harmonious in principle and, indeed, combine to form a powerful doctrine, worthy of careful study. By implication, we ought to abandon any thesis of 'two Mills', or of a strategic Mill seeking to fool people and win political power by hiding the true Mill, or of a totalitarian Mill lurking behind the façade of a champion of liberty.[18]

Suggestions for further reading

For details of the life of Mill, see Michael St J. Packe, *The Life of John Stuart Mill* (London, Secker and Warburg, 1954). A variorum edition of the *Autobiography* is included in John M. Robson and Jack Stillinger, eds, *Collected Works of J.S. Mill* (London and Toronto, Routledge and University of Toronto Press, 1981), Vol. 1, pp. 1–290. A focus on his years in Parliament is provided by Bruce L. Kinzer, Ann P. Robson and John M. Robson, *A Moralist In and Out of Parliament: J.S. Mill at Westminster 1865–68* (Toronto, University of Toronto Press, 1992). (The Governor Eyre affair is treated in Chapter 6, pp. 184–217.)

For further discussion of his father's view of education, see James Mill, 'Education' (1818?), in F.A. Cavenagh, ed., *James and John Stuart Mill on Education* (Westport, Conn., Greenwood Press, 1979), pp. 1–73. On John's relationship with his father, some insights may be gleaned from Alexander Bain, *John Stuart Mill: A Criticism* (London, Longmans, Green, 1882b) and Bain, *James Mill: A Biography* (London, Longmans, Green, 1882a).

On his relationship with Harriet, see F.A. Hayek, *John Stuart Mill and Harriet Taylor* (London, Routledge and Kegan Paul, 1951); and John M. Robson, 'Harriet Taylor and John Stuart Mill: Artist and Scientist', *Queen's Quarterly* 73 (Summer 1966): 167–86.

For perspectives on the social circles in which he moved, see M.L. Clarke, *George Grote: A Biography* (London, Athlone Press, 1962); Francis E. Mineka, *The Dissidence of Dissent: the Monthly Repository 1806–1838* (Chapel Hill, University of North Carolina Press, 1944), esp. Chapters 4–7, relating to W.J. Fox, Eliza Flower,

Robert Browning and others with whom Harriet and John Taylor were associated; Emery Neff, *Carlyle and Mill*, 2nd edn, rev. (New York, Octagon Books, 1964); Fred Kaplan, *Thomas Carlyle: A Biography* (Ithaca, Cornell University Press, 1983); E. Alexander, *Matthew Arnold and John Stuart Mill* (New York, Columbia University Press, 1965); Lotte and Joseph Hamburger, *Troubled Lives: John and Sarah Austin* (Toronto, University of Toronto Press, 1985); Graham Wallas, *The Life of Francis Place, 1771–1854*, 4th edn (London, George Allen and Unwin, 1951); and W. Robbins, *The Newman Brothers: An Essay in Comparative Intellectual Biography* (Cambridge, Mass., Harvard University Press, 1966).

The argument of the *Liberty* is self-contained. But it is usefully read in conjunction with Mill's essay on *Utilitarianism* (1861), especially Chapter 5 ('On the Connexion Between Utility and Justice'). See also his *Three Essays on Religion* (1874), especially 'The Utility of Religion' and 'Theism'. These companions to the 'text-book' are all reprinted in J.M. Robson, gen. ed., *Collected Works* (London and Toronto, Routledge and University of Toronto Press, 1969), Vol. 10, pp. 203–59, 369–489.

Also useful is to compare and contrast Mill's argument to some of those which he cites as similar in nature. Perhaps the most interesting are K. Wilhelm von Humboldt, *The Limits of State Action* (in German, 1851), ed. J.W. Burrow (London, Cambridge University Press, 1969); and Josiah Warren, *Equitable Commerce: A New Development of Principles, as Substitutes for Laws and Governments, for the Harmonious Adjustment and Regulation of the Pecuniary, Intellectual, and Moral Intercourse of Mankind: Proposed as Elements of a New Society* (1846), ed. S.P. Andrews (New York, Fowlers and Wells, 1852). Humboldt's book was first translated by J. Coulthard, as *The Sphere and Duties of Government*, in 1854, about the time Mill began to compose his essay. A quote from the translation serves as the frontispiece to the *Liberty*. Mill says he took the term 'sovereignty of the individual' from 'the Warrenites' (1873, p. 261).

A good selection of the early reviews of the *Liberty* is contained in A. Pyle, ed., *Liberty: Contemporary Responses to John Stuart Mill* (Bristol, Thoemmes Press, 1994).

Part two

The argument of
On Liberty

Chapter 2

Introductory
(Chapter I,
paras 1–16)

Stages of liberty (I.1–5)

Mill introduces his subject as 'the nature and limits of the power which can be legitimately exercised by society over the individual' (I.1, p. 217). That subject, though rarely treated in philosophical terms, 'is so far from being new', he says, 'that, in a certain sense, it has divided mankind, almost from the remotest ages' (ibid.). Even so, in the more advanced societies of his day (as well as our own), 'it presents itself under new conditions, and requires a different and more fundamental treatment' (ibid.). To clarify why the problem needs a novel philosophical treatment under 'new conditions' of large-scale industrial democracy, he identifies four stages of social development.

During the earliest stage, the struggle between liberty and authority was between subjects and rulers 'conceived (except in some of the popular governments of Greece) as in a necessarily antagonistic position to the people whom they ruled' (I.2, p. 217). '[L]iberty

... meant protection against the tyranny of the political rulers', in other words, limitations on the legitimate power of government (ibid.). Political liberty in this sense was secured, at first, 'by obtaining a recognition of certain ... political liberties or rights' which, if infringed by the rulers, justified individual 'resistance, or general rebellion'; and, later, by adding 'constitutional checks' which, by dividing government power and setting one group of rulers against another, helped the community to avoid injustice at the hands of its political leaders (I.2, p. 218).

It is important to see that this doctrine of balanced and limited government (exemplified by Machiavelli's *Discourses* (1531), Contarini's *Commonwealth and Government of Venice* (1543), and Locke's *Second Treatise* (1690)) does not necessarily involve a due regard for individual spontaneity. The doctrine is rather intended to secure the community from political oppression.

At a second stage of social progress, the struggle between liberty and authority was reinterpreted as a battle between a democratic party and other parties for the reins of political power: 'By degrees, this new demand for elective and temporary rulers became the prominent object of the exertions of the popular party, whenever any such party existed; and superseded, to a considerable extent, the previous efforts to limit the power of rulers' (I.3, p. 218). Liberty came to mean not limitation of government power but popular self-rule, if not by the people directly, by means of temporary representatives revocable at the majority's pleasure:

> What was now wanted was, that the rulers should be identified with the people; that their interest and will should be the interest and will of the nation. The nation did not need to be protected against its own will. There was no fear of its tyrannizing over itself.
>
> (ibid.)

Again, this doctrine of popular self-government (exemplified by Rousseau's *Of the Social Contract* (1762) or James Mill's essay on *Government* (1821)) does not necessarily involve any due respect for individual spontaneity. The doctrine is intended to make government reflect the will of the majority, on the assumption that 'the people have no need to limit their power over themselves' (I.4, p. 219).

At a third stage, entered first by the United States, it was recognized that the need to limit government power loses none of its importance when the government is controlled by the popular majority:

> [Popular] 'self-government' . . . is not the government of each by himself, but of each by all the rest. The will of the people, moreover, practically means the will of the most numerous or the most active *part* of the people; the majority, or those who succeed in making themselves accepted as the majority; the people, consequently, *may* desire to oppress a part of their number . . . The limitation, therefore, of the power of government over individuals loses none of its importance when the holders of power are regularly accountable to the community, that is, to the strongest party therein.
>
> (ibid., emphasis original)

The struggle for liberty became a struggle for limited democratic government, in which the rulers are accountable to the majority yet at the same time legitimate government power is limited by constitutional checks and a bill of fundamental political rights. Liberty now meant popular self-rule within certain fundamental legal limits designed to secure minorities against injustice by the popular majority and its elected representatives.[1]

But this doctrine still does not recognize the rightful liberty of the individual, in Mill's view. It is merely a combination of the two earlier doctrines of political liberty, neither of which manifests a due regard for individual spontaneity. The laudable purpose of the third doctrine is to make government accountable to the deliberate sense of the community, on the understanding that this 'deliberate sense' entails limitations on legitimate political power. In short, this kind of freedom demands that the *government* should limit its *legal* authority so as not to infringe on certain rights or liberties due equally to all citizens. But no limitations are placed in principle on the authority of popular *opinion* to enforce its standards of conduct. Although the government must not enact laws which violate the individual's rights to free speech and religious liberty, for example, the majority can interfere with those rights in other ways, by stigmatizing certain forms of speech and religious expression as unacceptable.[2]

Mill is concerned about a fourth stage of social development in which, as a result of technological improvements in mass transportation and communications, the popular majority has vastly expanded power to ensure, by means other than legal punishment, that all conform to its opinions and customs. As he emphasizes in his review of Tocqueville's *Democracy in America*, he fears the growing power of the 'middle class' to stamp its commercial type of character upon the rest of society because he associates any unduly homogeneous community with moral and cultural (and thus, eventually, material) stagnation and decline: 'the most serious danger to the future prospects of mankind is in the unbalanced influence of the commercial spirit' (1840b, p. 198; see also III.16–19, pp. 272–5). Indeed, he argues that Tocqueville's study properly documents the cultural and moral influences not of social equality but of a preponderant commercial class, influences which for the most part are also 'in full operation in aristocratic England' (1840b, p. 196).[3]

In any case, the struggle for liberty takes on a new dimension at this fourth stage. The individual requires protection not merely from government authority but also from increasingly oppressive popular opinion (mainly commercial in spirit) that achieves its meddlesome aims without relying on legislation or other government commands at all:

> Protection, therefore, against the tyranny of the magistrate is not enough: there needs protection also against the tyranny of the prevailing opinion and feeling; against the tendency of society to impose, by means other than civil penalties, its own ideas and practices as rules of conduct on those who dissent from them; to fetter the development, and, if possible, prevent the formation, of any individuality not in harmony with its ways, and compel all characters to fashion themselves upon the model of its own. There is a limit to the legitimate interference of collective opinion with individual independence: and to find that limit, and maintain it against encroachment, is as indispensable to a good condition of human affairs, as protection against political despotism.

(I.5, p. 220)

He concedes that most people by now would accept the general proposition that there is some limit to legitimate coercion – whether in the form of legal penalties or social stigma. Yet 'the practical question, where to place the limit – how to make the fitting adjustment between individual independence and social control – is a subject on which nearly everything remains to be done' (I.6, p. 220).

Absence of a general principle (I.6–8)

In his view, there is no recognized general rule or principle by which the legitimacy or illegitimacy of coercion can be consistently tested across different social contexts – ignoring 'backward states of society in which the race itself may be considered as in its nonage' (I.10, p. 224). Rather, men have usually decided the question by 'a mere appeal to a similar preference felt by other people' (I.6, p. 221). Little concern has been shown for an impartial principle, based on a rational assessment of the observed consequences of human behaviour. Rather, a remarkable variety of answers has been more or less arbitrarily dictated by social custom, and the limit placed on coercion by one society 'is a wonder to another':

> All that makes existence valuable to any one, depends on the enforcement of restraints upon the actions of other people. Some rules of conduct, therefore, must be imposed, by law in the first place, and by opinion on many things which are not fit subjects for the operation of law. What these rules should be, is the principal question in human affairs; but if we except a few of the most obvious cases, it is one of those which least progress has been made in resolving. No two ages, and scarcely any two countries, have decided it alike; and the decision of one age or country is a wonder to another. Yet the people of any given age and country no more suspect any difficulty in it, than if it were a subject on which mankind had always been agreed. The rules which obtain among themselves appear to them to be self-evident and self-justifying. This all but universal illusion is one of the examples of the magical influence of custom.
>
> (I.6, p. 220)

The magical influence of custom is 'all the more complete' in the present instance because most people are in the habit of thinking that existing rules of conduct do not require to be impartially justified by reason: 'People are accustomed to believe, and have been encouraged in the belief by some who aspire to the character of philosophers, that their feelings, on subjects of this nature, are better than reasons, and render reasons unnecessary' (ibid.).

Custom itself, in other words, has generally implanted 'the feeling in each person's mind that everybody should be required to act as he, and those with whom he sympathizes, would like them to act', without any further need for reasons (I.6, p. 221). Shared likings and dislikings, emanating from various sources (class interest, for example, or religious conviction), have thus been the usual standard of judgment, often glorified as common sense or moral sense. 'The likings and dislikings of society, or of some powerful portion of it, are thus the main thing which has practically determined the rules laid down for general observance, under the penalties of law or opinion' (I.7, p. 222).

Even intellectual leaders and social reformers have generally failed to recognize a general principle by which the propriety or impropriety of freedom from coercion can be tested: 'They have occupied themselves rather in inquiring what things society ought to like or dislike, than in questioning whether its likings or dislikings should be a law to individuals' (ibid.). These elites have not sought to place a limit in principle on society's authority to enforce, by means of social stigma or civil penalties, compliance with its rules of conduct. Rather, they have tried merely to rechannel that authority in directions of which they approved, by 'endeavouring to alter the feelings of mankind on the particular points on which they themselves were heretical' (ibid.)

The exceptional case of religious belief (I.7)

The only exceptional case, where 'the higher ground has been taken on principle and maintained with consistency', is that of religious belief: 'The great writers to whom the world owes what religious liberty it possesses, have mostly asserted freedom of conscience as an *indefeasible* right, and denied *absolutely* that a human being is accountable to others for his religious belief' (ibid., emphasis added). Among these great writers, he might have added, are Jefferson and Madison, who went well beyond Locke's doctrine of toleration to defend the full and free exercise of religion, first in the context of Virginia and later in the context of the United States.[4]

Madison claims, for example, that complete liberty of conscience is an 'unalienable' right because it is 'a duty towards the Creator': 'It is the duty of every man to render to the Creator such homage and such only as he believes to be acceptable to him' (1973, p. 299). Moreover, this unalienable right should never be subject to interference by law and opinion:

> This duty is precedent, both in order of time and in degree of obligation, to the claims of Civil Society ... We maintain therefore that in matters of Religion, no man's right is abridged by the institution of Civil Society and that Religion is *wholly* exempt from its cognizance.
>
> (ibid., emphasis added)

Thus, 'freedom of conscience' is 'a *natural and absolute right*' (Madison, in Adair, 1945, p. 199, emphasis original). In effect, the Creator, not man, draws the line that separates the individual's life into a private sphere of absolute religious liberty, and a public sphere to which social authority is properly confined.

Such a principle of religious liberty initially took root, Mill makes clear, when each church or sect was unable to win 'a complete victory' over its multiple competitors: 'minorities, seeing that they had no chance of becoming majorities, were under the necessity of pleading to those whom they could not convert, for permission to differ' (I.7, p. 222). Even so, the principle emerged victorious 'hardly anywhere' until 'religious indifference ... added its weight to the scale' (ibid.). By implication, any victory of this sort might prove to be short-lived. The right of the individual to religious liberty remains precarious, and might well crumble if a revival of religious enthusiasm sweeps over the majority: 'Wherever the sentiment of the majority is still genuine and intense, it is found to have abated little of its claim to be obeyed' (ibid.). There are ample signs in the essay that he takes seriously the possibility of such revivals of religious intolerance, and even fears the advent of despotic secular religions of the sort we now usually classify as 'totalitarianism'.

'One very simple principle' (I.9–10)

Excepting the case of religious belief, the lack of any general principle of liberty has resulted in frequent serious mistakes on both sides of the question. People's naked preferences are as often wrong about the impropriety of coercion, he suggests, as they are about its propriety (I.8, pp. 222–3; see also V.15, pp. 304–5). The purpose of his essay is to deal with the problem, by supplying the missing principle of liberty:

> The object of this essay is to assert one very simple principle, as entitled to govern *absolutely* the dealings of society with the individual in the way of compulsion and control, whether the means used be physical force in the form of legal penalties, or the moral coercion of public opinion. That principle is, that ... the only purpose for which power can be rightfully exercised over any member of a civilized community, against his will, is to prevent harm to others. His own good, either physical or moral, is not a sufficient warrant.
>
> (I.9, p. 223, emphasis added)

Thus, the principle states a necessary condition for legitimate use of coercion against any individual: his liberty of action should be restrained by law or opinion only if his action is reasonably expected to harm other persons. Put in other words, the principle states a sufficient condition for legitimate protection of individual liberty: the individual ought to be free from all forms of coercion if his action does not harm others. 'In the part [of his conduct] which merely concerns himself, his independence is, of right, *absolute*' (I.9, p. 224, emphasis added).

Mill expresses the caveat that his principle is meant to apply only to human beings capable of 'spontaneous progress', that is, self-development guided by their own judgment and inclinations: 'Liberty, as a principle, has no application to any state of things anterior to the time when mankind have become capable of being improved by free and equal discussion' (I.10, p. 224). Anyone who has not attained some minimal capacity for self-improvement should not be granted liberty, even if his conduct is harmless to others. Others must substitute their judgment and inclinations for his, to help him develop his capacities, or at least protect him from self-harm as well as injury at the hands of others. Thus, the liberty principle does not apply to 'children', 'young persons below the age which the law may fix as that of manhood or womanhood', 'those [including the mentally retarded and the insane] who are still in a state to require being taken care of by others' or 'barbarians' in 'backward states of society' (ibid.). But for most adults of civilized states of society (including our own), 'compulsion, either in the direct form or in that of pains and penalties for non-compliance, is no longer admissible as a means to their own good, and justifiable only for the security of others' (ibid.).

Utilitarian form of argument (I.11–12)

In addition to its apparent novelty, putative simplicity and restriction to adults capable of self-improvement, Mill points to several other distinctive features of the liberty principle. It is a utilitarian principle, for example, rather than a principle of 'abstract right' (I.11, p. 224). Its general limit on legitimate coercion is ultimately justified by general utility, he insists, 'but it must be utility in the largest sense, grounded on the permanent interests of man as a progressive being' (ibid.).

General utility thus understood authorizes social control over actions or inactions which are harmful to others, even if good reasons often exist for not bothering to exert the control. In particular, man's permanent interest in 'self-protection' or 'security' authorizes the establishment of impartial social rules designed to minimize if not prevent harm to others. Yet there are often good reasons for society not to enforce a rule:

> either because it is a kind of case in which [the individual] is
> on the whole likely to act better, when left to his own discretion, than when controlled . . . or because the attempt to exercise

control would produce other evils, greater than those which it would prevent.

(I.11, p. 225)

In these cases, where 'special expediencies' give society good reasons not to coerce the individual by law or opinion, 'the conscience of the agent himself should step into the vacant judgment seat, and protect those interests of others which have no external protection' (ibid.). The agent should enforce internally, as his own dictates of conscience, impartial rules which he thinks are generally expedient for all to follow in circumstances like his.

Apart from this, general utility in the largest sense also rules out social control altogether over actions or inactions which are harmless to other people, even if the others in question intensely dislike the relevant conduct. More specifically, man's permanent interest in 'self-development' or 'individuality' authorizes the absolute protection, by right, of individual liberty with respect to such actions. This leads us to a related feature of the liberty principle, what might be termed its practical bite.

Mill insists that the principle has bite because there really does exist conduct which is reasonably viewed as harmless to other persons:

> [T]here is a sphere of action . . . comprehending all that portion of a person's life and conduct which affects only himself, or if it also affects others, only with their free, voluntary, and unde-ceived consent and participation. When I say only himself, I mean directly, and in the first instance: for whatever affects himself may affect others through himself.

(I.12, p. 225)

Such conduct, which he refers to as 'private' or 'self-regarding' (I.14, p. 226), is harmless to others, apparently, because others are not directly 'affected' by it against their wishes. Without offering further clarification, he says merely that: 'This, then, is the appropriate region of human liberty' (I.12, p. 225). In short, freedom from coercion ought to be guaranteed, by right, for self-regarding actions and inactions.

The self-regarding region, he says, may be described as follows:

It comprises, first, the inward domain of consciousness; demanding liberty of conscience, in the most comprehensive sense; liberty of thought and feeling; *absolute* freedom of opinion and sentiment on all subjects, practical or speculative, scientific, moral, or theological. The liberty of expressing and publishing opinions may seem to fall under a different principle, since it belongs to that part of the conduct of an individual which concerns other people; but, being almost of as much importance as the liberty of thought itself, and resting in great part on the same reasons, is practically inseparable from it. Secondly, the principle requires liberty of tastes and pursuits; of framing the plan of our life to suit our own character; of *doing as we like*, subject to such consequences as may follow: without impediment from our fellow-creatures, so long as what we do does not harm them, even though they should think our conduct foolish, perverse, or wrong. Thirdly, from this liberty of each individual, follows the liberty, within the same limits, of combination among individuals; freedom to unite, for any purpose not involving harm to others: the persons combining being supposed to be of full age, and not forced or deceived.

(I.12, pp. 225–6, emphasis added)

Noteworthy even at this preliminary stage is his caveat that freedom of expression, though it really involves conduct which 'concerns others' (since publication of an opinion can harm another's reputation, for example, or mislead the public), is 'practically inseparable' from liberty of thought itself, and 'almost' as important. This may seem puzzling or worse. But he has already given us some hint of how it should be read.

Strictly speaking, expression is legitimately subject to social control, he seems to be saying, since it is conduct which can harm others. Even so, society should 'almost' never bother to exercise its control because laissez-faire is virtually always generally expedient here. In particular, the benefits of self-development associated with freedom 'almost' always outweigh the harms to others which can be prevented by regulation of expression. That utilitarian argument is similar in form to the one used to justify absolute freedom of thought itself. There is some difference because thought, unlike expression, *never* harms others, and thus is truly self-regarding. Social regulation of thought should never even be considered, whereas regulation of expression may be justified in special situations. Nevertheless, the reasons for granting liberty are 'in great part . . . the same' in the two sorts of cases, and allow us to treat expression in 'almost' all instances *as if* it were self-regarding. Moreover, as we will see, Mill has strategic reasons for assimilating expression to thought in this way. He wants to exploit the fact that liberties of conscience, of speech and of the press are already recognized to a large extent in advanced societies, so as to facilitate acceptance of his more general liberty principle.

Absolute priority of self-regarding liberty (I.7,10,13)

Yet another key feature of the liberty principle, which Mill points to in introducing it, is the *absolute* priority it gives to individual liberty over other moral or social considerations within self-regarding limits. As I have already tried to emphasize, he says repeatedly that the individual's liberty – in the sense of thinking and doing as he pleases, without fear of any coercive form of interference, legal or moral – is, by right, *absolute* with respect to self-regarding matters of no concern to others (because harmless to them). The agent's right to liberty can never be defeated by other considerations, if he is choosing among self-regarding actions. This feature of the liberty principle, whereby its prescription of liberty is indefeasible within the self-regarding region, gives it a foundational quality, a fundamental ethical status akin to that of the principle of utility from which, Mill insists, it directly flows.

This foundational quality of the liberty principle harkens back to a similar quality in the extraordinary principle of religious freedom, whose defenders, he claims, 'asserted freedom of conscience as an *indefeasible* right, and denied *absolutely* that a human being is accountable to others for his religious belief' (I.7, p. 222, emphasis added). Their common foundational character suggests that he sees his principle as a generalization of the religious liberty maxim already recognized by the US Constitution when he wrote. Without arguing the point here, there is evidence for such a view. In his *Notes on the State of Virginia*, for example, Jefferson does argue that absolute freedom should be extended to religion insofar as one person's convictions and practices do not harm other people:

> The legitimate powers of government extend to such acts only as are injurious to others. But it does me no injury for my neighbour to say there are twenty gods, or no god. It neither picks my pocket nor breaks my leg.
>
> (1982, p. 159)

Consistently with this, Madison says that the individual is entitled to the full and free exercise of his religion unless, under the guise of religion, he acts so as to disturb the peace or safety of society.

The fundamental status of Mill's liberty principle also implies that it should be accepted as a basic maxim by *every* civil society, whatever that society's cultural and moral circumstances: 'No society in which these liberties [in self-regarding matters] are not, on the whole, respected, is free, whatever may be its form of government; and none is completely free in which they do not exist absolute and unqualified' (I.13, p. 226). Thus, even if society advances toward intellectual and moral perfection, the liberty principle remains applicable. But its universal application to civil societies is possible only if the self-regarding sphere can be defined in a way that remains reasonable from the perspective of any civil society's cultural and moral norms. Otherwise, those norms may refuse to admit the feasibility of any actions that do not harm others. More specifically, harm to others, in the sense that others are directly affected against their wishes, must be recognizable by any human being who is capable of self-improvement, whatever his particular moral and cultural outlook. At the same time, all must recognize that some conduct does not give rise to harm in that sense.

What the liberty principle is not

The foregoing survey of its distinctive features allows us to emphasize what Mill's liberty principle is *not*, namely, a familiar liberal principle of equal basic rights or liberties, of the sort defended by

Rawls (1971, 1993), Dworkin (1977) or Harsanyi (1982, 1992). Certainly, all liberals (including Mill) will defend some such familiar principle, even if the nature of the rights defended varies with the defence under consideration. Classical liberals may defend private property rights and rights of contract, for example, as well as the rights enumerated in the US Bill of Rights. New liberals may deprecate private property and assign more importance to welfare rights, rights to a suitably participatory democratic political system, rights to clean air and a safe working environment, rights to non-discrimination on the basis of race, sex, ethnic background, age and so on. Myriad lists of rights and relative priorities are conceivable.

Mill is not arguing in his essay for rights to vote, own property, sell goods, receive subsistence from the state, be free from undue discrimination and the like. He surely defends such rights in some of his other writings. But his text-book is a defence of a special sort of equal basic rights, to wit, rights to liberty – in the sense of licence – of thought and of action in all modes not hurtful to others. It is a defence, in short, of the individual's right to have absolute control of what goes on within his self-regarding sphere. Such a defence is uncommon even within liberalism. Indeed, it is so rare that it makes his utilitarian liberalism distinct within the liberal family.

The growing danger of social repression (I.14–15)

After outlining his doctrine, Mill proposes to focus attention on the one division of his subject where the liberty principle is, 'to a certain point, recognized by the current opinions', namely, 'liberty of thought [including, of course, religious thought]: from which it is impossible to separate the cognate liberty of speaking and writing' (I.16, p. 227). The 'grounds' on which these liberties rest, 'when rightly understood, are of much wider application' (ibid.).

Before going on to clarify those grounds, however, he warns us that 'the general tendency of existing opinion and practice' is to meddle far more deeply into self-regarding matters (I.14, p. 226). The use of the law for this unduly meddlesome purpose has perhaps diminished relative to earlier ages, he admits, largely because of 'the greater size of political communities, and above all, the separation between spiritual and temporal authority' (ibid.). But the use of social stigma has not diminished: '[T]he engines of moral repression have been wielded more strenuously against divergence from the reigning opinion in self-regarding, than even in social matters' (ibid.). The main culprit seems to be traditional organized religion:

> [R]eligion [is] the most powerful of the elements which have entered into the formation of moral feeling, having almost always been governed either by the ambition of a hierarchy, seeking control over every department of human conduct, or by the spirit of Puritanism.
>
> (I.14, pp. 226–7)

Indeed, the liberties of thought and expression themselves might even be overwhelmed from this quarter in the future, a salient theme of the next chapter.

Although he evidently fears that religion will continue to spur tyrannical majority opinion and feeling, he also seems concerned about the rise of totalitarian social systems (such as that proposed by Auguste Comte) which, while strongly opposed to Christianity and other 'religions of the past', seek to establish 'a despotism of society over the individual, surpassing anything contemplated in the political ideal of the most rigid disciplinarian among the ancient philosophers' (I.14, p. 227; see also 1873, pp. 219–21). The general danger is that a new organic period will arrive, of a remarkably illiberal nature, to replace the critical period that was ongoing for the moment. He concludes his introduction with a dire prediction that all too soon proved prophetic in the twentieth century:

> The disposition of mankind, whether as rulers or as fellow-citizens, to impose their own opinions and inclinations as a rule of conduct on others, is ... hardly ever kept under restraint by anything but want of power; and as the power is not declining, but growing, unless a strong barrier of moral conviction can be raised against the mischief, we must expect, in the present circumstances of the world, to see it increase.
>
> (I.15, p. 227)

Suggestions for further reading

It makes good sense at this stage to study some literature relating to the history of the principle of religious liberty, given that Mill's principle appears to be a generalization of the religious principle. On the American argument for the sovereignty of the individual with respect to religious opinions and practices in all modes not harmful to others, see James Madison, 'Memorial and Remonstrance against Religious Assessments' (1785), in R. Rutland *et al.*, eds, *The Papers of James Madison*, (Chicago and London, University of Chicago Press, 1973), Vol. 8, pp. 295–306; and Thomas Jefferson, *Notes on the State of Virginia* (1785), ed. W. Peden (New York, Norton, 1982), Query XVII on 'Religion', pp. 157–61.

For further discussion of the historical context and consequences of the Virginia Statute for Religious Freedom, see T.E. Buckley, S.J., *Church and State in Revolutionary Virginia, 1776–1787* (Charlottesville, University Press of Virginia, 1977); and Merrill D. Peterson and Robert C. Vaughan, eds, *The Virginia Statute for Religious Freedom: Its Evolution and Consequences in American History* (Cambridge, Cambridge University Press, 1988).

Chapter 3

Of the liberty of thought and discussion (Chapter II, paras 1–44)

The grounds of some familiar liberties (II.1)

Mill thinks it convenient to begin with 'a thorough consideration' of the liberties of thought and discussion, partly because most people in advanced countries already take for granted that these freedoms are rightful: 'these liberties, to some considerable amount, form part of the political morality of all countries which profess religious toleration and free institutions' (I.16, p. 227). In England, for example, 'there is not . . . any intolerance of differences of opinion' on most of 'the great practical concerns of life', including politics and culture (II.36, p. 254).

Not so common is a proper understanding of the moral justification for these familiar liberties. Moreover, there *is* deep and growing intolerance of diversity of opinion on at least one great practical concern, he suggests, namely, principles of morality. An underlying theme is the grave danger to liberty of thought and discussion lurking in the increasingly popular claim that

'Christian morality . . . is the whole truth on that subject' (II.37, p. 254). Thus, he complains that the 'narrow' and 'one-sided' 'theological morality' which now passes for Christianity 'is becoming a grave practical evil' (II.38, p. 256). A 'revival of religion [of the sort under way in both Europe and America as he wrote] is always, in narrow and uncultivated minds, at least as much the revival of bigotry' (II.19, p. 240).

The central point of the chapter is that the considerable protection already extended to freedom of thought and discussion ought to be extended further, until it is, by right, *absolute* for all thought and 'almost' all expression. All thought is self-regarding, he makes clear, and virtually all expression is reasonably classified as self-regarding as well. In special circumstances, however, the expression of an opinion cannot be treated as self-regarding because it has 'at least a probable connexion' to an act which is seriously harmful to others. In those special cases, where expression is reasonably taken out of the self-regarding sphere, there is no moral right to liberty. Thus, he insists that 'there ought to exist the fullest liberty of professing and discussing, as a matter of ethical conviction, any doctrine, however immoral it may be considered' (II.1, p. 228, note), except in the relatively few situations where such expression is 'a positive instigation to some mischievous act' that is seriously harmful to others (III.1, p. 260).

It is important to keep in mind that Mill excludes some expression from the self-regarding sanctuary, so that his liberty principle does not pretend to grant absolute protection to *all* expression. With that caveat, his prescription of absolute liberty for what may be termed 'self-regarding expression' *is* compatible with his claim that society has legitimate authority to control expression in the special cases. Moreover, if 'almost' all expression is reasonably classed as harmless to others, his emphasis on liberty to the neglect of authority in this context is understandable, even though it may mislead the careless reader into a belief that an absolute right to liberty with respect to *all* expression of opinion is being defended. His liberty doctrine is radical enough, without going to that extreme.

Suppressing the caveat for ease of exposition, Mill denies 'the right of the people' to exert any power of coercion, by law or stigma, against the expression of opinion: 'The power itself is illegitimate' (II.1, p. 229). He 'altogether condemn[s]' even a reference to 'the immorality and impiety of an opinion' as such (II.11, p. 234). In support of his contention that the individual ought to enjoy absolute freedom from coercion, he argues that 'silencing the expression of an opinion is . . . a peculiar evil', namely, 'robbing the human race' of truth or, of 'what is almost as great a benefit, the clearer perception and livelier impression of truth' (II.1, p. 229). His argument provides, among much else, insights into the nature of his utilitarianism.

The harm of silencing an opinion which may be true (II.3–20)

The first step is to consider the peculiar evil of silencing an opinion which 'may possibly be true' (II.3, p. 229).

The assumption of infallibility (II.3–11)

Part of the problem is that the silencers make an unwarranted assumption of their own infallibility: 'All silencing of discussion is an assumption of infallibility' (ibid.). They not only deny the truth of the opinion for themselves; they also presume to know for certain that the opinion is false, thereby deciding the question for everyone else. But nobody can really have such absolute certainty in complex moral issues. By acting as if he had it, a silencer merely reveals his desire to impose his judgment on others, without letting them make up their own minds. That sort of undue moral coercion is what is *meant* by the assumption of infallibility:

> [I]t is not the feeling sure of a doctrine (be it what it may) which I call an assumption of infallibility. It is the undertaking to decide that question *for others*, without allowing them to hear what can be said on the contrary side.
>
> (II.11, p. 234, emphasis original)

It might be objected that 'there is no greater assumption of infallibility in forbidding the propagation of error, than in any other thing which is done by public authority on its own judgment and responsibility' (II.5, p. 230). Granted that all men are fallible, says the objector, the majority ought still to have the power to impose their 'conscientious convictions' on others when 'quite sure of being right' (ibid.). The power might sometimes be mistakenly exercised, resulting in the suppression of truth. Yet 'governments and nations have made mistakes in other things, which are not denied to be fit subjects for the exercise of authority' (II.5, p. 231). Bad taxes and unjust wars do not justify the denial of authority to lay taxes or make war. Similarly, occasional suppression of truth does not justify the denial of authority to 'forbid bad men to pervert society by the propagation of opinions which we regard as false and pernicious' (ibid.).

That objection, often made even by utilitarians, is treated seriously by Mill, as the very argument of his chapter suggests is appropriate. It leads him to reconsider the evil of silencing an opinion which might be true, when the silencer admits he lacks absolute certainty of the truth. His rejoinder is that silencing an opinion is inconsistent with that admission of fallibility: '[I]t is *not the feeling sure* of a doctrine (be it what it may) which I call an assumption of infallibility. It is *the undertaking to decide* that question *for others*, without allowing them to hear what can be said on the contrary side' (II.11, p. 234, emphasis added). Given fallibility, absolute liberty of thought and discussion is the only way in which warranted belief (as opposed to absolute certainty) can be acquired:

> Complete liberty of contradicting and disproving our opinion, is the very condition which justifies us in assuming its truth for purposes of action; and on no other terms can a being with human faculties have any rational assurance of being right.
>
> (II.6, p. 231)

Complete liberty is the *very test* of such truth as humans are capable of acquiring:

> The beliefs which we have most warrant for, have no safeguard to rest on, but a standing invitation to the whole world to prove them unfounded ... This is the amount of certainty attainable by a fallible being, and this is the sole way of attaining it.
>
> (II.8, p. 232)

Free and open discussion is essential so that fallible beings can rectify their mistakes: 'There must be discussion, to show how experience is to be interpreted' (II.7, p. 231).

Truth versus utility (II.10)

Mill also rejects any sharp distinction between truth and utility: 'In the opinion, not of bad men, but of the best men, no belief which is contrary to truth can be really useful' (II.10, pp. 233–4). Another way to put this is to say that utilitarianism in its best form will respect warranted belief and the liberty essential to it. Indeed, complete liberty of thought and discussion of alternative conceptions of utility is the test of a warranted conception of utility itself. As he makes clear toward the end of the chapter, he is urging us to recognize 'the necessity to the mental well-being of mankind (on which all their other well-being depends) of freedom of opinion, and freedom of the expression of opinion' (II.40, pp. 257–8).

The mischief illustrated and emphasized (II.11–17)

To illustrate the 'mischief' of silencing an opinion which might be true, Mill also identifies some 'instances memorable in history' when legal coercion has been used to suppress noble opinions widely regarded at the time as impious and immoral attacks on received doctrines of religion and morality. He points in particular to the condemnation of Socrates, the crucifixion of Christ, and the persecution of Christianity by the otherwise enlightened and impartial (even proto-Christian) Emperor Marcus Aurelius (II.12–14, pp. 235–7).[1]

Evidently, 'ages are no more infallible than individuals' (II.4, p. 230). Moreover, once-persecuted opinions have survived in one form or another to become the received doctrines of a later age, in which they are, 'as if in mockery', invoked to justify another round of persecution of dissenting opinions (II.11, p. 235). Under the circumstances, the people of any age (including our own) should not 'flatter' themselves that they can know when silencing an opinion is warranted or useful.

Nor should they indulge themselves in the 'pleasant falsehood' (associated with Samuel Johnson) that 'truth always triumphs over persecution', with the implication that coercion is justified because it only works against error anyway (II.17, p. 238). Coercion is as effective at silencing warranted opinions as unwarranted ones: 'Men are not more zealous for truth than they often are for error, and a sufficient application of legal or even of social penalties will generally succeed in stopping the propagation of either [at least for a time]' (II.17, pp. 238–9).

Lingering religious persecution (II.18–20)

Before going on to the second step of his argument in this chapter, Mill returns to his underlying theme of the serious and rising intolerance of diversity of religious and moral opinion in advanced societies. In contemporary England, he says, the silencing of opinions as impious and immoral is highly effective, even though coercion is usually in the form of stigma rather than legal punishment: 'It is the stigma which is really effective' (II.19, p. 241). That stigma results in 'a general atmosphere of mental slavery', an oppressive state of intellectual peace in which 'there is a tacit convention that [religious and moral] principles are not to be disputed' (II.20, p. 243). Many of even the best minds are too intimidated to engage in a 'fair and thorough discussion of heretical opinions', resulting in a false uniformity, an ill-considered conformity to conventional ideas (II.20, p. 242).

He mentions that there have been only three quite brief moments within the ongoing critical period stemming from the Reformation, when liberty of thought and discussion were encouraged and burst forth. The impulses given to self-development at these moments account for the relatively advanced state of contemporary European societies, he suggests. But it seems pretty clear that 'all three impulses are well nigh spent' (II.20, p. 243). No further social progress can be expected 'until we again assert our mental freedom' (ibid.).

The harm of silencing even a false opinion (II.21–33)

The second step of Mill's argument is to consider the 'peculiar evil' of silencing an opinion which, for the sake of argument, may be supposed entirely false.

Dead dogma versus living truth (II.21–3)

The problem now is that the silencers rob even themselves of the only warrant a fallible being can have of the truth: 'however true [the received opinion] may be, if it is not fully, frequently, and fearlessly discussed, it will be held as a dead dogma, not a living truth' (II.21, p. 243). Unless he can hear and answer objections to it, a person does not have any knowledge of the grounds of the true belief. Authority, as opposed to evidence, determines his judgment. He accepts the true opinion blindly, 'as a prejudice, a belief independent of, and proof against, argument' (II.22, p. 244). But 'this is not the way in which truth ought to held by a rational being ... Truth, thus held, is but one superstition the more, accidentally clinging to the words which enunciate a truth' (ibid.).

Someone might object that a person can be '*taught* the grounds' of a true opinion, without ever hearing what can be said on the other side (II.23, p. 244). The objection is decisive in the case of mathematical truths, Mill admits, where proof of a theorem negates the possibility of a reasonable difference of opinion. But on more complex subjects, including morals and religion, 'the truth depends on a balance to be struck between [at least] two sets of conflicting reasons', where the act of balancing consists in large measure of 'dispelling the appearances which favour some opinion' other than a warranted one (II.23, pp. 244–5). To carry out the balancing, it is imperative to hear and, where possible, refute what can be said by persons 'in earnest' on the different sides of the argument, so that one can identify a warranted opinion. Fully carried out, he implies, this process will distil the truth, that is, a belief warranted by the available evidence.

Mill is not content with the rational 'suspension of judgment' required when one is 'equally unable to refute the reasons' on different sides of a conflict (II.23, p. 245). Rather, he insists that 'those who have attended equally and impartially' to the different sides, will be able to gather together and reconcile the various parts of the truth that remain unrefuted. Thus, he speaks of the capacity of 'a completely informed mind' to acquire 'that part of the truth which turns the scale, and decides the judgment' (ibid.). But one can become completely informed about the available evidence only by throwing oneself 'equally and impartially' into the different mental positions of the combatants to hear and, where possible, refute their reasons.

> So essential is this discipline to a real understanding of moral and human subjects, that if opponents of all important truths do not exist, it is indispensable to imagine them, and supply them with the strongest arguments which the most skilful devil's advocate can conjure up.
>
> (ibid.)

A utilitarian elite? (II.24–6)

Even if this process of free thought and discussion is accepted as the sole way in which truth can be acquired by a rational being, however, someone might go on to object that it is only necessary for some instructed elite, rather than 'mankind in general', to go through the process (II.24, p. 246). Conceding for the sake of argument that there is nothing to be said against such a division of society into a rational elite and non-rational mass, that objection still does not touch the claim that complete liberty of thought and expression is essential for the elite:

> If not the public, at least the philosophers and theologians who are to resolve the difficulties, must make themselves familiar with those difficulties in their most puzzling form; and this cannot be be accomplished until they are freely stated, and placed in the most advantageous light which they admit of.
>
> (II.25, p. 246)

But there is much to be said against the relevant social hierarchy. If forced to adopt warranted opinions merely on the authority of the elite, the public will be left ignorant not only of the grounds of the truth but also, eventually, of its very meaning: 'not only the grounds of the opinion are forgotten in the absence of discussion, but too often the meaning of the opinion itself' (II.26, p. 247). Free discussion is in effect mental *exercise*, the absence of which causes the powers of the mind to atrophy, until at last the person cannot really grasp the truth behind the words:

The words which convey it, cease to suggest ideas, or suggest only a small portion of those they were originally employed to communicate. Instead of a vivid conception and a living belief, there remain only a few phrases retained by rote; or, if any part, the shell and husk only of the meaning is retained, the finer essence being lost.

(ibid.)

Lurking in the background is Mill's concern that, unless mental exercise of this sort is widespread, neither competent government nor tolerant public opinion can be expected as the balance of power shifts toward the working-class majority. Without widespread free discussion, democracy is likely to be incompetent and oppressive, as words and ideas lose their significance. At the same time, an ignorant majority is easily manipulated and misled by false prophets and leaders, whose ability to flatter and pander to the crowds negates any attempt by instructed minorities to offer criticism.

Hierarchy and dogma (II.27, 30)

Absence of free discussion facilitates the emergence of 'dead dogma', perhaps actively propagated by some influential minority, charged with the care and study of its ideas and maxims. Such a creed is received 'passively' by most people: it 'remains as it were outside the mind, incrusting and petrifying it against all other influences addressed to the higher parts of our nature' (II.27, p. 248). Thus, organic periods, it seems, have typically involved a settled social hierarchy and dogma.

Mill insists that the tendency of living beliefs to degenerate into dead dogma through absence of free discussion, is 'illustrated in the experience of almost all ethical doctrines and religious creeds' (II.27, p. 247). They are 'full of meaning and vitality' to their originators and expounders who struggle to defend them against their critics, yet they lose their animating force as controversy dies, until, eventually, they take their place as dead dogma, 'if not as a received opinion, as one of the admitted sects or divisions of opinion' which excite little interest and are no longer really understood (II.27, pp. 247–8).

The example of Christianity again (II.28–30)

Such is the experience of Christianity itself, he remarks. The New Testament was 'assuredly' full of meaning and vitality to 'the early Christians', whose conduct and character largely reflected its principles during their struggle to establish their doctrine as the received 'religion of the Roman empire' (II.29, p. 249). But what passes for Christianity in modern Europe or America is something much different. Those who are called Christians now, he points out, do not really believe the doctrine of the New Testament 'in the sense of that living belief which regulates conduct' (II.28, p. 249). It is rare to see anybody give away their wealth to become one of the 'blessed', for example, or to observe people loving their neighbours as themselves (a suspiciously communistic outlook). Rather, most so-called Christians believe and act upon the rules of the true Christian doctrine just up to the point at which it is *customary* at the moment to do so. 'They have an habitual respect for the sound' of the words (ibid.). But 'whenever conduct is concerned, they look round for Mr. A and B to direct them how far to go in obeying Christ' (ibid.). In a predominantly commercial culture, he might have added, the conventional directions given and accepted by most will tend to be imbued with a commercial spirit, yielding a so-called 'Christian' dogma whose rules are bent to fit capitalistic expectations rather than anything Christ and his early followers had in mind.[2]

Evidently, with that example, Mill has sounded the alarm among those of his readers who consider themselves Christians. But the point he wants to illustrate is that even the Christian religion has not been immune from the evil caused by suppression of allegedly false opinions. Christianity has lost its meaning for most of those who still profess to believe in it, for want of free discussion of the ideas held out as 'Christian' by church authorities. Original Christian maxims of morality, even if entirely warranted, no longer motivate most so-called Christians, who now mistakenly apply the term 'Christianity' to quite different ideas: 'The fatal tendency of mankind to leave off thinking about a thing when it is no longer doubtful, is the cause of half their errors' (II.30, p. 250). He is trying to provoke modern Christians to examine whether they might be in error to call themselves Christians. Such self-examination requires them to think and discuss their 'living beliefs' with their critics. Before anyone can really be said to believe in the New Testament, he must have learned the meaning and grounds of its doctrine, defended that doctrine from its critics and shaped his conduct in accord with its maxims. Until they are committed to all that, he implies, people should desist from calling themselves Christians and see themselves in a truer light.[3]

Unanimity versus truth? (II.31–3)

Yet even a non-Christian might object that the argument at this stage carries an unwelcome implication, namely, that unanimous agreement among people on a warranted belief causes the meaning of the opinion to 'perish within them' (II.31, p. 250). Without critics who 'persist in error', the essential process of free thought and discussion apparently comes to a halt, causing the truth to waste away.

But the objection is too quick, Mill replies. Even if unanimity were achieved, the essential process would remain necessary for fallible beings to retain the meaning of their warranted opinions. Complete liberty of thought and discussion can be carried on by a 'contrivance' such as 'the Socratic dialectics', in which skilled devil's advocates take the place of committed critics (II.32–3, pp. 251–2).

The harm of silencing an opinion which may be only partly true (II.34–6, 39)

Mill now turns to the last step of his argument, where he considers a third case, 'commoner . . . than either' of the other two (III.34, p. 252). In this case, the opinion to be silenced is neither entirely warranted nor completely refutable. Rather, it shares the truth with received opinion. The 'peculiar evil' of silencing such an opinion is thus a conjunction of the evils already considered, to wit, the failure to acquire all sides of the truth, united with the lack of a lively appreciation of the grounds and meaning of even that portion of truth found in received opinion.

His discussion of this case allows him to clarify some aspects of his argument before returning to the particular problem that concerns him most in practice, that is, intolerance of diversity of opinion on religious and moral principles.

Popular opinion is generally biased (II.34)

Received opinions 'on subjects not palpable to sense' are generally one-sided, containing only part of the truth, Mill suggests, because heretical opinions which contain complementary parts of the truth are silenced at any given time. History is viewed by him not as a victorious march of inevitable improvement but rather as a largely cyclical process in which different parts of the truth repeatedly supersede one another, one part setting as another rises:

> Even progress, which ought to superadd, for the most part only substitutes, one partial and incomplete truth for another; improvement consisting chiefly in this, that the new fragment of truth is more wanted, more adapted to the needs of the time, than that which it displaces.
>
> (II.34, pp. 252–3)

Truth and toleration (II.34–6)

Given the 'partial character' of any received ideas on complex subjects (including religion and morality), heretical opinions that perhaps embody some neglected side of the truth 'ought to be considered precious' by fallible beings, 'with whatever amount of error and confusion that truth may be blended' (II.34, p. 253). Those who seek to learn the many sides of a warranted opinion on morality or politics, that is, ought to be grateful even to one-sided critics and committed ideologues who attempt to 'explode' the 'compact mass' of received opinion, 'forcing its elements [of truth] to recombine in a better form and with additional ingredients' (II.35, p. 253).

A case in point, he remarks, is Rousseau's romantic attack on the received opinion among eighteenth-century Europeans that the civility and enlightenment of their culture made it wholly superior to simpler states of society (ibid.). Another illustration is provided by a freely competitive party system, which has the generally beneficial effect of keeping received political opinion 'within the limits of reason and sanity' (II.36, pp. 253–4).

Complete liberty of discussion is utilitarian (II.36, 39)

More generally, Mill re-emphasizes his argument that complete liberty of thought and discussion is the *only* way fallible beings can hope to develop the capacities required to infer, and retain a lively understanding of, warranted beliefs (see II.6–10, 22–3, 31–3). Complete liberty is essential because we cannot expect impartial observers with warranted beliefs to appear like magic in its absence:

> Truth, in the great practical concerns of life, is so much a question of the reconciling and combining of opposites, that very few have minds sufficiently capacious and impartial to make the adjustment with the approach to correctness, and it has to be made by the rough process of a struggle between combatants fighting under hostile banners.
>
> (II.36, p. 254)

He is under no illusions that complete freedom of discussion somehow automatically leads the combatants themselves to grasp many-sided truths: 'I acknowledge that the tendency of all opinions to become sectarian is not cured by the freest discussion', he says, 'but is often heightened and exacerbated thereby; the truth which ought to have been, but was not, seen, being rejected all the more violently because proclaimed by persons regarded as opponents' (II.39, p. 257). Despite its costs, however, the 'rough process' is utilitarian because there is no other way for impartial persons (including the combatants themselves upon reflection) to acquire the truth and sustain a lively appreciation for it:

> [I]t is not on the impassioned partisan, it is on the calmer and more disinterested bystander, that this collision of opinions works its salutary effect. Not the violent conflict between parts of the truth, but the quiet suppression of half of it, is the formidable evil . . . And since there are few mental attributes more rare than that judicial faculty which can sit in intelligent judgment between two sides of a question, of which only one is represented by an advocate before it, truth has no chance but in proportion as every side of it, every opinion which embodies

any fraction of the truth, not only finds advocates, but is so advocated as to be listened to.

(ibid.)

Minority opinions, unpopular with the majority, ought nevertheless to be encouraged by the majority, and their free expression protected by right, because otherwise there is no hope of finding warranted opinions.

The crucial case of Christian moral beliefs (II.37–8)

But someone may still object that some received beliefs, for example, Christian principles, are special in the sense that they comprise 'the whole truth' on the vital subject of morality. That objection returns Mill to what he considers the crucial test case for his principle of absolute liberty of thought and discussion: 'As this is of all cases the most important in practice, none can be fitter to test the general maxim' (II.37, p. 254). His strategy is to show that Christian principles contain only a part of the truth about morality, so that a fully adequate morality (utilitarian or otherwise) requires them to be modified and supplemented by non-Christian elements.

In the first place, there is doubt about the meaning of 'Christian morality'. If it means the maxims of the New Testament, he argues, then it was clearly intended to be only a part of moral truth: 'The Gospel always refers to a pre-existing morality, and confines its precepts to the particulars in which that morality was to be corrected, or superseded by a wider and higher [one]' (ibid.). It can only be completed by specifying the relevant 'pre-existing' rules. But the usual suggestions, including codes drawn from the Old Testament, for example, or from the Greeks and Romans, are 'in many respects barbarous', even going so far (in Saint Paul's case) as to give 'an apparent sanction to slavery' (II.37, pp. 254–5). Granted, better suggestions can be made. Indeed, the 'sayings of Christ' can be reconciled with everything which 'a comprehensive morality requires' (II.38, p. 256). But this does not alter the point that Christian principles in this sense 'contain, and were meant to contain, only a part of the truth' (ibid.).[4]

If 'Christian morality' means the 'theological morality' gradually devised by the early Catholic church and subsequently modified by 'moderns and Protestants', then, apart from the fact that this is distinct from the maxims of the New Testament, 'it is ... incomplete and one-sided' (II.37, p. 255). Mill affirms that 'mankind owe a great debt to this [so-called Christian] morality' (ibid.). But 'it is, in great part, a protest against Paganism', and requires to be modified and completed by that part of the truth which Paganism contains:

> Its ideal is negative rather than positive; passive rather than active; Innocence rather than Nobleness; Abstinence from Evil, rather than energetic Pursuit of Good ... It is essentially a doctrine of passive obedience; it inculcates submission to all authorities found established; who indeed are not to be actively obeyed when they command what religion forbids, but who are not to be resisted, far less rebelled against, for any amount of wrong to ourselves.
>
> (ibid.)

A complete morality must make room for so-called Pagan ideals, for example, 'duty to the state' and the associated virtues of public service and honour (II.37, pp. 255–6).

The incomplete theological morality hardly notices the idea of constitutional obligation, looking instead beyond this life for the motives to virtue. In so doing, it tends to

> give to human morality an essentially selfish character, by disconnecting each man's feelings of duty from the interests of his fellow-creatures, except so far as a self-interested inducement [hope of heaven or threat of hell] is offered to him for consulting them.
>
> (II.37, p. 255)[5]

Even the New Testament largely ignores the idea of constitutional obligation on the parts of political leaders and citizens alike, he insists.[6]

However we define it, Mill argues, Christian morality must be supplemented by non-Christian principles if we hope to get a complete picture of the many different sides of warranted moral opinion: 'the

Christian system is no exception to the rule, that in an imperfect state of the human mind, the interests of truth require a diversity of opinions' (II.38, p. 257). The insistence by so-called Christians, contrary to Christ's own intentions, that their religious doctrine provides 'a complete rule for our guidance' is 'a great error' and is 'becoming a grave practical evil' (II.38, p. 256). Unless the requisite Pagan elements are given freedom to breathe, he fears, 'there will result, and is even now resulting, a low, abject, servile type of character' in the majority (ibid.). Complete liberty of religious thought and expression is essential to avoid this result, for otherwise the Pagan elements of truth will be silenced:

> If Christians would teach infidels to be just to Christianity, they should themselves be just to infidelity. It can do truth no service to blink the fact . . . that a large portion of the noblest and most valuable moral teaching has been the work, not only of men who did not know, but of men who knew and rejected, the Christian faith.
>
> (II.38, p. 257).[7]

Must free expression be fair and temperate? (II.44)

Before moving on to examine more generally the extent to which men ought to be free from coercion when acting upon their opinions, Mill considers briefly the objection that complete freedom of expression is permissible only if 'the manner be temperate, and do not pass the bounds of fair discussion' (II.44, p. 258). Such a requirement of fair and temperate discussion has lately enjoyed a revival in our own age, as a requisite of political liberalism. He rejects the requirement for several reasons. People commonly take offence whenever their opinions are subjected to a 'telling and powerful' attack, for example, and are liable to brand a skilled opponent an intemperate one.

Even more importantly, legal penalties or stigma can never be employed effectively against the 'gravest' sorts of unfairness, namely, 'to argue sophistically, to suppress facts or arguments, to misstate the elements of the case, or misrepresent the opposite opinion' (ibid.). The problem is that people do this sort of thing all the time 'in perfect good faith', mistakenly rather than with the intention to harm others. As for the use of 'invective, sarcasm, personality, and the like', these are weapons which are generally advantageous only to the defenders of received opinion, as minorities have little incentive to give unnecessary offence to majorities (II.44, p. 259). In any case, law and stigma 'have no business' in restraining vituperative expressions of opinion (ibid.).

'[T]he real morality of public discussion', he emphasizes, involves a disposition to distinguish between what a person says and how he says it. Complete liberty ought to be granted to both the content and the manner of expression, with the usual caveat about expression which is not reasonably classed as self-regarding. But observers must develop the capacity to see the truth in what a person says, and separate that truth from how he says it. At the same time, observers ought to make up their own minds as to whether a person's manner of discussion reveals an unjust intent to defraud others of the truth, by deliberately misrepresenting opposing arguments and so on.

Suggestions for further reading

There is no finer argument than Mill's for freedom of thought and discussion. His views continue to inspire many liberal writers today, although his utilitarian underpinnings are usually rejected and there is some disagreement about what his views really are. See, e.g., C.L. Ten, *Mill on Liberty* (Oxford, Clarendon Press, 1980), Chapter 8; Thomas Scanlon, 'A Theory of Freedom of Expression', *Philosophy and Public Affairs* 1 (1972): 204–26; Scanlon, 'Freedom of Expression and Categories of Expression', *University of Pittsburgh Law Review* 40 (1979): 519–50; and Cass Sunstein, *The Partial Constitution* (Cambridge, Mass., Harvard University Press, 1993).

At the same time, it is important to remember that Mill admits acts of 'expressing and publishing opinions' are not truly self-regarding acts, since they always pose some risk of harm to other people (if for no other reason than others may be misled against their wishes about the facts or warranted conclusions of relevant issues). Such acts do not really fall within the ambit of the liberty principle, apparently, which prescribes complete liberty of thought and self-regarding action.

But he treats them as 'practically inseparable' from the liberty of thought itself, and suggests that they should be given 'almost' as much protection as the absolute protection afforded to thought. Interference with the content and perhaps even manner of public expression is rarely generally expedient, it seems, even if society may have legitimate authority to consider intervention.

An interesting general issue is whether social conditions in countries like Britain and the US are now so different from Mill's times that he might reasonably change his mind about how often interference with the content of public expression is expedient. Given the rise of global motion picture, television and computer networks with which he was not familiar, for example, perhaps he would admit more opportunities for censorship of such visual forms of expression as violent movies, pornographic films and racist Web-sites. The issue of when it is expedient to censor public expression evidently overlaps with the more general issue of when it is expedient to employ coercion against indecent or unruly behaviour in public. Yet, unfortunately, he doesn't say much to clarify his views in the *Liberty* (cf. V. 7, pp. 295–6). We return to these questions below in Chapters 6, 8 and 9.

Chapter 4

Of individuality, as one of the elements of well-being (Chapter III, paras 1–19)

The grounds of liberty of action (III.1)

With his case made for absolute liberty of expression, Mill next considers 'whether the same reasons do not require that men should be free to *act* upon their opinions' (III.1, p. 260, emphasis added). He says immediately that 'no one pretends that actions should be as free as opinions', and then reminds us that even expression is subject to legitimate social control in special circumstances which render unreasonable its classification as a self-regarding act (ibid.). Specifically, in rare situations where it is 'a positive instigation' to violence, molestation or other serious damage, expression can no longer be reasonably treated as harmless to others. Yet, just as 'almost' all expression is reasonably treated as self-regarding, a significant field of action is also reasonably treated thus, he suggests, and for the same reasons:

> [I]f [the individual] refrains from molesting others in what concerns them, and merely acts

according to his own inclination and judgment in things which concern himself, the same reasons which show that opinion should be free, prove also that he should be allowed, without molestation, to carry his opinions into practice at his own cost . . . As it is useful that while mankind are imperfect there should be different opinions, so is it that there should be different experiments of living; that free scope should be given to varieties of character, short of injury to others.

(III.1, pp. 260–1)

By implication, absolute liberty ought to be guaranteed, by right, with respect to certain 'self-regarding' acts, which do not harm others.

Individuality and happiness

By analogy with the case of thought and discussion, such liberty of action is essential for the individual to acquire, and sustain a lively appreciation of, a many-sided truth, namely, that of *his own nature or character*. The only way to gather this sort of warranted opinion about oneself, it seems, is to think, express, and act as one likes, 'short of injury to others'. Choosing spontaneously, in accord with one's own judgment and inclinations, is a constitutent element, apparently, of what Mill means by 'individuality' and (what is 'the same thing') self-development (III.10, p. 267). As such, '[i]t is desirable', he says,

that in things which do not primarily concern others, individuality should assert itself. Where, not the person's own character, but the traditions and customs of other people are the rule of conduct, there is wanting one of the principal ingredients of human happiness, and quite the chief ingredient of individual and social progress.

(III.1, p. 261)

The main purpose of his discussion in this chapter is to underline the high value of individuality, and thereby make clear why the complete liberty of self-regarding acts essential to its realisation is justified.

Before proceeding with his discussion, it is worth noting a large ambiguity which has cropped up at this stage. Although he clears it up by the final chapter, and, indeed, has already given some hint of the way he will do so, the ambiguity is one which continues to baffle many readers. The problem is this. Mill has assimilated freedom of acting upon one's opinion to freedom of expressing it. Yet we know that expression is something of an exceptional case from the perspective of his liberty doctrine, to wit, expression is really *other-regarding* conduct which, though it concerns others and can be legitimately prevented through coercion, is 'almost' always reasonably treated *as if* it were self-regarding conduct, harmless to others. The question then arises: is the sphere of self-regarding action that comes within the purview of his 'very simple principle' *really* self-regarding (in the sense that no harm to others is involved), or is it really other-regarding, yet treated as if it were not (in the sense that, although harm to others is involved, regulation is generally inexpedient for one reason or another, so that laissez-faire should prevail)? How we answer that question is extremely important.

If there are no truly self-regarding actions, for example, then the simple liberty principle is arguably a sham since we must await (possibly complex) utilitarian calculations before we can determine which other-regarding acts ought to be treated 'as if' they are self-regarding. If there truly are actions which are harmless to other people, on the other hand, actions with respect to which the agent ought to be perfectly free to do as he likes, independently of any further social calculation relating to their consequences, then which actions are these? That last question of identification raises the vexed issue of the definition of 'harm', about which Mill appears rather cavalier. Even if we confine our attention to the first couple of pages of this chapter, he seems to use interchangeably with 'harm' such terms as 'mischief', 'nuisance', 'molestation', and the like (III.1, pp. 260–1).

Despite this ambiguity, which will linger with us until the final chapter, it is also worth recalling Mill's remark that liberty of expression 'rest[s] in great part on the same reasons' as liberty of thought itself, where, he makes clear, thought truly *is* self-regarding. So, the distinction between the two forms of reasoning might not be that crucial at this stage of his argument. His present focus is on the great importance of individuality as a component of well-being. Perhaps for ease of exposition, if for no other reason, he decided to postpone clarifying some key distinctions which were not needed for the moment.

The worth of spontaneous action (III.2–6)

Mill begins by insisting on the 'intrinsic worth' of 'individual spontaneity' because it 'is hardly recognised', he feels, by either defenders or critics of received opinions and practices:

> The majority, being satisfied with the ways of mankind as they now are (for it is they who make them what they are), cannot comprehend why those ways should not be good enough for everybody; and what is more, spontaneity forms no part of the ideal of the majority of moral and social reformers.
>
> (III.2, p. 261)

He points to Wilhelm von Humboldt as a notable exception, and applauds his doctrine that '"the end of man"' ought to be seen as the cultivation of individuality, in other words, '"the highest and most harmonious development of his powers to a complete and consistent whole"' (ibid., quoting from Von Humboldt, 1969, p. 16). As the quotation makes clear, a fully cultivated individuality – the most complete idea of individuality, individuality in all its glory – is in effect an ideal type of moral character, a character in which the many different sides of the individual's true nature have a chance to flourish as much as possible in mutually compatible ways.[1]

Mill's subsequent remarks are directed at clarifying what he thinks are warranted inferences about the different sides of the relevant character ideal, and how they are combined into a 'consistent whole'. This brings him back to his earlier claim that the part of the truth contained in the Christian (also Platonic) ideal of 'passive obedience' must be integrated with the distinct part that is contained in a non-Christian (or Pagan) ideal of 'energetic' self-assertion (II.37–8, pp. 255–7; cf. III.8–9, 265–6). At the same time, in the course of providing this clarification, he says more about the high utility of self-assertion, or, in other words, of liberty itself, in the sense of doing as one likes. Liberty is essential not only to sustain the ideal many-sided character once it has been developed. Liberty is also necessary to self-development, the process of cultivating and acquiring that ideal.

He devotes quite a lot of time to his point that complete liberty of choosing as we like, 'short of injury to others', is essential to individuality and its cultivation. Rather than blindly follow the customs of the majority, without any inclination to consider and experiment with alternatives, the individual should desire to make up his own mind and choose for himself, at least when harm to others is not involved:

> The human faculties of perception, judgment, discriminative feeling, mental activity, and even moral preference, are exercised only in making a choice. He who does anything *because* it is the custom [rather than because he chooses to do it, in accord with his own judgment and inclinations], makes no choice.
>
> (III.3, p. 262, emphasis added)

Just as a licence to think and discuss is needed to develop one's capacities to identify, and retain an understanding of, warranted opinions, a licence to choose (at least among self-regarding acts) is needed to develop one's capacities to acquire, maintain and *act upon* warranted opinions about one's own enjoyments, desires, loves and plans of life.

> The mental and moral, like the muscular powers, are improved only by being used. The faculties are called into no exercise by doing a thing merely because others do it, no more than by believing a thing only because others believe it.
>
> (ibid.)

The worth of obedience to social rules (III.3–6,9,17)

But his emphasis on the worth of liberty and spontaneity should not make us lose sight of other valuable ingredients in the ideal type of moral character, which he insists is the true 'end of man', and, thus, for him, the best conception of personal happiness. That character-ideal, he makes clear, involves a 'complete and consistent' blend of human powers or capacities, implying some sort of harmony between the general ability to obey social rules (designed to prevent, or at least control, acts harmful to others), and the capacity to think and choose as one likes, in accord with one's own judgment and desires.

He emphasizes that individuality should be cultivated 'within the limits imposed by the rights and interests of others' (III.9, p. 266). Some 'compression' of individual spontaneity 'is necessary to prevent the stronger specimens of human nature from encroaching on the rights of others' (ibid.). But social control for that purpose is justified even if we restrict attention to 'human development', he points out, because such control allows every person (including the weaker) to cultivate his individuality without fear of injury by others. Indeed, the requisite compression is justified even from the perspective of any agent's *self-development*:

> [E]ven to himself there is a full equivalent in the better development of the social part of his nature, rendered possible by the restraint put upon the selfish part. To be held to rigid rules of justice for the sake of others, develops the feelings and capacities which have the good of others for their object.
>
> (ibid.)

It helps the individual (including the strongest) along the road to an ideal moral character, to be forced (if necessary) to develop the 'feelings and capacities' of goodwill toward others, at least to the extent of not doing them serious injury. But for the individual 'to be restrained in things not affecting [the] good [of others], by their mere displeasure, developes [*sic*] nothing valuable' (ibid.).

Within an ideal type of character, then, self-restraint in accord with general rules is consistently mixed with self-assertion in self-regarding matters.

Self-assertion not the sole source of improvement (III.5,17)

The propriety of a balance between spontaneity and rule-abidingness is made clear by him at other points as well. For example, he argues for different self-regarding experiments of living so that people may learn from their own and others' experiences which of the many different desires and impulses possible to human nature are best for *them*. People are capable of self-improvement, in the sense that they can choose to acquire or strengthen some desires and weaken or discard others, if they judge such a change to be desirable for them. But liberty of self-regarding experiments, while it may be 'the only unfailing and permanent source of improvement' in morality and personal plans of life, is *not* the only source of it: 'the spirit of improvement is not always a spirit of liberty, for it may aim at forcing improvements on [the] unwilling' (III.17, p. 272). Rather, improvement may require coercion in some contexts, to force the recalcitrant to obey rules designed to secure others from serious harm.

Consistently with this, Mill does not advocate free scope for *other-regarding* experiments of living incompatible with a due regard for the rights and interests of other people. Rather, he calls for development of an ideal moral character involving a 'proper balance' of strong desires and impulses:

> [S]trong impulses are only perilous when not properly balanced; when one set of aims and inclinations is developed into strength, while others, which ought to co-exist with them, remain weak and inactive. It is not because men's desires are strong that they act ill; it is because their consciences are weak. There is no natural connexion between strong impulses and a weak conscience. The natural connexion is the other way.
>
> (III.5, p. 263)

Such a character is depicted as 'energetic', embodying an array of strong desires and impulses under the self-government of a powerful rational will (III.5, p. 264). A strong conscience, or desire to do right by others, is an essential ingredient.

Coercion may be needed to help cultivate conscience

To foster self-development in that direction, society must encourage the individual to cultivate a 'proper balance' of strong desires and impulses. In part, this is done by giving free scope to self-regarding experiments of living: there is no other way to gain warranted opinions about the 'proper balance'. But society can also legitimately use coercion where need be, to enforce general rules of other-regarding conduct. Threats of legal penalties and social stigma may be useful to encourage the unwilling to acquire or strengthen a desire to do right. This remains so even if coercion alone can never lead the individual to develop his conscience.

Obedience and individuality

It emerges that there is no necessary conflict between the cultivation of individuality and obedience to expedient social rules. A person ought to think freely for himself and choose his own lifestyle rather than *blindly* imitate other people. But that does not preclude him from choosing, after reflection, to imitate others to the extent implied by common obedience to reasonable rules governing conduct harmful to others. Indeed, he *ought* to choose to obey laws and customs which most people think are reasonable means of governing other-regarding conduct (even if he thinks better rules might be devised). He *ought* to suppress, by means of his own moral will power (which must be developed), those of his desires and impulses which, if he acted upon them, would harm other people in unreasonable ways. He *ought* to develop his capacity to recognize when he is likely to cause serious injury to others, and he *ought* to develop a sufficiently strong conscience, or desire to do right, that he chooses to respect their rights, pay his fair share of taxes and otherwise suitably 'compress' his behaviour. Until he develops the requisite will power and character (habits of acting), however, the individual may legitimately be coerced to do as he ought.

Society has legitimate authority to coerce the individual (if need be) to follow whichever rules of other-regarding conduct are in the majority's estimation generally expedient. No person is infallible – nobody is absolutely sure what an ideal code looks like in this respect. But, provided complete liberty of discussion of the alternatives is guaranteed, the majority is warranted in establishing such laws and customs as it (at least tacitly) considers reasonable. That does not mean that the individual must *agree* with the existing rules governing other-regarding conduct (let alone any which meddle with self-regarding acts), or that he must sit quietly rather than work at social reform. But it does mean that society has legitimate authority to punish him for deviations from those of its existing rules which are designed to control conduct harmful to others. Society has no legitimate authority, however, to enforce rules of self-regarding conduct.

Even with respect to self-regarding conduct, the individual should consult 'traditions and customs', which he is properly taught in youth, 'to find out what part of recorded experience is properly applicable to his own circumstances and character' (III.3, p. 262). Those customs include, of course, the prevailing conventions of warranted inference *per se*. As Mill remarks, 'it would be absurd to pretend that people ought to live as if nothing whatever had been known in the world before they came into it' (ibid.). Consistently with this, however, any person capable of self-improvement should be granted complete liberty of thought and action, short of injury to others.

An ideal type of individual character (III.5–9)

Mill's emphasis on liberty and individuality, as opposed to compression and rule-abidingness, reflects his view that the 'proper balance' has been tipped dangerously against individuality in the present age, and is likely to get even worse: 'In our times, from the highest class of society down to the lowest, every one lives as under the eye of a hostile and dreaded censorship' (III.6, p. 264). In 'some early states of society' the balance was tipped too much the other way: 'But society has now fairly got the better of individuality' (ibid.). Even 'in what concerns only themselves', people blindly follow custom rather than consider what they would most like to try: 'I do not mean that they *choose* what is customary, in preference to what suits their own inclination. It does not occur to them to have any inclination, except for what is customary' (III.6, pp. 264–5, emphasis added). Moreover, just as lack of free thought and discussion can result in loss of any acquired understanding of the grounds and even meaning of warranted opinions, so lack of self-regarding choices and experiments can cause people to lose all desire to depart from custom, since they no longer have any idea of what might be suitable to their own nature: 'their human capacities are withered and starved' (III.6, p. 265).

Self-denial of that sort exhausts the so-called Christian interpretation (now referred to as 'the Calvinistic theory') of an ideal moral character, Mill argues: 'All the good of which humanity is capable, is comprised in obedience', whether to the will of God or some other authority sanctioned by the divine (III.7, p. 265). He ties this in with his earlier theme of the rising danger of religious intolerance of competing moral ideals: 'In some such insidious form there is at present a strong tendency to this narrow theory of life, and to the pinched and hidebound type of human character which it patronizes' (III.8, p. 265). That Christian theory contains a part of the truth. But it must be modified and supplemented by other warranted opinions concerning what besides obedience comprises an ideal moral character.

In particular, account must be taken of the value of self-assertion, not merely the importance of obedience to rules: '"Pagan self-assertion" is one of the elements of human worth, as well as "Christian self-denial"' (III.8, p. 266; quoting from Sterling, 1848, I, p. 190). He points to a 'Greek ideal' which apparently combines these different sides of the truth into a 'complete and consistent whole'. Since he explicitly mentions Pericles, that warranted character-ideal might be referred to as *Periclean*. It apparently involves liberty and spontaneity, duly balanced with self-government in the sense of freely choosing to obey rules. Moreover, the cultivation of this Periclean ideal presupposes individual rights to liberty within the self-regarding sphere, consistently mixed with legitimate social enforcement of reasonable rules of conduct outside that sphere.

Evidently, this 'Greek ideal' of character is not purely 'Platonic' since Mill equates the latter with the 'Christian ideal of self-government' (III.8, p. 266). Rather than Periclean, it is sometimes labelled as Aristotelian, even though the golden age of Pericles in Athens ended with the coming of the Peloponnesian War about 431BC. Aristotle was born in 384BC, almost half a century after the death of Pericles is recorded. The ideal might be referred to as Socratic, since Socrates was a contemporary of Pericles. Yet Mill chooses to speak of Pericles. A major reason for this may be that, in his view, Pericles anticipates the liberty doctrine during the course of his great funeral oration (see Mill, 1853, pp. 333–4; for further discussion, see Riley, forthcoming b, Conclusion).

Another reason may be to call attention to the fact that Pericles, in addition to his attainments as a great political leader and orator, seems to have done as he pleased in his self-regarding matters. As already mentioned in Part I, he seems to have sustained a passionate love affair with Aspasia, a foreigner, outside the marriage conventions of Athens. She was also apparently his trusted political and philosophical adviser, as well as a teacher and confidante of Socrates. Indeed, she seems to have advocated true love between equals as a model for all intimate relationships (heterosexual and homosexual). Her unusual position, as a woman not bound by social conventions and treated as an equal by men such as Pericles and Socrates, apparently made her the object of severe criticism as a whore, a manipulator of men, another Helen who instigated wars and so on. Like Socrates, she was even formally charged with impiety, though her trial ended in acquittal (after Pericles wept in open court for her release, so Plutarch tells us). Perhaps Mill was even reminded by all this of his own beloved Harriet, and of the hostility and stigma they faced as a result of their own unconventional relationship.

Utilitarian case for the equal right to liberty (III.10–19)

Mill goes on to clarify his utilitarian form of argument for giving the individual absolute liberty, by right, to choose among opinions and self-regarding acts in accord with his own judgment and inclinations.

Self-development and true happiness (III.10)

For those who seek warranted opinions about their own feelings, who want knowledge of which of their desires and impulses to strengthen and which to weaken, the utility of liberty within the self-regarding sphere is clear: it is essential to their self-development. Such persons recognize that choosing as they like is essential to their progress toward an ideal moral character, which reflects a *warranted belief about their own happiness*.

Complete liberty of self-regarding action is the very test of a true conception of their personal utility, just as complete liberty of discussion is the test of warranted opinions in general. Moreover, equal rights to liberty in self-regarding matters would maximize social development without causing harm to others, if each member of society sought his self-development and desired liberty.

But, as Mill recognizes, not all people do value self-development and the liberty essential to it. Thus,

> it is necessary [for a utilitarian] further to show that these developed [and truly happy] human beings are of some use to the undeveloped – to point out to those who do not desire liberty, and would not avail themselves of it, that they may be in some intelligible manner rewarded for allowing other people to make use of it without hindrance.
>
> (III.10, p. 267)

He offers at least four related reasons to persuade 'the undeveloped', that is, the majority whose religion is infused with the spirit of commercial society rather than any Periclean ideal of self-development.

Better social customs and practices (III.11–12)

First, 'they might possibly learn something' (III.11, p. 267). Even if they do not develop habits of free inquiry and free experimentation themselves, they might benefit as new warranted opinions (including opinions about lifestyles) are put into practice and converted into customs through imitation of the developed persons who originated them:

> There is always need of persons not only to discover new truths, and point out when what were once truths are true no longer, but also to commence new practices, and set the example of more enlightened conduct, and better taste and sense in human life.
>
> (ibid.)

In short, there is always need of individuals with a passion for liberty to point out to the majority over time which 'uncustomary things . . . are fit to be converted into customs' (III.14, p. 269). This applies not only to self-regarding matters, where respect for liberty ought to be made the custom. It applies as well to other-regarding matters where, for example, new warranted beliefs about other people's interests and rights, or about what harms them, should be put into general practice.

Admittedly, only a relatively few persons will actually discover new truths worthy of adoption by the majority. But, since we cannot know beforehand who these 'salt of the earth' will be, the general '*atmosphere* of freedom' which they need to breathe and flourish ought to be secured (III.11, p. 267, emphasis original). Equal rights to liberty of self-regarding choices must be distributed, therefore, so that individuals who desire liberty, and will 'avail themselves of it', can choose in accord with their own judgment and inclinations. Otherwise, even that portion of the truth embodied in existing practices will tend to lose its significance, and may eventually lose its very meaning for the majority, who have nothing to contrast it with or to defend it from: 'There is only too great a tendency in the best beliefs and practices to degenerate into the mechanical' (ibid.).

More effective government (III.13)

Second, the undeveloped cannot expect fair and reasonable government in the absence of a body of developed individuals. 'Mediocrity' is 'the ascendant power among mankind', Mill insists: ill-considered popular opinions, spewed at the majority by 'men much like themselves' through the mass media, are everywhere gaining political influence as democracy takes hold in advanced commercial societies (III.13, pp. 268–9; see also III.18–19, pp. 274–5). To counteract this and promote competent government, it is essential to have competent individuals, with complete liberty to advise and cajole the majority:

> No government by a democracy or a numerous aristocracy . . . ever did or could rise above mediocrity, except in so far as the sovereign Many have let themselves be guided (which in their best times they always have done) by the counsels and influence of a more highly gifted and instructed One or Few.
>
> (III.13, p. 269)

He emphasizes that he does not countenance Carlyle's (1841) brand of 'hero-worship', whereby the 'strong man of genius' seizes power and uses it to coerce the masses to behave in accord with some ideal code (ibid.). Rather than such a power of coercion, the developed should merely have 'freedom to point out the way' (ibid.). He seems to have in mind something like Coleridge's (1818, 1839) notion of a 'clerisy', a national corps of intellectuals, ministers and professors, suitably independent of the government, accessible to the people and serving them (as well as political leaders) as a source of learning and friendly advice.[2]

More generally, to help 'break through' the tyranny of majority opinion, he thinks it expedient for society to encourage 'exceptional individuals' to deviate as they like from majoritarian ideas and practices, short of injury to others. The point, it seems, is that such deviations help remind people that popular opinion often reflects mediocrity rather than excellence, and unfairness to minorities rather than justice. Effective government is thus facilitated by the mere example of non-conformity: 'In this age, the mere example of nonconformity, the mere refusal to bend the knee to custom, is itself a service ... That so few now dare to be eccentric, marks the chief danger of the time' (ibid.).

Diversity more congenial than forced uniformity (III.14–16)

A third reason for the undeveloped to welcome a free scope for individuality within the self-regarding sphere is that they too (not the developed alone) will generally be happier than they would be if society tried to make everyone conform to a code of self-regarding conduct: 'If a person possesses any tolerable amount of common sense and experience, his own mode of laying out his existence is the best, not because it is the best in itself, but because it is his own mode' (III.14, p. 270). People have different tastes and 'also require different conditions for their spiritual development' (ibid.). General rules laying out how everyone ought to act in their self-regarding concerns could never effectively take account of such diversity:

> Such are the differences among human beings in their sources of pleasure, their susceptibilities of pain, and the operation on them of different physical and moral agencies, that unless there is a corresponding diversity in their modes of life, they neither

> obtain their fair share of happiness, nor grow up to the mental, moral, and aesthetic stature of which their nature is capable.
>
> (ibid.)

Moreover, rules in this context have no justification in terms of preventing harm to others.

Mill returns yet again at this point to his theme of rising religious intolerance, arguing that the public is currently 'more disposed than at most former periods' to try to make everyone behave as if his desires and impulses are moderate or weak: the 'standard, express or tacit, is to desire nothing strongly' (III.15, p. 271). He is evidently referring to the 'movement' by Christians (so-called) to make their standard of self-denial into a complete guide of conduct:

> Its ideal of character is to be without any marked character; to maim by compression, like a Chinese lady's foot, every part of human nature which stands out prominently, and tends to make the person markedly dissimilar in outline to commonplace humanity.
>
> (III.15, pp. 271–2)

Pagan self-assertion and diversity of lifestyles are to be stamped out. Everyone is to obey whichever rules the majority decides are needed for all alike to mould for themselves the same maimed character. That character's defining feature is 'obedience', that is, 'Platonic and Christian . . . self-government' in accord with the social rules (III.7–8, pp. 265–6).

He thinks that the religious movement has already gone too far in England, though its unintended effect has been to produce an 'outward conformity' to religion and morality with little genuine interest in either (III.16, p. 272). Strong desires and impulses, or what is left of them, have largely been redirected elsewhere: 'There is scarcely any outlet for energy in this country except business' (ibid.). This emerging pattern, of 'outward conformity' to an incomplete moral ideal conjoined with a passion for commerce, leads him to his fourth reason for the undeveloped to respect liberty and individuality within the self-regarding sphere: the spectre of social stagnation and even decline.

Prevention of social stagnation and decline (III.17–19)

Liberty and individuality are necessary not merely for social improvement, he insists, but to prevent a kind of social paralysis associated with the complete 'despotism of custom' (III.17, p. 272). He speaks of China, 'stationary' in its customs 'for thousands of years' and no longer capable of progress without foreign intervention, as 'a warning example' (III.17, p. 273). But he thinks the despotism of custom which threatens Europe (and, in all likelihood, America) will take a somewhat different form, more consonant with advanced industrial society and its consumption possibilities. The threat is 'not precisely stationariness' but rather endless changes of fashion, 'change . . . for change's sake' in self-regarding matters like dress and opinions on all subjects, 'provided all change together' (ibid.). A constant flux of mass desires and impulses, a continual grabbing and tossing away of commercial products and ideas, an habitual restlessness with little consideration or discussion of alternative ways of life, awaits the majority unless steps are taken immediately to protect self-regarding liberty and individuality by right.

Holes in the case?

Mill evidently does make a rather elaborate utilitarian case for the rights of liberty and individuality, then, despite the familiar chorus of protests that he fails even to address the question. Warranted opinions about personal happiness are possible, he insists, only if complete liberty is granted to self-regarding experimentation. Consistently with that, developed individuals are warranted up to now in believing that their happiness is associated with the Periclean character ideal, which integrates liberty and spontaneity in self-regarding matters with rule-abidingness and self-government in other-regarding ones. The individual who has developed such an ideal character will, of course, voluntarily govern himself in accord with an ideal code restricted to other-regarding concerns. But before he attains that character, during the development process when he lacks the strong conscience that governs him to do right, he may be legitimately coerced by society to obey its existing rules of other-regarding conduct.

Apart from those who desire liberty and seek self-perfection, individuals who do not desire to develop themselves beyond some modicum of common sense separating the barbarian from the person capable of rational persuasion, are also given utilitarian reasons for respecting liberty and individuality, short of harm to others.

But are there holes in the case? Before we can make an attempt to answer, several related issues of interpretation cry out to be cleared up, namely: are there *truly* self-regarding acts, or is the self-regarding category merely an artifical utilitarian construction in the seamless web of other-regarding conduct? If there really are acts harmless to others, what is meant by harm? If all acts are really harmful to others to some degree, on the other hand, why all the fuss about self-regarding acts? Is his talk of these merely a subterfuge, a way to hide from the reader of liberal sympathies the utilitarian form of reasoning at the heart of the argument? These sorts of questions begin to receive more attention in his next chapter.

Suggestions for further reading

Mill's admiration for the ancient Athenian way of life, as envisioned by Pericles in his great funeral oration near the beginning of the long Peloponnesian War, is discussed further in J. Riley, *Mill's Radical Liberalism: An Essay in Retrieval* (London, Routledge, forthcoming), Conclusion. On Pericles, see George Grote, *A History of Greece*, 12 vols (London, John Murray, 1846–56), Vol. 6; Philip Stadter, *A Commentary on Plutarch's Pericles* (Chapel Hill, University of North Carolina Press, 1989); and Donald Kagan, *Pericles of Athens and the Birth of Democracy* (New York, Free Press, 1991). A rich discussion of Aspasia and her biographical tradition is provided by Madeleine Henry, *Prisoner of History: Aspasia of Miletus and her Biographical Tradition* (Oxford, Oxford University Press, 1995).

Mill's Periclean ideal of self-development or individuality, which attempts consistently to combine Christian virtues with Pagan self-assertion, found many echoes in Victorian culture. Others who imagined such character-ideals included Matthew Arnold and Walter Pater. See, e.g., Arnold, 'Marcus Aurelius' (1863), in his *Essays in Criticism: First Series* (1865), ed. Sister T.M. Hoctor (Chicago and

London, University of Chicago Press, 1968), pp. 204–24; and Pater, *Marius the Epicurean* (1885), ed. M. Levey (Harmondsworth, Penguin, 1985).

Arnold glorifies Christianity as a supreme moral ideal, and extols the Stoicism of Marcus Aurelius as an approximation to that Christian idealism. Unlike Mill, he seems to see a suitably revitalized Christianity as a *complete* morality, requiring nothing else to supplement it. He rejects any right to choose as one pleases in self-regarding matters, as well as hedonistic utilitarianism more generally.

Pater also elaborates on Mill's discussion of Aurelius (II.14, pp. 236–7), in a way that emphasizes a potential harmony between Millian utilitarianism and Christian idealism. His 'Marius' follows a course of self-development through which his simple youthful Epicureanism or Cyrenaicism is transformed into a 'noble' version of that doctrine. That noble Cyrenaicism is (like Mill's utilitarianism) a hedonistic philosophy which affirms the development of a beautiful character, involving a complete harmony of human virtues. At the same time, the ideal character is identified (as in Arnold's idealism) with true Christian virtue. Pater seems more open than Arnold to something like a right to pursue aesthetic personal ideals as one pleases.

On the mixture of Greek and Christian cultural influences in Britain and America more generally, see D.J. DeLaura, *Hebrew and Hellene in Victorian England: Newman, Arnold, Pater* (Austin, University of Texas Press, 1969); Peter Hinchcliff, *Benjamin Jowett and the Christian Religion* (Oxford, Clarendon Press, 1987); Frank M. Turner, *The Greek Heritage in Victorian Britain* (New Haven, Yale University Press, 1981); and Turner, 'The Triumph of Idealism in Victorian Classical Studies', in his *Contesting Cultural Authority: Essays in Victorian Intellectual Life* (Cambridge, Cambridge University Press, 1993), pp. 322–61.

Of the limits to the authority of society over the individual (Chapter IV, paras 1–21)

The nature of utilitarian coercion (IV.1–3)

Mill now starts to lend more precision to his general doctrine of 'the nature and limits' of legitimate coercion. He has made his utilitarian case for the right to absolute liberty in self-regarding matters, so that those who desire self-development may make use of the freedom of thought and action essential to its achievement. More needs to be said, however, not only about the general boundary of the self-regarding realm within which coercion should not even be considered, but also about how coercion should be exercised by society in the other-regarding realm where its use is legitimate. His attempt to clarify these things preoccupies him for the remaining two chapters.

In return for the valuable general security which society provides, he says, all individuals have a duty to obey its rules of other-regarding conduct: 'every one who receives the protection of society owes a return for the benefit, and the fact of living in society renders it indispensable that each should be bound to observe a certain line of conduct towards the rest' (IV.3, p. 276).

First, the individual ought not to injure 'certain interests' of other people, 'which, either by express legal provision or by tacit understanding, ought to be considered as rights' (ibid.). Second, he ought to 'bear his share (to be fixed on some equitable principle) of the labours and sacrifices incurred for defending the society or its members from injury and molestation' (ibid.). 'These conditions society is justified in enforcing *at all costs to those who endeavour to withhold fulfilment*' (ibid., emphasis added).

But third, the individual ought also to refrain from hurting others in ways that do not 'go the length of violating any of their constituted rights' (ibid.). In that type of case, '[t]he offender may . . . be justly punished by opinion, though not by law' (ibid.).

Utilitarian coercion thus has the following nature and limits, as Chapter 5 of Mill's *Utilitarianism* confirms. Legal coercion, the form symbolic of society's deepest contempt and the most costly to implement, is expediently used to prevent *only* the most serious kinds of harms to others. Suitable legal penalties (including death, incarceration, fines and the like) ought to be enforced by government officials only to prevent a person from violating others' moral rights, including the rights of officials to perform their legitimate public duties. Officials must have a right to collect a fair share of taxes, for example, and a right to draft citizens into military service when necessary for the defence of the country.

Social stigma, but not legal punishment, ought to be used to prevent less serious kinds of harms which do not rise to the level of rights-violations. Public contempt (including *displays* of condemnation, publicized messages intended to humiliate their targets, and so on) ought to be showered on the individual who repeatedly disappoints others' conventional expectations for help when he can afford to help, for example, or who otherwise exhibits unusually bad will toward others, without due cause.

Of course, the conduct which is legitimately subject to these forms of coercion is other-regarding. It 'affects prejudicially the interests of others' (ibid.); it 'affects others' *without* 'their free, voluntary, and undeceived consent' (I.12, p. 225, emphasis added); and it is 'the part [of life] which chiefly interests society' (IV.2, p. 276). Moreover, it is not merely harmful to others. It is so harmful that coercion to prevent it is generally expedient. Coercion should not merely be *considered* in these cases. It ought to be *employed*.

In contrast, 'there should be perfect freedom' from all forms of coercion, Mill says, 'when a person's conduct affects the interests of no persons besides himself, or needs not affect them unless they like (all the persons concerned being of full age, and the ordinary amount of understanding)' (IV.3, p. 276). Coercion should not even be 'open to discussion' in such cases.

It is worth remarking, however, that a third possibility is still being ignored at this stage of his argument, namely, other-regarding conduct which, though legitimately open to coercion, is not so harmful to others as to render coercion *expedient*. This raises yet again the ambiguity noted earlier in the context of freedom of expression. Is the third possibility, where social control of conduct admittedly harmful to others is not generally expedient, really distinct from the self-regarding sphere of liberty? Or is the self-regarding sphere just another name for that part of the seamless web of other-regarding conduct where coercion is not expedient? He does not give a complete answer until his final chapter. But he lays much of the groundwork in the present one.

The nature of self-regarding acts (IV.4–7)

'Selfish indifference' to others in their self-regarding concerns, Mill insists, is no part of his doctrine (IV.4, pp. 276–7). Absence of coercion does not imply absence of all forms of interaction. People should try to persuade each other to cultivate 'self-regarding virtues' such as prudence, moderation and self-respect. They should advise and warn each other to think more carefully and to act more wisely. But, ultimately, the individual must choose in accord with his own judgment and desires in his self-regarding concerns because '[h]e is the person most interested in his own well-being' (IV.4, p. 277). 'Considerations to aid his judgment, exhortations to strengthen his will, may be offered to him, even obtruded on him, by others; but he himself is the final judge' (ibid.).

Self-regarding acts, he admits, can and should affect *the feelings* of other people. It is 'neither possible nor desirable' for others to remain unaffected altogether by the individual's conduct, even though that conduct is harmless to them (IV.5, p. 278). By implication, *harm* to others cannot mean merely affecting their feelings, or causing them to feel aversion, without any injury or damage beyond that. Others are reasonably expected to like or dislike self-regarding acts, as the case may be. Self-degrading conduct, for example, can and should occasion intense dislike in other people: 'Though doing no wrong to any one, a person may so act as to compel us to judge him, and feel to him, as a fool, or as a being of an inferior order' (ibid.).

Moreover, others are properly free to act upon their contempt for the individual's self-regarding conduct. They have 'a right to avoid' him, for example, as well as a right (and perhaps a duty) to warn others to avoid him (ibid.). But nobody has a right to 'parade the avoidance', in other words, make a public display of their contempt as would be justified if he were guilty of an other-regarding fault such as lack of charity (ibid.).

Natural penalties (IV.5–7)

It emerges that the agent may suffer *harm* 'at the hands of others' as a result of his self-regarding conduct:

> In these various modes a person may suffer very severe penalties at the hands of others, for faults which directly concern only himself; but he suffers these penalties only in so far as they are the natural, and, as it were, the spontaneous consequences of the faults themselves, not because they are purposely inflicted on him for the sake of punishment.
>
> (ibid.)

These natural penalties are apparently 'strictly inseparable from the unfavourable judgment of others', in the sense that no deliberation or will is required to bring them about (ibid.). They flow immediately from others' dislike: 'the natural penalties . . . cannot be prevented from falling on those who incur the distaste or the contempt of those who know them' (IV.11, p. 282). Thus, a self-regarding act, although harmless to others, can trigger their aversion and thereby result in harm to the agent himself.

Mill contends that the natural penalties 'are the only ones to which a person should ever be subjected' for his self-regarding conduct (IV.6, pp. 278–9). Nevertheless, the fact that such penalties are inseparable from mere dislike may seem to pose a problem for his earlier suggestion that harm must mean something other than mere dislike. Self-regarding acts cannot be said to be harmless, someone might object, because they inspire dislike and the harms that are inseparable from it. But this is not an insurmountable objection. Self-regarding acts *can* be said to be harmless *to others*. There are really two aspects to consider.

On the one hand, self-regarding acts admittedly can cause self-harm through the actions of others, but that is not harm to them. Indeed, these natural penalties are largely self-inflicted, Mill seems to be saying, because they are direct consequences of self-regarding conduct itself. Others do not really want to inflict punishment on the person, apart from that which is implied in the exercise of their own liberty. Rather, they feel *compelled* to avoid his company by what they consider his self-regarding vices. He in effect brings these harms on himself because any reasonable person can foresee the likely consequences of his displays of obstinacy, intemperance and the like. Thus, 'it is not *our part* to inflict any suffering on him except what may incidentally follow from our using the same liberty in the regulation of our own affairs, which we allow to him in his' (IV.7, p. 280, emphasis added).

On the other hand, what about the suffering implied for *others* by the natural penalties which flow from a self-regarding act? Don't the other people who feel compelled to avoid a person's company suffer the loss of his friendship and all which that may entail? Evidently so. Yet they are not directly affected against their wishes. They do choose, however reluctantly, to avoid him, and what they choose to do cannot be said to cause them harm: 'volenti non fit injuria' (see Mill, 1861b, p. 253, quoting Ulpian).

Equal rights to complete liberty of self-regarding acts are thus compatible with natural penalties because such harms are not harms *to others*. Liberty is choosing in accord with one's own judgment and likes; natural penalties are inseparable from dislike of another's self-regarding act; and so natural penalties are inseparable from the self-regarding exercise of liberty itself. Other-regarding actions are simply not involved.

Natural penalties versus artificial punishment (IV.7)

Mill insists on a distinction, then, between natural penalties which are not harms to others, and artificial penalties which are harms to others. The latter are deliberately inflicted on the individual because society decides to retaliate against his *immoral* conduct, that is, conduct which the majority judges causes serious harm to other people by damaging their rights and other essential interests.[1] This distinction between natural and artificial penalties calls to mind Hume, whose influence on Mill's philosophy is not sufficiently appreciated in the literature.[2]

This 'is not a merely nominal distinction', Mill says (IV.7, p. 279). Two distinct psychological phenomena are involved. If we become aware of another person's self-regarding faults, for example, then we recognize that the harmful consequences of his acts fall on himself. Thus:

> [W]e may express our distaste, and we may stand aloof ... but we shall not therefore feel called on to make his life uncomfortable. We shall reflect that he already bears, or will bear, the whole [natural] penalty of his error; if he spoils his life by mismanagement, we shall not, for that reason, desire to spoil it further: instead of wishing to punish him, we shall rather endeavour to alleviate his [self-inflicted] punishment, by showing him how he may avoid or cure the evils his [self-regarding] conduct tends to bring upon him. He may be to us an object of pity, perhaps of dislike, but not of anger or resentment.
>
> (IV.7, pp. 279–80)

But 'it is far otherwise' if we become aware of another person's moral vices (IV.7, p. 280). For 'the evil consequences of his acts do not then fall on himself, but on others' (ibid.). We feel anger and resentment toward anyone whose conduct has caused, or is likely to cause, harm to another's essential interests. Moreover, his other-regarding misconduct is a reason for deliberately punishing him. Thus, society rightfully imposes suitable artificial penalties on any person 'of mature years' who infringes its moral rules of other-regarding conduct:

> [I]f he has infringed the rules [of justice and of charity] neces-
> sary for the protection of his fellow-creatures, individually or
> collectively ... [then] society, as the protector of all its
> members, must retaliate on him [by law or by opinion]; must
> inflict pain on him for the express purpose of punishment, and
> must take care that it be sufficiently severe.
>
> (ibid.)

Those artificial penalties are strictly separable from anybody's mere dislike of the other-regarding conduct *per se*. Their rationale is the prevention of harm to others, which is something other than mere dislike and the natural penalties which flow from it.

Beyond morality (IV.6)

Mill is careful to highlight his view that 'self-regarding faults ... are not properly immoralities, and to whatever pitch they may be carried, do not constitute wickedness' (IV.6, p. 279).[3] Such faults by them-selves do not harm other people. We may have self-regarding duties to correct such faults but the duties are

> not socially obligatory, unless circumstances render them at the
> same time duties to others. The term duty to oneself, when it
> means anything more than prudence, means self-respect or self-
> development; and for none of these is any one accountable to
> his fellow creatures.
>
> (ibid.)

But certain *other-regarding* faults *are* properly immoralities *because* they seriously harm other persons. Immoral acts include

> encroachment on [the] rights [of other persons]; infliction on
> them of any loss or damage not justified by [the agent's] own
> rights; falsehood or duplicity in dealing with them; unfair or
> ungenerous use of advantages over them; even selfish abstinence
> from defending them against injury.
>
> (ibid.)

97

'And not only these acts, but the dispositions which lead to them, are properly immoral' (ibid.). Immoral dispositions include cruelty, malice, envy, dishonesty, love of domineering, habitual egotism, vain enjoyment of others' misfortunes and so on: 'these are moral vices, and constitute a bad and odious moral character' (ibid.). Society legitimately has jurisdiction over morality thus understood, and should impartially interfere with immoral conduct as a means of promoting each person's permanent interests. But society has no legitimate authority over self-regarding matters.

The meaning of harm

It seems quite clear, then, that Mill believes there are truly self-regarding acts, 'properly' beyond morality, which do not harm other people. Such acts can and should affect others' feelings. Others may feel intense dislike, for example, and thus seek to avoid the agent. But none of this amounts to harm to them. Harm is something other than mere dislike, namely, 'perceptible damage' suffered against one's wishes. (By implication, self-harm must be unintentional on this view.) It may appear in myriad forms, including physical injury (not excepting death), forcible confinement, financial loss, damage to reputation, broken promises (contractual or otherwise) and so on. Unlike self-regarding choices, other-regarding conduct directly harms others in one of these ways, or carries a reasonable probability of doing so.

An important caveat is that society must not artificially distort this simple notion of harm, by recognizing (in law or custom) rights not to suffer the mere pain or dislike which anyone may feel at another's purely self-regarding conduct. Violation of such recognized rights would, after all, constitute a type of perceptible damage suffered against the right-holder's wishes (ignoring cases of forfeiture or voluntary waiver). Unfortunately, societies generally have recognized such rights and correlative duties, and have thereby hidden truly self-regarding acts, by transforming them into fake other-regarding acts that cause no harm other than to violate the rights in question. Mill's claim is that a civilized society ought never to interfere with purely self-regarding conduct, by recognizing such illiberal rights and duties.

Rather, equal absolute rights to liberty of self-regarding conduct ought to be recognized.

The idea of harm, around which the argument of the *Liberty* seems to cohere, is this simple idea of perceptible damage experienced against one's wishes, with the caveat that the perceptible damage must exist independently of any rights and correlative duties recognized by the majority or its representatives.

The self–other distinction: some objections answered (IV.8–12)

Mill certainly recognizes that 'many persons will refuse to admit' the distinction he wants to draw between self-regarding and other-regarding conduct (IV.8, p. 280). He identifies three general objections. First, critics will object that 'no person is an entirely isolated being' (ibid.). By harming himself, he may harm his dependents and creditors. Moreover, he may become incapable of rendering the customary level of help to others, and eventually depend entirely on their charity for his subsistence.

Second, the individual's self-injurious conduct will be said to set a bad example to others. Thus, he 'ought to be compelled to control himself, for the sake of those whom the sight or knowledge of his conduct might corrupt or mislead' (ibid.).

Third, even supposing for the sake of argument that 'the consequences of misconduct could be confined to the vicious or thoughtless individual', critics will still object that society should interfere for the same reasons, admittedly dispositive, in the case of children or mental defectives:

> There is no question here (it may be said) about restricting individuality, or impeding the trial of new and original experiments in living. The only things it is sought to prevent are things which [are known] ... not to be useful or suitable to any person's individuality. There must be some length of time and amount of experience, after which a moral or prudential truth may be regarded as established; and it is merely desired to prevent generation after generation from falling over the same precipice which has been fatal to their predecessors.
>
> (IV.9, p. 281)

He takes these three objections seriously but insists that they are not fatal to his doctrine.

No person is entirely isolated (IV.10–11)

Concerning the first objection, he begins by saying that if a person's self-injurious conduct causes him at the same time 'to violate a distinct and assignable obligation to any other person or persons, the case is taken out of the self-regarding class, and becomes amenable to moral disapprobation in the proper sense of the term' (IV.10, p. 281). Thus, if self-harm is inseparable from violation of some other person's rights, or from violation of the agent's own duty to pay his taxes or serve as a public official, then the misconduct is properly identified as *other-regarding* misconduct – indeed, unjust action – properly subject to legal and moral interference. Mill gives some illustrations, including the man whose extravagant personal consumption leads him to violate his creditors' rights; and the soldier or policeman whose drunkenness prevents him from performing the duties which society has a right to expect from him (IV.10, pp. 281–2).

Moreover, he says, self-injurious conduct is also properly seen as other-regarding misconduct – more specifically, uncharitable action – if the self-injury is inseparable from a failure to observe the customary level of beneficence towards others: 'Whoever fails in the consideration generally due to the interests and feelings of others, not being compelled by some more imperative duty, or justified by allowable self-preference, is a subject of moral [but not legal] disapprobation for that failure' (IV.10, p. 281). If a cocaine addict harms others through his extraordinary unkindness in situations where his assistance is reasonably expected under existing customs, for example, then 'he deserves reproach' for his failure to give due consideration, 'but not for the cause of it, nor for the errors, merely personal to himself, which may have remotely led to it' (ibid.).

Thus, where circumstances conjoin self-regarding faults to unjust or uncharitable conduct (so that the conduct is not properly seen as self-regarding), the person is legitimately punished by law or by opinion for his breach of duty:

Whenever, in short, there is a definite damage, or a definite risk of damage, either to an individual or to the public, the case is taken out of the province of liberty, and placed in that of morality or law.

(IV.10, p. 282)

But the province of liberty is not thereby rendered empty because, in many situations, self-regarding faults remain separable from other-regarding misconduct. The point is that the extravagant man who nevertheless is able to pay his debts, the public servant who is drunk only while off duty and the cocaine addict who is as kind and helpful to others as they may reasonably expect under prevailing social conventions, should remain perfectly free from legal or social penalties.

The question arises, however, whether those putatively self-regarding acts are, like expression, really other-regarding ones which, when violations of others' rights and other interests are absent, may be treated as if they were self-regarding because coercion is generally inexpedient. The answer, it seems, is that these acts are not like the case of expression. Expression always carries a risk of harm to others, by damaging their reputations, or misleading them, and so on. It remains other-regarding even outside the special situations where its suppression is held to be expedient. But drinking on duty, or drinking with a known tendency to become violent toward others when drunk, is arguably a different type of act than merely drinking with other consenting adults, of the usual tendencies, on a free evening. Merely consuming alcohol does not pose any risk of harm to others beyond their mere dislike. To be removed from the self-regarding class, drinking, it seems, must, unlike expression, be conjoined with some additional factor from which the drinking itself is logically separable. The drinker must have some pre-existing tendency to harm others, for example, or he must have voluntarily incurred certain duties of employment, marriage, loan repayment and so on, none of which are necessarily associated with drinking.

What about the damage to society occasioned when self-indulgent behavior eventually leads to a complete dependence on the taxpayer? In Mill's view, that 'merely contingent, or, as it may be called, constructive injury which a person causes to society . . . is one which society can afford to bear, for the sake of the greater good of human freedom' (IV.11, p. 282). He argues that society has better means than coercion to influence its members to be prudent and temperate workers:

> Armed not only with all the powers of education, but with the ascendency which the authority of a received opinion always exercises over the minds who are least fitted to judge for themselves; and aided by the natural penalties which cannot be prevented from falling on those who incur the distaste or the contempt of those who know them; let not society pretend that it needs, besides all this, the power to issue commands and enforce obedience in the personal concerns of individuals.
>
> (ibid.)

He apparently assumes that, in general, an ordinary person, capable of 'being acted on by rational consideration of distant motives', will not voluntarily become dependent on others for his subsistence (ibid.). If society fails to educate 'any considerable number of its members' up to this threshold level of rationality, then it has only 'itself to blame for the consequences' (ibid.).

That assumption is also implicit in his responses to the other two objections.

Bad examples (IV.11)

Mill admits that 'a bad example may have a pernicious effect, especially the example of doing wrong to others with impunity to the wrong-doer' (IV.11, p. 283). But he emphasizes that 'we are now speaking of conduct which, while it does no wrong to others, is supposed to do great harm to the agent himself' (ibid.). Such self-regarding misconduct must generally set 'a more salutary than hurtful' example to other people capable of self-improvement (ibid.). For 'if [the example] displays the misconduct, it displays also the painful or degrading consequences which, if the conduct is justly censured, must be supposed to be in all or most cases attendant on it' (ibid.).

Paternalism (IV.12)

As for the third objection, Mill argues in effect that the majority is far more likely than the individual to be wrong about what is useful or suitable to him in his self-regarding concerns. The lessons drawn from experience by the majority are more likely to be right when it comes to other-regarding concerns:

> On questions of social morality, of duty to others, the opinion of the public, that is, of an overruling majority, though often wrong, is likely to be still oftener right; because on such questions they are only required to judge of their own interests; of the manner in which some mode of conduct, if allowed to be practised [by everyone], would affect themselves.
>
> (IV.12, p. 283)

In short, majoritarian laws and customs of other-regarding conduct are more likely than not to be generally expedient because most adults can be expected to make reasonable judgments about harm to their own interests. But majoritarian rules of self-regarding conduct are 'quite as likely' to be generally inexpedient because 'in these cases public opinion means, at the best, some people's opinion of what is good or bad for *other* people' (ibid., emphasis added).

Interference with self-regarding conduct *denies* the assumption that most adults capable of self-improvement can be expected to make reasonable judgments about harm to their own interests. Since he wants to maintain that key assumption, he argues that society should never interfere with liberty and individuality in purely self-regarding matters.

'Gross usurpations upon the liberty of private life' (IV.13–21)

Mill concludes the chapter with several examples of the majority's tendency to encroach on individual spontaneity in self-regarding concerns. He says he is 'not writing an essay on the aberrations of existing moral feeling' (IV.13, p. 284). But he wants to show that his principle of liberty 'is of serious and practical moment', as opposed to 'a barrier against imaginary evils' (ibid.).

The public's tendency to translate its mere likes and dislikes into rules of self-regarding conduct, rules which are improperly called moral rules at all because they are not designed to prevent harm to others, is easy to illustrate: 'one of the most universal of all human propensities . . . [is] to extend the bounds of what may be called moral police' (ibid.). After considering some cases of religious intolerance which, though not actually found in English-speaking societies at the time, would be unobjectionable if the majority has authority to regulate self-regarding conduct, he discusses three cases drawn from those societies, presumably to drive home the point that no 'superior excellence' (III.18, p. 274) inheres in English-speaking majorities, which keeps them from committing 'gross usurpations upon the liberty of private life' (IV.18, p. 287).

His three examples are: legal prohibition (except for medical purposes) of 'fermented drinks' in New Brunswick and 'nearly half the United States' (the so-called Maine laws, after the state which first enacted prohibition in 1851), which the United Kingdom Alliance was pressing to have similarly enacted in the United Kingdom (despite the beginnings of repeal throughout North America) when he was writing (IV.19, pp. 287–8); Sabbatarian legislation, re-enacted in Britain in 1850 to forbid the greater part of work and public amusements on Sundays (IV.20, pp. 288–9); and the relentless persecution of Mormonism, chiefly on account of 'its sanction of polygamy', despite the attempt of the Mormons to voluntarily remove themselves from the larger American society by relocating during the 1840s to the remote Utah Territory (IV.21, pp. 290–1).

As these cases make clear, he has returned to his earlier theme of rising religious intolerance. All of them illustrate a revivified religious bigotry put into practice by (so-called) Christian majorities in the English-speaking societies. Needless to add, similar cases can still be drawn from the practices of English-speaking countries in our own time. Laws prohibiting the sale and possession of drugs, Sabbatarian legislation and legal bans on polygamy are all found in the United States today, for example, among many other rules meddling with self-regarding conduct.

During the course of his discussion, he makes some remarks relating to the application of his doctrine. Although he presents a more sustained treatment of problems of application in his final chapter, it seems useful to highlight those remarks now, to facilitate study of the three cases.

Consumption versus trading (IV.19)

When discussing temperance laws, Mill suggests that 'the act of drinking fermented liquors' is self-regarding, whereas 'selling fermented liquors . . . is trading, and trading is a social act' (IV.19, p. 288). This distinction between consumption and 'trading' or marketing is of great importance in understanding his doctrine. The individual ought to be given complete liberty, by right, to consume alcohol, or any other product, in accord with his own judgment and desires. Other people may intensely dislike his consumption activities, but mere dislike is not harm. Marketing those same products, however, is *not* self-regarding conduct, and thus is *not* covered by his liberty principle. Market competitors can cause each other unwanted financial loss through their selling activities. Society thus has legitimate authority to regulate the market, in his view, even if general expediency usually recommends a policy of laissez-faire rather than legal or social coercion.

Personal lifestyle versus marketing of labour (IV.20)

A similar distinction is at work in his discussion of Sabbatarian legislation. '[S]elf-chosen occupations' are self-regarding activities, he suggests, whereas contractual employer–employee relationships are other-regarding because they involve the selling of labour on the market. The individual ought to have absolute liberty to employ himself in whatever productive activities he pleases, assuming he has a legal right or permission to use any natural resources he proposes to use. Others may dislike what he does. But they can avoid him and his products, without harm to themselves.

In contrast, self-interested behaviour by some workers in the labour market can directly affect other workers against their wishes. By breaking a customary agreement not to work on one day of the week, for example, some workers can increase their own wages while tending to depress the weekly wage rate for others: 'The operatives are perfectly right in thinking that if all worked on Sunday, seven days' work would have to be given for six days' wages' (IV.20, p. 289).[4] Society thus has legitimate authority to control the labour market by enforcing a day of leisure. But Mill goes on to provide strong arguments for concluding that Sabbatarian legislation, or, more generally, legislation forcing *all* workers to take the *same* day off, is not generally expedient. 'The only ground, therefore, on which restrictions on Sunday amusements can be defended, must be that they are religiously wrong; a motive of legislation which can never be too earnestly protested against' (ibid.).

Contracts in perpetuity (IV.21)

When discussing the Mormons, he says, despite his general conclusion that they should be left alone under the cirumstances, that the institution of polygamy 'is a direct infraction' of his liberty principle (IV.21, p. 290). The problem, it seems, is that any contract in perpetuity, including a marriage contract, polygamous or otherwise, is incompatible with his doctrine of liberty. This can be inferred from his discussion of slavery contracts in the next chapter (V.11, pp. 299–300). He also makes a general case against contracts in perpetuity elsewhere (Mill, 1870; 1871, pp. 953–4).

Given that they can never be revoked by one of the parties without the consent of the other(s), such contracts (including international treaties) bind the parties together in a permanent relationship, despite the possibility of unforeseen changes of circumstances leading to subsequent changes of mind not shared by all. Agreements of this sort are commonly an unreasonable restriction on individual liberty (or, by analogy, a country's liberty), he argues, and thus on self-development (or national development):

> if [the law] ever does sanction them, it should take every possible security for their being contracted with foresight and deliberation; and in compensation for not permitting the parties themselves to revoke their engagement, should grant them a release from it, on a sufficient case being made out before an impartial authority.
>
> (1871, p. 954)

'These considerations are eminently applicable to marriage', he goes on to emphasize as of 1852 (just after his own marriage had taken place), 'the most important of all cases of engagement for life' (ibid.).

Even so, he recognizes that Mormon contracts of polygamous marriage, like other marriage contracts in perpetuity, are made by willing participants in the given culture. Thus, there is no ground, aside from religious intolerance, for interfering with the Mormon community on this score, given that the community is not aggressive toward others, grants complete freedom of exit to its dissatisfied members and is not otherwise roiled by internal dissensions in which appeals for external intervention are made by those whose liberty is being repressed:

> So long as the sufferers by the bad law do not invoke assistance from other communities, I cannot admit that persons entirely unconnected with them ought to step in and require that a condition of things with which all who are directly interested appear to be satisfied, should be put an end to because it is a scandal to persons some thousands of miles distant, who have no part or concern in it.
>
> (IV.21, p. 291)

Foreign intervention (IV.21)

Elsewhere, in *Representative Government* (1861a, pp. 546–77) and 'A Few Words on Non-Intervention' (1859a, pp. 118–24), Mill clarifies the conditions under which he thinks intervention by one community in the affairs of another is justified. Among other things, he says that one country can rightfully intervene in the affairs of another, to counter the previous intervention of a third party determined to support the side of despotism against that of free institutions (including political democracy and market capitalism): 'Intervention to enforce non-intervention is always right, always moral, if not always prudent' (1859a, p. 123). If a foreign despot offers financial or military support to an oppressive government, for example, the friends of liberty have a moral right to interfere similarly on the side of domestic rebels fighting for their freedom, with some prospect for success were it not for the initial foreign interference, in the context of a civil war. This includes a civil war between different ethnic groups in the same state, of course, one of which is fighting the other for national liberation and its own free institutions.

Suggestions for further reading

As a prelude to identifying and analysing current examples of 'gross usurpations upon the liberty of private life', it is useful to read more about the three examples discussed by Mill. There is a large literature on nineteenth-century temperance crusades in general, and the Maine laws in particular. See, e.g., Neal Dow, *The Reminiscences of Neal Dow, Recollections of Eighty Years* (Portland, Maine, The Evening Express Publishing Company, 1898); J.K. Chapman, 'The Mid-Nineteenth-Century Temperance Movement in New Brunswick and Maine', *Canadian Historical Review* 35 (1954): 43–60; J.S. Blocker, *American Temperance Movements: Cycles of Reform* (Boston, Twayne, 1989); J. Noel, *Canada Dry: Temperance Crusades Before Confederation* (Toronto, University of Toronto Press, 1995); L.L. Shiman, *Crusade Against Drink in Victorian England* (New York, St Martin's Press, 1988); and I.R. Tyrrell, *Sobering Up: From Temperance to Prohibition in Ante-Bellum America, 1800–1860* (Westport, Conn., Greenwood Press, 1979), pp. 252–89.

For the career of the United Kingdom Alliance, see Brian Harrison, *Drink and the Victorians: The Temperance Question in England 1815–72* (Pittsburgh, University of Pittsburgh Press, 1971); and A.E. Dingle, *The Campaign for Prohibition in Victorian England: The United Kingdom Alliance, 1872–95* (New Brunswick, NJ, Rutgers University Press, 1980).

The history of Sabbatarian legislation is analysed by D.N. Laband and D.H. Heinbuch, *Blue Laws: The History, Economics, and Politics of Sunday Closing Laws* (Amherst, Lexington Books, 1987).

The Mormons are of special interest, as a Christian sect founded as recently as 1830, by Joseph Smith, who led his followers from New York to settle initially around Nauvoo, Illinois. Quickly driven into Missouri, they faced more harassment and violence there, and eventually relocated to Utah. Their trials were far from over when Mill wrote. During the 'Mormon Wars' of 1857–8, President James Buchanan sent federal troops to occupy the Utah Territory. By 1862, in the midst of the larger Civil War, the Republican majority in Congress had enacted anti-bigamy legislation. Although the law was largely ignored until the 1879 *Reynolds* decision of the Supreme Court sanctioned federal enforcement, the US government conducted an intense campaign of persecution against the Mormons thereafter, with popular majority support. Mormons were repeatedly prosecuted for bigamy (a felony) and 'cohabitation' (an ambiguous misdemeanour), they were effectively stripped of the franchise (under the power of Congress to regulate the territories) and, finally, their church was driven into bankruptcy, with the Court upholding federal seizure of its assets in an infamous 1890 decision, *Church of Jesus Christ of Latter-day Saints* v. *US*. Shortly after the decision, church leaders issued a manifesto which abandoned polygamy as an article of the official Mormon faith, although polygamy continues to be practised even today by scattered 'fundamentalists'. By 1893, Mormon polygamists were given a general amnesty by presidential proclamation. In 1896, Congress granted Utah admission into the union as a state. Further discussion can be found in L.J. Arrington and D. Bitton, *The Mormon Experience: A History of the Latter-Day Saints*, 2nd edn (Champaign, University of Illinois Press, 1992); E.L. Lyman, *Political Deliverance: The Mormon Quest for Utah Statehood* (Champaign, University of Illinois Press, 1986); K.D. Driggs, 'The Mormon Church–State Confrontation in Nineteenth-Century America', *Journal of Church and State* 30 (1988): 273–89; Driggs, 'After the Manifesto: Modern Polygamy and Fundamentalist Mormons', *Journal of Church and State* 32 (1990): 367–89; R.L. Jensen and M.R. Thorp, eds, *Mormons in Early Victorian Britain* (Salt Lake City, University of Utah Press, 1990); and R.S. Van Wagoner, *Mormon Polygamy: A History*, 2nd edn (Salt Lake City, Signature Books, 1992).

For a discussion of some general lessons for liberalism to be drawn from Mill's approach to the Mormons, see C.L. Ten, 'Mill's Place in Liberalism', *The Political Science Reviewer* 24 (1995): 179–204, esp. pp. 185–7.

For a helpful commentary on Mill's still-influential approach to foreign intervention, see G.E. Varouxakis, *J.S. Mill on French Thought, Politics, and National Character*, Ph.D. thesis in History, University College, London, 1995.

Chapter 6

Applications
(Chapter V,
paras. 1–23)

Mill's doctrine and its application (V.1–2)

It has emerged that the principle of liberty is directed at opinions and truly self-regarding acts, which are harmless to others in the sense that others do not suffer any perceptible damage against their wishes. Others may intensely dislike the self-regarding conduct. But mere dislike, without any evidence of perceptible damage, does not constitute harm. Others may *choose* to avoid the agent as a result of their dislike, thereby imposing possibly severe natural penalties on him and even themselves. But any loss which others may suffer because of their decision to avoid the agent is not suffered against *their* wishes.

Of course, the liberty principle has as its corollary what may be termed the social authority principle. The authority principle says that society has legitimate power to enforce rules of other-regarding conduct. The individual has no right to choose as he pleases with respect to conduct which *is* harmful to others, in the

sense that it directly causes them perceptible damage beyond their mere dislike. Rather, he ought to obey the general rules accepted by the majority, and is justifiably subject to coercion for that purpose.

When introducing the concluding chapter, Mill reminds the reader that he is arguing for this 'one very simple principle' of liberty and its logical complement. After referring to 'the two maxims which together form the entire doctrine of this Essay', he restates the maxims:

> The maxims are, first, that the individual is not accountable to society for his [self-regarding] actions . . . Advice, instruction, persuasion, and avoidance by other people if thought necessary by them for their own good, are the only measures by which society can justifiably express its dislike or disapprobation of his conduct. Secondly, that for [other-regarding] actions . . . the individual is accountable, and may be subjected to social or to legal punishment, if society is of opinion that the one or the other is requisite for its protection.
>
> (V.2, p. 292)

His remaining discussion is intended to clear up remaining ambiguities surrounding his doctrine, and to illustrate how the maxims can be consistently applied.

Many situations arise in practice, he suggests, where it is not immediately clear which of the maxims applies. He offers 'specimens of application' to help us learn how to go about arriving at reasonable practical conclusions in these sorts of situations. The sample cases are chosen, he says, with a view 'to assist the judgment in holding the balance between [the two maxims], in the cases where it appears doubtful which of them is applicable to the case' (V.1, p. 292). As it turns out, he invariably argues that a reasonable balance can be struck, as we would expect in light of his comments in Chapter II about the decisiveness of 'a completely informed mind' (II.23, p. 245). Even in hard cases where he himself cannot make up his own mind between conflicting answers, both of which appear reasonable, he suggests that further debate and discussion among the members of a given society would lead to a contextual resolution of the conflict.

It is important to emphasize at the outset that there is no doubt in any of these cases about the meaning of self-regarding acts, or about the logical distinction between self-regarding and other-regarding spheres upon which the doctrine of the essay depends. Rather, any doubts are inherent in the practical situation, and they generally vanish once certain reasonable distinctions are made to deal with the situation. In short, further reflection usually reveals what was not immediately apparent, namely, which of the two maxims applies, or, to be more precise, whether the conditions are satisfied for application of the liberty maxim or for the authority principle. Even where doubts are expressed by Mill himself about what to do, the integrity of the principle of liberty is not compromised.

Harm to others not sufficient for coercion (V.3)

He begins by reminding us of an important point already touched on in his introductory chapter (I.11, pp. 224–5). The propriety of individual liberty is *not* confined, he re-emphasizes, to self-regarding acts: 'it must by no means be supposed, because damage, or probability of damage, to the interests of others, can alone justify the interference of society, that therefore it always does justify such interference' (V.3, p. 292). In many situations, acts which directly harm other people should nevertheless be free from legal or social coercion: 'In many cases, an individual, in pursuing a legitimate object, necessarily and therefore legitimately causes pain or loss to others, or intercepts a good which they had a reasonable hope of obtaining' (ibid.).

Liberty should be granted in these cases not because the acts are of a type harmless to others, but because social control of the acts, though it can be legitimately considered, is commonly admitted to be generally inexpedient:

> Whoever succeeds in an overcrowded profession, or in a competitive examination; whoever is preferred to another in any contest for an object which both desire, reaps benefit from the loss of others, from their wasted exertion and their disappointment. But it is, by common admission, better for the general interest of mankind, that persons should pursue their objects undeterred by this sort of consequences.
>
> (V.3, pp. 292–3)

There is no denying that the successful agent harms his unsuccessful competitors by directly causing them perceptible damage beyond their mere dislike, to wit, 'wasted exertion' and the loss of valuable things which they had 'a reasonable hope of obtaining'. Nevertheless, coercion for the purpose of preventing such harms would, 'by common admission', result in even more damage to the interests of the members of society than the alternative of laissez-faire. In other words, the harms suffered by losing competitors are of a less weighty kind, which does not justify enforcement of social rules:

> society admits no right to immunity from *this kind* of suffering; and feels called on to interfere, only when means of success have been employed which it is contrary to the general interest to permit – namely, fraud or treachery, and force.
>
> (V.3, p. 293, emphasis added)

At least two implications must be kept in mind if Mill's doctrine is to be consistently applied 'with any prospect of advantage' (V.1, p. 292).

The expedient scope of individual liberty

First, the liberty principle is not intended to determine the expedient scope of individual liberty. The liberty maxim says that each individual ought to enjoy complete liberty, by right, with respect to those of his acts which are harmless to others. The purely self-regarding sphere, to which the maxim applies, is a *minimum* domain of individual liberty, the violation of which ought to be considered an injustice in any civil society. In general, the expedient field of liberty will include more than that inviolable minimum.

What *additional* domain is called for, beyond the self-regarding minimum, is not the subject of the liberty principle. Rather, it falls within the legitimate jurisdiction of majority opinion in any social context, recognizing that majoritarian notions of general expediency may well vary across contexts. In this regard, the social authority maxim, which applies only to other-regarding acts, does not imply that society ought invariably to exercise its legitimate power to coerce the individual to prevent harm to others. Liberty of other-regarding action is not necessarily illegitimate. Rather, a policy of laissez-faire is commonly held to be generally expedient in many cases. Enforcement of rules of other-regarding conduct is viewed as inexpedient in such cases,

> either because it is a kind of case in which [the individual] is on the whole likely to act better, when left to his own discretion ... or because the attempt to exercise control would produce other evils, greater than those which it would prevent.
>
> (I.11, p. 225)

In short, absence of harm to others, while sufficient, is not necessary for individual liberty to be generally expedient. Thus, the expedient scope of liberty may extend beyond the ambit of the liberty principle, which tells us where the individual has an inviolable moral right to choose as he pleases.

The realm of private action

A second implication is that, for analogous reasons, the expedient domain of private action may extend beyond the purely self-regarding sphere, if by private action we mean any action (including competitive market behaviour) that individuals are morally at liberty to perform, without interference by others (including government officials). Some private actions may well be harmful other-regarding acts.

Note that what is then called private action may take place 'in public', as many market transactions do. This alerts us to the vagaries of any private–public distinction, and should make us suitably cautious when using these terms. But, more importantly, it also tells us that the mere performance of an action 'in public' cannot be sufficient to justify interference with that action. On the other hand, it leaves open the possibility that acts which, when performed behind closed doors, are purely self-regarding, are brought into the other-regarding class when performed 'in public', without ceasing to be considered private! Sex 'in public' between consenting adults might perhaps be shown to pose some sort of perceptible damage to others against their wishes, for example, so that consensual sex in that case loses its otherwise purely self-regarding character (cf. V.7). Yet the majority might nevertheless view coercion against sex in public as inexpedient, so that it would continue to be private in that sense.

The liberty principle distinguished from laissez-faire (V.4)

We can now make sense of Mill's claim that his liberty maxim must not be conflated with the economic doctrine of laissez-faire: 'the principle of individual liberty is not involved in the doctrine of free trade' (V.4, p. 293). Market sales are *not* self-regarding acts, and thus do *not* fall within the ambit of his liberty maxim. Rather,

> trade is a social act. Whoever undertakes to sell any description of goods to the public, does what affects the interest of other persons, and of society in general; and thus his conduct, in principle, *comes within the jurisdiction of society.*
>
> (ibid., emphasis added)

Selling goods to others is an other-regarding act within the ambit of the social authority maxim. Society can legitimately consider imposing rules of exchange and production, yet, 'by common admission', laissez-faire is often (though not always) more expedient than social regulation:

> [I]t is now recognised, though not till after a long struggle, that both the cheapness and the good quality of commodities are most effectually provided for by leaving the producers and sellers perfectly free, under the sole check of equal freedom to the buyers for supplying themselves elsewhere. This is the so-called doctrine of free trade, which rests on grounds different from, though equally solid with, the principle of individual liberty asserted in this essay.
>
> (ibid.)

Social control of exchange and production is not illegitimate in principle: 'the restraints in question affect only that part of conduct which society is competent to restrain' (ibid.). But it is 'now recognised' that such control is often inexpedient – it causes more harm than it prevents. The restraints directly harm producers and suppliers, by preventing them from transacting on the terms they wish; taxpayers, who must bear enforcement costs; and even consumers, who face higher prices and lower quality goods as compared to laissez-faire. Thus, the restraints 'are wrong solely because they do not really produce the results which it is desired to produce by them' (ibid.).

Mill argues in his *Political Economy* that there are various 'large exceptions' to the laissez-faire doctrine (1871, pp. 936–71). But 'most of the questions which arise respecting the limits of that doctrine' also have nothing to do with his liberty maxim (V.4, p. 293). '[H]ow far sanitary precautions, or arrangements to protect workpeople employed in dangerous occupations, should be enforced on employers', for example, are questions of general expediency relating to other-regarding conduct (ibid.).

Yet 'there are questions relating to interference with trade, which are essentially questions of liberty' (ibid.). The liberty maxim is involved in 'all cases . . . where the object of the interference is to make it impossible or difficult to obtain a particular commodity', for example, temperance laws, 'prohibition of the importation of opium' and 'restriction of the sale of poisons' (ibid.). In these cases, society violates the right of the individual to buy or use any products he likes, short of harm to other people: 'These interferences are objectionable, not as infringements on the liberty of the producer or seller, but on that of the buyer' (ibid.).

The clear implication is that the liberty principle can be applicable to consumer choices, whereas the laissez-faire doctrine applies to the activities of producers and sellers. It does not follow that all consumption behaviour is purely self-regarding. That claim is highly implausible. Rather, there is some field of consumption activity which can be seen as self-regarding. Mill suggests later in this chapter that the individual should have a right to spend his income as he wishes on any good which can be used in ways harmless to other people. Even a product such as poison, which in some uses poses danger to others, ought not to be forbidden to consumers, because it also has innocent uses. Still, if a commodity is designed solely to cause injury to others, he allows, its use may be prohibited consistently with the liberty maxim.

Granting all this, there must be more to the story, even though he does not tell it in this place. For even if a product has innocent uses, someone may object that its purchase and consumption by one person can directly injure another against his wishes, by denying that other person the opportunity to use that particular scarce commodity. But the objection is, in general, misplaced. One way to answer it might be to draw a distinction between harm and the denial of goods or benefits which a person had a reasonable hope of obtaining. But such an avenue is closed to Mill, who, after all, admits that the losing competitors for jobs and the like do suffer perceptible hurts at the hands of the winners.

A far more persuasive answer is available in any event: the consumption of a product by one person does not, in general, preclude its consumption by others at the same price. Given that a good can be reproduced indefinitely at a competitive cost of production, its use by one individual in no way prevents others from acquiring like goods. Moreover, in reasonably competitive markets characterized by free entry and exit (though not necessarily by large numbers of sellers or buyers at any one time), one person's consumption choices have no perceptible impact on market prices. Current market supply is determined by producers' expectations, at a previous time, of potential market demand. Any person's current consumption cannot affect past producer decisions, but can only help to call forth an adequate market supply at competitive cost in the future.

No doubt there are exceptions. Harm to others may be caused by large-scale purchases, which temporarily disrupt competitive market prices, for example, or by the use of irreplaceable objects which are in fixed supply. But these special cases do not alter the fact that many acts of consumption do belong in the self-regarding realm.

It transpires that, according to the liberty principle, the individual ought to be given complete liberty, by right, to consume any product which, first, has uses harmless to other people and, second, can be reproduced indefinitely at a competitive cost. But no person has a moral right to produce or sell anything as he wishes. Society has legitimate authority to organize production and exchange as the majority thinks expedient. Should scarce inputs of natural resources, labour and capital be employed to create this type of product or that? Should production and allocation be organized in terms of central planning or decentralized markets? Should market enterprises be organized as socialistic co-operatives or capitalistic corporations? Should these enterprises be left alone to buy their inputs and sell their products on any terms they agree to negotiate without force or fraud, or should government intervene for various reasons to regulate market prices? These are all questions of general expediency, legitimately within the purview of social authority. At the same time, Mill emphasizes, general expediency is commonly held to dictate a continuing reliance on capitalistic firms and free markets, at least for the foreseeable future. Private ownership of the means of production ought to be conjoined with a general presumption in favour of laissez-faire. (For further discussion and caveats relating to these points, see Riley, 1996.)

When applying Mill's doctrine, then, we must not suppose that there is a neat correspondence between the expedient scope of individual liberty (or private conduct) and the liberty maxim on the one hand, and between the expedient scope of public coercion and the authority maxim on the other. The laissez-faire doctrine implies that some liberty of other-regarding acts is utilitarian, whereas the liberty maxim says the same of complete liberty of purely self-regarding acts.

Why draw the distinction?

The question arises whether there is really much point in distinguishing between the liberty maxim and a laissez-faire principle. In both cases, it might be said, the value of individuality or self-development outweighs competing considerations, even if harm to others is involved in the one case and not in the other.

Nevertheless, there are crucial differences. The liberty maxim prescribes equal rights to complete liberty of self-regarding actions. Equal rights of this sort can be enjoyed in harmony, since one person's exercise of his right does not directly affect other people against their wishes. The laissez-faire doctrine says, in contrast, that individuals have no moral obligations to each other with respect to some other-regarding activities. Rather, individuals have moral permission (and perhaps legal rights founded on that permission) to compete under certain terms and conditions. But an equal permission to compete is a much weaker moral claim than an equal right to do as one likes. Indeed, it is impossible to guarantee self-interested producers and sellers an equal right to choose as they wish in a competitive scramble for scarce resources. Some competitors can succeed only at the expense of others. Thus, society needs good reasons – the efficient production and allocation of resources, for example – for permitting the individualities of some to flourish at the expense of others under laissez-faire. The form of reasoning that justifies the liberty maxim, namely, that it affords an equal opportunity for the cultivation of individuality without harm to others, is simply not available.

The extraordinary case of expression

Before considering a second sort of practical insight offered by Mill, we should return briefly to the ambiguity which has been lingering around his treatment of expression. The ambiguity must be resolved, it seems, by saying that expression is an extraordinary case.

In general, unlike expression, self-regarding acts are truly harmless to others. Such acts are not really other-regarding acts which, because interference with them is calculated to be generally inexpedient, are treated *as if* they are harmless to others, when in fact they are harmful (or carry a significant risk of harm) to others.

Expression is extraordinary because, although truly other-regarding, it is virtually never the object of expedient coercion: the risks and perils to others (to their reputations and the like) are 'almost' always outweighed by the expected benefits of self-development. Thus, expression can be seen as a peculiar element of the other-regarding class. Since it is 'almost' self-regarding, it may conveniently be treated in general as if it were self-regarding, and practically inseparable from thought.

The proper limits of society's police authority (V.5–6)

Mill next turns to another practical issue, opened up, as he says, by the example of 'the sale of poisons' touched on in his treatment of the laissez-faire doctrine. The 'new question' is 'the proper limits of what may be called the functions of police; how far liberty may legitimately be invaded for the prevention of crime, or of accident' (V.5, pp. 293–4). It is indisputable, he says, that social authority is legitimately employed to prevent crimes, understood as acts involving serious harms to others, and accidents, including unintentional self-injury. Public officials may interfere with 'any one evidently preparing to commit a crime', for example, and may also prohibit the manufacture and sale of any product which is only ever used to commit crimes (V, p. 294). Moreover, they, 'or any one else', may prevent a person from 'attempting to cross a bridge which had been ascertained to be unsafe', if 'there were no time to warn him of his danger' (ibid.). Such interference does not constitute 'any real infringement of his liberty' when the bridge is *known* to be unsafe, because his attempt to cross it will result with *certainty* in an accident: '[L]iberty consists in doing what one desires, and he does not desire to fall into the river' (ibid.). Note that Mill does not allow for special cases where a suicidal person does wish to plunge into the river. Perhaps he thinks that such a person must be 'a child, or delirious, or in some state of excitement or absorption incompatible with the full use of the reflecting faculty' (ibid.). In any case, the desire for self-annihilation is evidently at odds with self-development or individuality, the cultivation of which is the very purpose of protecting the individual's liberty, by right, in self-regarding matters.

Practical uncertainties (V.5)

These more or less clear-cut cases are not, however, the only ones in practice. It may be unclear whether a person is preparing to commit a crime, for example, because the products which he has bought have 'innocent' and 'useful purposes' as well as criminal ones. The buyer of poison might be preparing to murder his wife, or he might be intending to use it to help protect the plants in his garden from insects. Such situations seem problematic because we are uncertain about whether a person intends to perform an other-regarding action or a self-regarding action. If we could know beforehand how he will act, we could decide in a straightforward way whether the social authority maxim or the liberty maxim applies. But we do not know what he will do.

Again, it may be unclear just how unsafe a bridge is, in which case a person's attempt to cross it will result in an accident only with some probability less than unity. He might be an adventuresome soul fully aware of the danger to himself, or he might be someone who is ignorant of the risk and who would not wish to take it once suitably informed. Such situations seem problematic because we are uncertain about how much information the person has concerning the probable consequences of his behaviour. If we could know beforehand how much he knows, we could again quite easily decide which of the two maxims applies to the case. But we do not know his state of knowledge, and will never know unless we seize him at the entry of the bridge. What to do?

The problem in these situations is to find a reasonable balance between the maxims with which to resolve the uncertainty inherent in the situation itself. Precisely because we do not know enough at the moment to be able to say whether conditions justify application of one maxim or the other, we must give due weight to both until we have acquired the relevant knowledge. Otherwise, if we dismiss either maxim *ex ante*, we preclude ourselves from gaining the very information required to decide which of the two properly applies *ex post*. In order to resolve our ignorance in a way that allows for due application of whichever maxim is called for in the situation as it materializes, we must place certain restrictions on the individual's right to choose as he wishes in what may ultimately prove to be his self-regarding concerns (though we cannot be sure of this when the restrictions are imposed). The restrictions are reasonable in light of society's legitimate authority to take precautions against crimes and accidents whose burdens will fall on unwilling victims as well as the general taxpayer.

Reasonable compromises (V.5)

Mill thinks a reasonable balance can be struck in these cases without any real encroachment on the individual's freedom to choose as he wishes in his self-regarding concerns. Society can legitimately take precautions against accidents, for example, by forcing the individual to attend to a warning of the risk he incurs when he crosses a dangerous bridge or uses toxic drugs. Once warned, however, the person should be free to choose as he likes, as long as self-injury is not a certainty: 'when there is not a certainty, but only a danger of mischief, no one but the person himself can judge of the sufficiency of the motive which may prompt him to incur the risk' (ibid.). Society properly has authority to assure itself that he is informed about the possibly grave consequences of his self-regarding acts. But the informed individual should not be 'forcibly prevented from exposing himself to [risks]' which he *desires* to undertake (ibid.).

Similarly, society can legitimately take precautions against crimes by forcing the individual to observe 'certain formalities' as a condition of sale in the case of 'articles adapted to be instruments of crime' (V.5, p. 295). A buyer of poisons or guns should be required to provide what 'Bentham . . . called "preappointed evidence"' of how he intends to use these products:

> The seller, for example, might be required to enter in a register the exact time of the transaction, the name and address of the buyer, the precise quality and quantity sold; to ask the purpose for which it was wanted, and record the answer he received.
>
> (ibid.)

The provision of such evidence is no 'material impediment' to the buyer's freedom to do as he likes short of injury to others. But it may help to ward off crimes, by facilitating their detection: 'Such regulations would in general be no material impediment to obtaining the article, but a very considerable one to making an improper use of it without detection' (ibid.).

Special instances of legitimate police authority (V.6)

Mill goes on to argue that society's legitimate power, to 'ward off crimes against itself by antecedent precautions', can even extend to coercion against what seems to be self-regarding action in special circumstances. It is 'perfectly legitimate', for example,

> that a person, who had once been convicted of any act of violence toward others under the influence of drink, should be placed under a special legal restriction, personal to himself; that if he were afterwards found drunk, he should be liable to a penalty, and that if when in that state he committed another offence, the punishment to which he would be liable for that

> other offence should be increased in severity.
>
> (V.6, p. 295)

Such a person's consumption of alcohol, although apparently self-regarding, carries a significant probability, based on his own special experience, of becoming in fact a violent act toward others. What looks like a self-regarding act is really an other-regarding one, posing a risk of evil to others: 'The making himself drunk, in a person whom drunkenness excites to do harm to others, is a crime against others' (ibid.). But most consumers are not similarly excited by alcohol, even if they drink it in excessive amounts. Thus, the extraordinary interference with his liberty, though justified in his case, is not justified in general.

For analogous reasons, Mill thinks it perfectly legitimate that an idle person, who has a special financial obligation towards others as a result of contractual arrangements or kinship, should be coerced to fulfil that obligation, 'by compulsory labour, if no other means are available' (ibid.).

Society's authority to enforce 'good manners' (V.7)

Mill completes his discussion of 'obvious limitations' of this extraordinary sort to the liberty maxim, by claiming that 'purely self-regarding misconduct' can often properly be meddled with when it takes place in public:

> there are many acts which, being directly injurious only to the agents themselves, ought not to be legally interdicted, but which, if done publicly, are a violation of good manners, and coming thus within the category of offences against others, may rightfully be prohibited.
>
> (V.7, p. 295)

The claim is puzzling as it stands, and he provides virtually no clarification. 'Of this kind are offences against decency', he says, yet 'the objection to publicity' is 'equally strong in the case of many actions not in themselves condemnable, nor supposed to be' (V.7, pp. 295–6). He seems to be saying that publicity as such can lend a special quality to what is otherwise a self-regarding act, transforming it into other-regarding conduct harmful to others. Examples might include self-mutilation in public, sexual intercourse between consenting adults in public or the publication of intimate details of one's personal relationships contrary to the wishes of the others involved. The last case might be read broadly, to include publication of gossip about one's friends and their acquaintances, as communicated in private conversations, letters and the like.

Harm in these instances apparently involves the violation of certain conventions of goodwill and polite behaviour, which constitute 'good manners' in a particular social context. Such rules might be viewed as reasonable contrivances for protecting each individual's interest in his good reputation, for example, in which case a violation of the rules could be seen as harmful to others' reputations. Perceptible damage to reputation, suffered against one's wishes, would be a form of harm. Even if Mill has something like this in mind, however, it cannot be the whole story. More needs to be said. The line between mere dislike and harm may well vanish for acts performed in public, if harm can include whatever most people feel is too rude or impolite to be suffered in public. This admittedly hard case requires further discussion (see VIII.3).

Liberty of public solicitation and its limits (V.8)

Mill next considers practical cases that are prompted by the question: 'what the agent is free to do, ought other persons to be equally free to counsel or instigate?' (V.8, p. 296). Given that the individual should be completely free, by right, to engage in self-regarding misconduct which is disliked by most, should others be equally free to encourage such self-regarding misconduct? 'This question', he admits, 'is not free from difficulty' (ibid.). Strictly speaking, soliciting another to do an act is not a self-regarding action: 'To give advice or offer inducements to any one, is a social act, and may, therefore, like actions in general which affect others, be supposed amenable to social control' (ibid.). Yet he argues that, like expression, it can reasonably be treated as if it were self-regarding, since it is practically inseparable from deliberation over self-regarding acts:

> If people must be allowed, in whatever concerns only them-
> selves, to act as seems best to themselves at their own peril,
> they must equally be free to consult with one another about what
> is fit to be so done; to exchange opinions, and give and receive
> suggestions. Whatever it is permitted to do, it must be permitted
> to advise to do.
>
> (ibid.)

The benefits of self-development made possible by liberty of advice
and consultation generally outweigh any harms to others' interests.

Nevertheless, just as complete liberty of expression is not
recommended, so exceptions ought to be admitted to liberty of solicitation. Mill argues that treating solicitation as if it were self-regarding
becomes dubious 'only when the instigator derives a personal benefit
from his advice; when he makes it his occupation, for subsistence
or pecuniary gain, to promote what society and the state consider
to be an evil' (ibid.). The 'new element of complication' in these
exceptional cases is the existence of classes of producers and sellers,
'with an interest opposed to what is considered as the public weal'
(ibid.). Ought society to regulate these sellers, or adopt a policy of
laissez-faire? 'Fornication, for example, must be tolerated, and so must
gambling; but should a person be free to be a pimp, or to keep a
gambling house?' (ibid.). This is a hard case, he admits, which 'lie[s]
on the exact boundary line between two principles, and it is not at
once apparent to which of the two it belongs' (ibid.).

On the one hand, it may be argued that such a case ought to be
assimilated to the liberty principle, since that principle admittedly
applies already to the *buyer* of the product or service which the pimp
or casino-owner is promoting and offering to sell.

> On the side of toleration it may be said, that the fact of follow-
> ing anything as an occupation, and living or profiting by the
> practice of it, cannot make that criminal which would other-
> wise be admissible; that the act should be either consistently
> permitted or consistently prohibited; that if the principles which
> we have hitherto defended are true, society has no business,
> as society, to decide anything to be wrong which concerns
> only the individual; that it cannot go beyond dissuasion, and

that one person ought to be as free to persuade, as another to dissuade.

(ibid.)

In short, a policy of laissez-faire ought to apply to the producers and marketers because the consumer admittedly has complete freedom, by right, to buy and use the products or services in question. It cannot be wrong for people to make a living trying to persuade the individual to consume that which he has a right to consume as he wishes.

On the other hand, it may be argued that such a case is properly covered by the social authority maxim, because society has legitimate power to try

to exclude the influence of solicitations which are not disinterested, of instigators who cannot possibly be impartial – who have a direct personal interest on one side, and that side the one which the state believes to be wrong, and who confessedly promote it for personal objects only.

(V.8, p. 297)

Given that all are fallible, the majority is justified in assuming that the individual ought to decide for himself, with as little influence as possible from biased sellers, whether the product or service is good or bad for his purposes:

There can surely, it may be urged, be nothing lost, no sacrifice of good, by so ordering matters that persons shall make their election, either wisely or foolishly, on their own prompting, as free as possible from the arts of persons who stimulate their inclinations for interested purposes of their own.

(ibid.)

To minimize the influence of biased advertising, so the argument goes, public brothels and casinos should be prohibited. This would confine the self-regarding activities to private establishments, out of view of the general public: 'all persons should be free to gamble [or buy sex] in their own or each other's houses, or in any place of meeting established by their own subscriptions, and open only to the members and their visitors' (ibid.). Even 'the prohibition [against public establishments] is never effectual', he admits (ibid.). Yet it serves its purpose. Public brothels and gambling-houses can only be carried on 'with a certain degree of secrecy and mystery, so that nobody knows anything about them but those who seek them' (ibid.).

Mill apparently leans in favour of the social authority maxim here. Social control of the sellers, to prevent their public advocacy of fornication and gambling, is properly conjoined, he suggests, with complete liberty of the buyers. The liberty maxim applies, then, whereas the laissez-faire principle does not, in this type of case. The police can legitimately shut down public brothels and casinos, and also make sure that private establishments operate according to the terms and conditions of their licences, for example, they must be open only to paying members and their guests.

At the same time, he 'will not venture to decide' whether social authority ought to extend to '*punishing* the accessary, when the principal is (and must be) allowed to go free; of fining or imprisoning the procurer, but not the fornicator, the gambling-house keeper, but not the gambler' (ibid., emphasis added). Police action to prevent public solicitation is justified, but it remains unclear whether society ought to punish those who engage in it, beyond shutting down their enterprises. Presumably, this is a question of general expediency which may reasonably be decided either way, depending on social context. Yet Mill does seem reluctant to opt for punishment, as he speaks of it as a 'moral anomaly' when the principal must be allowed to go free (ibid.).

He clearly rejects any claim that 'the common operations of buying and selling [ought] to be interfered with on analogous grounds' (ibid.). The sellers of virtually every commodity 'have a pecuniary interest in encouraging' excess consumption of it. But 'no argument' in favour of prohibition 'can be founded on this', because the sellers are essential to consumers who have a right to buy and use articles as they wish, short of harm to others. Temperance laws cannot be justified on that basis, for example, 'because the class of dealers in strong drinks, though interested in their abuse, are indispensably required for the sake of their legitimate use' (ibid.).

This does not preclude special regulations, akin to those imposed on pimps and casino operators, which are designed to prevent public encouragement of alcohol consumption: 'The interest, however, of these dealers in promoting intemperance is a real evil, and justifies the state in imposing restrictions and requiring guarantees which, but for that justification, would be infringements of legitimate liberty' (ibid.). The public authorities might properly require that dealers post warnings against abuse of alcohol, for example, and refuse to serve apparently intoxicated patrons. Repeated violation of these conditions would result in revocation of the licence to sell drinks to the public.

Legitimate authority to tax sales and limit the number of sellers (V.9–10)

Mill now turns to yet another question, namely, 'whether the state, while it permits, should nevertheless indirectly discourage [purely self-regarding] conduct which it deems contrary to the best interests of the agent' (V.9, p. 297). He asks, for example, whether government 'should take measures to render the means of drunkenness more costly, or add to the difficulty of procuring them by limiting the number of the places of sale' (V.9, pp. 297–8). To give an adequate answer, he insists, 'many distinctions require to be made' (V.9, p. 298).

Special taxation of stimulants (V.9)

On the one hand, it is an illegitimate use of social authority to tax 'stimulants' solely for the purpose of limiting their consumption: 'Every increase of cost is a prohibition, to those whose means do not come up to the augmented price; and to those who do, it is a penalty laid on them for gratifying a particular taste' (ibid.). The individual should be free to spend his income on alcohol and drugs as he likes, provided he does not harm others.

On the other hand, taxation for purposes of revenue is a legitimate exercise of social authority, if only because revenues are evidently required to maintain government and run the legal system which any civilized society creates as an important component of its moral code. Since 'in most countries it is necessary that a considerable part of that taxation should be indirect', society 'cannot help imposing penalties, which to some persons may be prohibitory, on the use of some articles of consumption' (ibid.). Given that such penalties are inevitable, society properly has the right to focus taxation on those commodities 'of which it deems the use, beyond a very moderate quantity, to be positively injurious [to the consumer]' (ibid.). Thus, special taxation of stimulants for revenue purposes is 'not only admissible, but to be approved of' (ibid.).

Mill's argument here distinguishes between legitimate and illegitimate purposes of special taxes on self-regarding acts of which the majority disapproves. Specifically, taxation of self-regarding conduct is legitimate for the purpose of raising revenues needed by the state to carry out certain generally expedient functions.[1] But it is illegitimate when employed merely to interfere with consumption, raising no necessary revenues. This distinction may seem very fine in the context of the modern welfare state, where government's appetite for funds appears virtually unlimited. Note, however, that in addition to taking for granted a liberal theory of government as limited to certain expedient functions, Mill does not rule out the possibility that indirect taxation for fiscal purposes will cease to be necessary. In advanced societies with massive wealth, for example, necessary revenues might be raised entirely through direct taxation of income and wealth. If so, because it is not needed to raise revenues, special taxation of stimulants is an illegitimate interference with individual liberty in that social context.

Limits on supply (V.10)

As for social authority to limit the number of sellers of intoxicants, its propriety also depends on the purpose of its exercise. On the one hand, it is illegitimate to set a 'limitation in number, for instance, of beer and spirit houses, for the express purpose of rendering them more difficult of access, and diminishing the occasions of temptation' (V.10, p. 298). Such paternalism treats as children those (notably workers) who want to drink, and violates the right of the individual to spend his income as he likes, short of harm to others.

On the other hand, some limitation in the number of sellers may be a justified by-product of society's exercise of legitimate authority to regulate the market and take precautions against crime:

All places of public resort require the restraint of a police, and places of this kind peculiarly, because offences against society are especially apt to originate there. It is, therefore, fit to confine the power of selling these commodities (at least for consumption on the spot) to persons of known or vouched-for respectability of conduct; to make such regulations respecting hours of opening and closing as may be requisite for public surveillance, and to withdraw the licence if breaches of the peace repeatedly take place through the connivance or incapacity of the keeper of the house, or if it becomes a rendez-vous for concocting and preparing offences against the law.

(ibid.)

Again, there is no absolute right to sell commodities, free of all forms of coercion, because marketing is not a purely self-regarding act. The doctrine of laissez-faire is distinct from the principle of liberty. The latter is implicated only to the extent that society interferes in the market for the sole purpose of prohibiting the consumption of particular commodities. The individual does have a right to spend his income on whatever he wants, short of harm to others.[2] Note that an indefinite number of places of drink, open at all hours, could be justified if sufficient keepers of good repute were available and round-the-clock police surveillance were not inexpedient.

Voluntary association and the enforcement of contracts (V.11)

Mill next turns to the question of applying his two maxims in cases where 'any number of individuals' choose 'to regulate by mutual consent such things as regard them jointly, and regard no persons but themselves' (V.11, p. 299). It is straightforward that any such group ought to have complete liberty, by right, to conduct its self-regarding affairs in accord with the unanimous wishes of its members. But, recognizing that their unanimity may not persist, the members may choose to negotiate contracts of various sorts with one another, and rely on society to enforce the contracts: 'it is often necessary, even in things in which they alone are concerned, that they should enter into engagements with one another; and when they do, it is fit, as a general rule, that those engagements should be kept' (ibid.). Failure to keep to the terms of a contract harms other parties, by disappointing legitimate expectations raised by the contract itself. Society properly has authority to coerce all parties, by law or opinion, to satisfy contractual obligations which have been voluntarily incurred.

Even though society legitimately has authority to enforce the terms of all contracts, however, it is, by common admission, not always generally expedient for society actually to exercise that enforcement authority: 'in the laws, probably, of every country, this general rule [that engagements should be kept] has some exceptions' (ibid.). Indeed, 'it is sometimes considered a sufficient reason for releasing [persons] from an engagement, that it is injurious to themselves' (ibid.).

Voluntary slavery

One example, an 'extreme case', is slavery contracts: 'an engagement by which a person should sell himself, or allow himself to be sold, as a slave, would be null and void; neither enforced by law nor by opinion' (ibid.). The reason why society ought to interfere with such contracts is 'apparent', Mill says, even though harm to third parties is not involved. The seller ought to be prevented from alienating his liberty:

> [B]y selling himself for a slave, he abdicates his liberty; he fore-goes any future use of it beyond that single act. He therefore defeats, in his own case, the very purpose which is the justification of allowing him to dispose of himself. He is no longer free; but is thenceforth in a position which has no longer the presumption in its favour, that would be afforded by his voluntarily remaining in it.
>
> (V.11, pp. 299–300)

If slavery contracts are enforced, a person who sells himself as a slave can no longer freely choose whether to remain in that position. Because he can no longer make a voluntary choice, his subsequent conduct provides no evidence that his continuing slave status is 'desirable, or at the least endurable, to him' (V.11, p. 299). *A fortiori*, there can be no presumption that his remaining a slave is conducive to his self-development, the essential ingredient of his well-being which is '[t]he reason for not interfering, unless for the sake of others, with [his] voluntary acts' in the first place (ibid.). Thus, no society which purports to value liberty and individuality can properly enforce slavery contracts: 'The principle of freedom cannot require that he should be free not to be free. It is not freedom, to be allowed to alienate his freedom' (V.11, p. 300).

Mill's claim that society can legitimately interfere with voluntary slavery has puzzled many commentators, since it seems to contradict his liberty doctrine. Admittedly, society has every right to regulate the sellers of any commodity in the market: 'trade is a social act' (V.4, p. 293). Society can even properly prohibit the sale of any commodity whose only possible uses involve harm to others: buyers have no right to use such commodities. In the slavery case, however, the marketed commodity, namely, the seller's very person, need not be used by the buyer to harm other people. Thus, it seems that the buyer should be free to use voluntary slaves short of injury to others, in which case prohibition of selling oneself into slavery is not only inexpedient but illegitimate.

Nevertheless, Mill does not seem to be guilty of inconsistency in this case. There are other pertinent considerations. What is peculiar about a slavery contract is that the seller is marketing his very person, including his liberty to act in accord with his own judgment and inclinations. This poses no problem so long as the seller-slave wishes to act as his buyer-master wishes him to act. If he comes to regret his slave status, however, and wishes to recover his freedom against the master's wishes, unanimous consent no longer exists between the parties to the slavery contract. The difficulty is that society, if it has recognized the contract in the first place, is then committed to enforcing involuntary servitude. For, once authority is exercised to enforce the individual's contractual promise to give up his liberty completely, society can no longer legitimately intervene on behalf of the slave.

Application of the liberty maxim is complicated in this situation by the fact that there is uncertainty about the nature of the durable commodity which the buyer is purchasing. Is he buying a voluntary slave who will always wish to remain a slave, or a voluntary slave who will sooner or later become an unwilling slave? Given such uncertainty, we cannot simply say that the buyer should have complete liberty to use voluntary slaves, short of harm to others. Rather, the real issue is how to balance that liberty against society's legitimate authority to prohibit involuntary slavery. But to speak of balancing in this extreme case is misleading. Society must decide either permanently to enforce slavery contracts (since, once such contracts are recognized, no distinction can be drawn in practice between voluntary and involuntary slavery), or never to enforce them. Evidently, any society which values individuality, and the moral right of the individual to choose as he likes in self-regarding matters which is essential to its cultivation, must decide not to recognize slavery contracts. In such a society, the individual's choice to alienate his liberty to another is not a purely self-regarding act. Rather, it is a challenge to social authority, in particular, society's enforcement of equal rights to liberty in self-regarding matters.

Mill seems correct, then, to insist that a society committed to his liberty doctrine must prohibit any practice of selling oneself into slavery. There cannot be any liberty, by right, to buy and control another's very person. Slavery contracts are by their nature irrevocable. Society cannot recognize them without sacrificing all means of discriminating between voluntary and involuntary servitude on the part of the seller-slave. Unless prepared to enforce in perpetuity a state of absolute vulnerability, which the once-willing slave may have come to regret and now wish to alter, society must refuse to enforce slavery contracts.

It might be suggested that such a refusal would not achieve its intended purpose. But non-enforcement has the practical effect of a prohibition against selling oneself into slavery. No reasonable buyer can be expected to pay a price to a seller who has permission from society to remove what has been sold (namely, himself) from the buyer's hands at will. Of course, if anyone tries to coerce another into slavery, society retains legitimate authority to prevent such harm to others.

It is true that a person may yet freely sell his services or promise his love (rather than give up his very person) to another for some time. But employment contracts, marriage contracts and the like must be distinguished from the resignation of liberty involved in slavery contracts. Subsistence, affection and other 'necessities of life ...

continually require, not indeed that we should resign our freedom, but that we should consent to this and the other limitation of it' (V.11, p. 300). Moreover, as we have already seen in our earlier discussion of the Mormon case (IV.21, pp. 290–1), Mill is reluctant ever to recommend contracts-in-perpetuity. Employment contracts, marriage contracts, international treaties and the like ought to include automatic termination ('sunset') clauses that come into effect after a suitably expedient fixed period, he suggests, at which time they would be open to renegotiation.

Voluntary release and the permission to break contracts (V.11)

Mill goes on to point out that his liberty maxim implies that the parties to all contracts in self-regarding matters should have complete liberty, by right, to release each other by mutual consent: 'those who have become bound to one another, in things which concern no third party, should be able to release one another from the engagement' (V.11, p. 300). '[E]ven without such voluntary release', he continues, 'there are perhaps no contracts or engagements, except those that relate to money or money's worth, of which one can venture to say that there ought to be no liberty whatever of retraction' (ibid.).

Evidently, dissolving an engagement against the wishes of another party is not a self-regarding act. Society properly has authority to prohibit an individual from harming others by disappointing their expectations, which he himself has encouraged, 'either by express promise or by conduct' (ibid.). Even though society has legitimate authority to enforce contracts, however, general expediency might sometimes dictate letting a party disappoint the contractual expectations of others. Such a laissez-faire policy is quite distinct from the liberty maxim.

To illustrate his view that social authority generally ought to be applied to force unwilling parties to observe the terms of their contracts, Mill briefly discusses, and rejects as simplistic, Von Humboldt's conviction that all 'engagements which involve personal relations or services' should be of limited legal duration, and that marriage in particular 'should require nothing more than the declared will of either party to dissolve it' (ibid.). Against Von Humboldt, he argues that social stigma, if not legal punishment, ought to be used to prevent people from ignoring their moral obligations to their sexual partners, for example, as well as to third parties such as children peculiarly associated with the partnership:

> When a person, either by express promise or by conduct, has encouraged another to rely upon his continuing to act in a certain way – to build expectations and calculations, and stake any part of his plan of life upon that supposition – a new series of moral obligations arises on his part toward that person, which may possibly be overruled, but cannot be ignored. And again, if the relation between two contracting parties has been followed by consequences to others; if it has placed third parties in any peculiar position, or, as in the case of marriage, has even called third parties into existence, obligations arise on the part of both the contracting parties toward those third parties ... [E]ven if, as Von Humboldt maintains, [these obligations] ought to make no difference in the *legal* freedom of the parties to release themselves from the engagement (and I also hold that they ought not to make *much* difference), they necessarily make a great difference in the *moral* freedom. A person is bound to take all these circumstances into account, before resolving on a step which may affect such important interests of others; and if he does not allow proper weight to those interests, he is morally responsible for the wrong.
>
> (V.11, pp. 300–1, emphasis original)

There may be situations where society ought to allow a person to dissolve her marriage, because enforcing the contract harms her more than it benefits the other relevant parties. Even so, the individual should not have complete liberty, by right, of divorce.

'Misapplied notions of liberty' (V.12–15)

Mill next discusses cases in which individual liberty cannot be justified by application of his liberty maxim, even though prevailing majority sentiment 'in the modern European world' is strongly in favour of granting liberty in these cases. The most important of these 'in its direct influence on human happiness', he says, is 'family relations', where it is commonly held that a husband should be virtually free to do as he likes in acting for his wife and children, 'under the pretext that the affairs of the other are his own affairs' (V.12, p. 301). But the moral right to *liberty* in self-regarding matters must not be conflated with a right to dominate, or exercise *power* over, others.[3] No individual should have any power at all, for example, to coerce other adults in their respective self-regarding concerns. Rather, all adults should have equal rights to liberty of self-regarding action. Thus, no utilitarian argument exists for the 'almost despotic power of husbands over wives' (ibid.). Rather, 'wives should have the same rights, and should receive the protection of the law [including enforcement of contracts] in the same manner, as all other persons' (ibid.).[4]

Moreover, although public officials and even private citizens must be legally entrusted to exercise legitimate social authority to prevent harm to others, general expediency recommends a democratic political system with checks and balances, such that no person has unfettered power to lay down rules of other-regarding conduct as he likes: 'The state, while it respects the liberty of each in what specifically regards himself, is bound to maintain a vigilant control over his exercise of any power which it allows him to possess over others' (ibid.).[5]

Mill is even more preoccupied with 'misapplied notions of liberty' in the case of parents' control over their children (ibid.). His liberty maxim evidently does not apply to children *per se*: anyone not yet capable of rational persuasion and self-development requires to be taken care of by others, for his own good. Society properly has authority to make sure that those (including parents) who are entrusted to take care of children, act in ways which society deems essential for the good of the children.

Education (V.12–14)

In particular, society has every right to compel parents by law to provide a suitable education:

> It still remains unrecognised, that to bring a child into existence
> without a fair prospect of being able, not only to provide food
> for its body, but instruction and training for its mind, is a moral
> crime, both against the unfortunate offspring and against society;
> and that if the parent does not fulfil this obligation, the state
> ought to see it fulfilled, at the charge, as far as possible, of the
> parent.
>
> (V.12, p. 302)

This does not imply that government must monopolize the
provision of education, or even provide any schools at all:

> It might leave to parents to obtain the education where and how
> they pleased, and content itself with helping to pay the school
> fees of the poorer classes of children, and defraying the entire
> school expenses of those who have no one else to pay for them.
>
> (V.13, p. 302)

Indeed, Mill rejects the idea that government should direct 'the whole
or any large part of the education of the people', unless society is 'so
backward' that there is no alternative (V.13, pp. 302–3).

But it does imply that government must administer 'public
examinations, extending to all children, and beginning at an early age',
as a means of enforcing the law which makes education compulsory
(V.14, p. 303). In his view, such examinations, given annually, should
cover a 'gradually extending range of subjects' and require 'a certain
minimum of general knowledge' to pass. To give them an incentive
to fulfil their obligations, parents might be subjected to 'a moderate
fine' for the failure of their children to pass an exam (ibid.).

In addition to these compulsory minimum examinations, 'there
should be *voluntary* examinations on all subjects, at which all who
come up to a certain standard of proficiency might claim a certificate'
(ibid., emphasis added). Even these 'higher classes of examinations'
are expediently 'confined to facts and positive science exclusively',
to prevent government from having 'an improper influence over
opinion' on 'disputed topics' such as religion and politics (ibid.).

Given his view that the state should not monopolize or control
the schools, Mill sees no problem with children 'being taught religion,

if their parents chose, at the same schools where they were taught other things', provided they are 'not required to profess a belief' (V.14, pp. 303–4). Despite his concerns over rising religious bigotry, he apparently thinks that the state can even administer public examinations in religion, without unduly interfering with the religious liberty of the individual.

Examinations 'in the higher branches of knowledge', including knowledge of religion, should, however, be 'entirely voluntary' (V.14, p. 304). Persons who attain advanced certificates and degrees in any subject might thereby gain an advantage over competitors for professional employment of one sort or another. Yet there is no improper government influence, so long as government does not have power to 'exclude any one from professions, even from the profession of teacher, for alleged deficiency of qualifications' (ibid.; see also Mill, 1842).

Birth control (V.15)

Mistaken notions of liberty also obscure the recognition of society's legitimate authority to regulate the act of 'causing the existence of a human being' (V.15, p. 304). Society has every right legally to prevent couples from bestowing a life of misery on another person, by bringing him into the world without 'the ordinary chances of a desirable existence' (ibid). It can properly 'forbid marriage', for example, 'unless the parties can show that they have the means of supporting a family' (ibid.). By extension, it can also force couples to use suitable birth control devices to prevent the creation of wards of the state.

Even if couples have the requisite means to raise a child, society can properly enact such laws to prevent harm to the working classes, resulting from excess supply of labour:

> [I]n a country either overpeopled, or threatened with being so, to produce children, beyond a very small number, with the effect of reducing the [long-run] reward of labour by their competition, is a serious offence against all who live by the remuneration of their labour.
>
> (ibid.)

Whether expedient or not, such measures 'are not objectionable as violations of liberty' (ibid.). Nobody has a moral right to produce children as he likes. 'Such laws are interferences of the state to prohibit a mischievous act – an act injurious to others, which ought to be a subject of reprobation, and social stigma, even when it is not deemed expedient to superadd legal punishment' (ibid.).

Yet prevailing majority sentiment rebels against those interferences, as illegitimate infringements of liberty:

> When we compare the strange respect of mankind for liberty, with their strange want of respect for it, we might imagine that a man had an indispensable right to do harm to others, and no right at all to please himself without giving pain to any one.
>
> (V.15, pp. 304–5)

Liberty to refuse to co-operate (V.16–23)

By way of conclusion, Mill turns to cases 'which, though closely connected with the subject of this essay', he says, 'do not, in strictness, belong to it' (V.16, p. 305). These cases do not involve any interference by society with the individual's freedom to act as he wishes. *A fortiori*, the right of the individual to liberty of self-regarding action is not compromised.

> [T]he question is not about restraining the actions of individuals, but about helping them: it is asked whether government should do, or cause to be done, something for their benefit, instead of leaving it to be done by themselves, individually, or in voluntary combination.
>
> (ibid.)

Strictly speaking, these cases do not involve acts harmful to other people. Rather, to the extent that spontaneous acts do occur, one person's act directly confers perceptible advantages on others, instead of causing them perceptible damage against their wishes. Now, if people act this way toward each other with mutual consent, and the benefits are confined to the parties concerned, this is indistinguishable from jointly self-regarding behaviour. If benefits spill over onto third parties without their consent, however, a species of other-regarding conduct is implicated. Yet, there seems to be little reason why a third party would wish to refuse advantages (such as public goods) conferred on him by the acts of others.[6] In any case, there is no question that individuals ought to be inclined to help each other, and that society ought to advise and educate people to develop the requisite motivations.

But suppose that people have not learned to co-operate to mutual advantage, and thus fail to act accordingly. The question is whether society ought to employ its authority to ensure that mutually beneficial acts will be performed when citizens lack the requisite norms of mutual co-operation. In particular, should government intervene, either to perform the beneficial actions itself, or to force people to perform them in accord with its laws and policies? Or should individuals be left alone to learn to co-operate among themselves, with advice and encouragement but no coercion?

These cases are 'closely connected with the subject of this essay', it seems, because, although no interference with the individual's liberty of action is contemplated, interference with his *failure to act* is under consideration. The question is whether government should intervene to prevent certain harms of inaction, namely, forgone benefits of mutual co-operation which some government officials (if nobody else) do not wish to forgo, and which all members of society, were their intellectual and moral capacities more developed, would not wish to forgo.

Mill counsels against government intervention in these cases, except as a last resort. Admittedly, society has legitimate authority to compel its members to perform all sorts of mutually beneficial actions, either directly, or indirectly through tax contributions to support a suitably active government. But general expediency apparently dictates a presumption in favour of something like laissez-faire.[7]

Rationale for laissez-faire (V.18–22)

He identifies three sorts of arguments in favour of letting individuals or groups learn to help each other with their projects, rather than relying on government to help them.

Relative inefficiency of government (V.18)

Non-intervention is expedient 'when the thing to be done is likely to be better done by individuals than by the government' (V.18, p. 305). Since those whose material self-interest is tied to a business are generally the most fit to manage its operations or at least choose the managers, for example, government ought not to interfere with 'the ordinary processes of industry' by forcing some people to subsidize others through the tax system (ibid.). But this economic doctrine of laissez-faire is treated in detail by him elsewhere, in his *Political Economy* (1871, Book V, Chapter XI), and, as he has already made sufficiently clear, 'is not particularly related to the principles of this essay' (ibid.; cf. V.4).

Cultivation of individuality (V.19)

Even if government officials might do the thing more competently 'on the average', non-intervention can still be expedient because it is desirable that individuals should do the thing 'as a means to their own mental education' (V.19, p. 305). This is a major reason for trial by jury rather than trial by judge alone, for example, and for voluntary philanthropic associations rather than government departments which provide support for the welfare of the individual beyond some minimum level of subsistence. It is also a strong argument for co-operative industrial enterprises of all sorts, and for voluntary associations of firefighters, street cleaners and other providers of local and municipal services, rather than government agencies set up for those purposes.

The individual's performance of such beneficial other-regarding actions, though generally not the same thing as choosing as he likes in his self-regarding concerns, similarly promotes self-development, more specifically, the development of his capacities to understand 'joint interests', manage 'joint concerns' and act habitually 'from public or semi-public motives' in pursuit of 'aims which unite' rather than isolate him from his fellows (ibid.). 'Without these habits and powers, a free constitution can neither be worked nor preserved' (ibid.).

By leaving individuals and voluntary associations alone to experiment in various ways to discover what can be accomplished through mutual co-operation, government can promote, among other things, the cultivation of that Periclean character ideal which is also the target of the basic right to liberty in self-regarding concerns.

> What the state can usefully do, is to make itself a central depository, and active circulator and diffuser, of the experience resulting from many trials. Its business is to enable each experimentalist to benefit by the experiments of others; instead of tolerating no experiments but its own.
>
> (V.19, p. 306)

Prevention of totalitarian state (V.20–2)

A final, 'and most cogent', reason for non-intervention in these cases 'is the great evil of adding unnecessarily to [government] power' (V.20, p. 306). Mill dismisses the idea that a utilitarian society would involve a large-scale bureaucracy comprised of the most able persons in society. If an attempt were made to run society by means of such a 'numerous bureaucracy' of the most skilled and ambitious, he insists, there would cease to be any social support for critics of the bureaucratic elite. Rather than help each other with their various projects in their own ways, everyone would look to the bureaucracy, 'the multitude for direction and dictation in all they had to do; the able and aspiring for personal advancement' (V.20, p. 307).

A bureaucratic despotism would tend to arise, involving some uniform system of rules and regulations governing all the details of life: 'where everything is done through the bureaucracy, nothing to which the bureaucracy is really adverse can be done at all' (V.21, p. 308). 'And the evil would be greater, the more efficiently and scientifically the administrative machinery was constructed – the more skilful the arrangements for obtaining the best qualified hands and heads with which to work it' (V.20, p. 306). The 'more perfect' the organization and discipline of the bureaucracy, 'the more complete is the bondage of all, the members of the bureaucracy included' (V.21, p. 308). At an extreme, virtually nobody would even consider acting in opposition to the customs and standards of the bureaucracy, as in

Russia, where the 'Czar himself is powerless against the bureaucratic body' (V.20, p. 307), or in China, where a 'mandarin is as much the tool and creature of a despotism as the humblest cultivator' (V.21, p. 308).

In contrast, where individuals and voluntary associations are accustomed to undertake various co-operative ventures without government intervention, as in America and to some extent in France, the danger of bureaucratic tyranny recedes: 'No bureaucracy can hope to make such a people as this do or undergo anything that they do not like' (ibid.). This is not to say that there will be no danger of majority despotism, in the form of illegitimate interference, by stigma if not law, with individual liberty of self-regarding action. But the majority will not suffer the government to gather power beyond certain limits, under the guise of helping the people to do what they can more expediently do by themselves, through mutual co-operation.

Mill also emphasizes that a society run by a bureaucratic elite would inevitably suffer stagnation and decline: 'the absorption of all the principal ability of the country into the governing body is fatal, sooner or later, to the mental activity and progressiveness of the body itself' (V.22, p. 308). Unless subject to external 'watchful criticism of equal ability', the bureaucracy will tend to sink into 'indolent routine' or embrace 'some half-examined crudity which has struck some leading member of the corps' (ibid.). To promote a spirit of individuality and improvement within the bureaucracy and society, it is imperative to let various independent groups serve as an expedient check on the administration. Independent associations should be empowered to criticize the bureaucracy freely, for example, and to experiment with their own co-operative ventures: 'if we would not have our bureaucracy degenerate into a pedantocracy, this body must not engross all the occupations which form and cultivate the faculties required for the government of mankind' (ibid.).

A maxim of liberal utilitarian government (V.23)

A utilitarian society must balance the benefits of social order and co-ordination which an active bureaucracy can provide, against the evils of oppression and stagnation which will result if that bureaucracy discourages individuals and voluntary associations from transacting with each other to mutual advantage. Without laying down any 'absolute rule' akin to the liberty maxim, Mill calls for 'the greatest dissemination of power consistent with efficiency; but the greatest possible centralization of information and diffusion of it from the centre' (V.23, p. 309). He seems particularly concerned that a central bureaucracy should limit itself, beyond enforcing certain general rules of justice enacted by the legislature, to the collection and dissemination of knowledge which will facilitate co-operation to mutual advantage by people outside the bureaucracy: 'A government cannot have too much of the kind of activity which does not impede, but aids and stimulates, individual exertion and development' (V.23, p. 310). But the bureaucracy should not force individuals into some pattern of co-operative activities in accord with certain administrative criteria:

> The mischief begins when, instead of calling forth the activity and powers of individuals and bodies, it substitutes its own activity for theirs; when, instead of informing, advising, and, upon occasion, denouncing, it makes them work in fetters, or bids them stand aside and does their work instead of them.
>
> (ibid.)

It is worth recalling that this recommendation, that government should provide relevant information but otherwise leave individuals alone to pursue various collectively beneficial projects freely, is, 'in strictness', distinct from the liberty maxim. Both are directed at the cultivation of individuality or development. Whereas the liberty maxim urges complete liberty of self-regarding action, however, the present recommendation is for government to refrain from undertaking collectively beneficial projects, or from forcing individuals to undertake them, prior to the emergence of the relevant norms of mutual co-operation. By refusing to exercise coercion, society makes possible the development of the norms in question by its members. Until the individual acquires such dispositions, however, he will fail to act co-operatively with others.

At the same time, there is a 'close connection' between the liberty maxim and the present recommendation. For, once individuals have learned norms of mutual co-operation, spontaneous acts to mutual advantage will be included among their self-regarding acts. Prior to that time, these people simply do not choose to perform such beneficial acts, for want of the essential intellectual and moral capacities.

This co-operative aspect of self-development seems to be the decisive consideration underlying Mill's recommendation for laissez-faire in this context. It might have turned out, contrary to his reasoning, that social benefits could be maximized by government intervention rather than laissez-faire with respect to mutually beneficial actions. Thus, the general expediency of laissez-faire requires further argument, to show why people are benefited more than they would be under mandated projects of mutual co-operation. His answer seems to turn on the idea that most people who are left alone to spontaneously help themselves, will develop norms of mutual co-operation which they would not otherwise develop in the presence of legal coercion.[8]

Suggestions for further reading

Much of the literature relating to application of the liberty doctrine is unhelpful. Some commentators are so hostile and/or confused that they claim Mill perversely abandons his 'one very simple principle' in this fifth chapter, leading them roundly to dismiss his whole approach. See, e.g., Bernard Bosanquet, *The Philosophical Theory of the State* (1899), 4th edn (London, Macmillan, 1923), esp. pp. 55–63, 117–19; and Gertrude Himmelfarb, 'Liberty: "One Very Simple Principle?"' in her *On Looking Into the Abyss: Untimely Thoughts on Culture and Society* (New York, Knopf, 1994), pp. 74–106.

A more careful discussion is provided by C.L. Ten, *Mill on Liberty* (Oxford, Clarendon Press, 1980), esp. Chapters 6–8. Even those as sympathetic as Ten clearly is to the spirit of Mill's liberalism, however, tend to reinterpret his 'text-book', in such a way that we lose sight of any clear connection between his stated doctrine and what he tells us are its practical implications. For the most elaborate of these influential attempts, see Joel Feinberg, *The Moral Limits to the Criminal Law*, 4 vols (Oxford, Oxford University Press, 1984–8). The respective approaches of Ten and Feinberg are taken up below in Chapters 7–9, where I try to spell out some of the main points of contrast with the approach favoured in this GuideBook.

For further discussion of Mill's views on the economic doctrine of laissez-faire, on the need for birth control duly to restrict the general supply of labour in the long run, and on capitalism versus socialism, see J. Riley, 'Justice Under Capitalism', in J. Chapman and J.R. Pennock, eds, *Markets and Justice: NOMOS XXXI* (New York, New York University Press, 1989, pp. 122–62; Riley, 'Introduction', in J. Riley, ed., *John Stuart Mill: Principles of Political Economy and Chapters on Socialism* (Oxford, Oxford University Press, 1994), pp. vii–xlvii; and Riley, 'J.S. Mill's Liberal Utilitarian Assessment of Capitalism Versus Socialism', *Utilitas* 8 (1996): 39–71.

For an important public disclaimer, consistent with his liberty doctrine, that Mill added to his own marriage contract, see 'Statement on Marriage' (1851), in J.M. Robson, gen. ed., *Collected Works of J.S. Mill* (London and Toronto, Routledge and University of Toronto Press, 1984), Vol. 21, pp. 97–100.

For further discussion of his views on education, see, e.g., Mill, 'Inaugural Address at St Andrews' (1867), in Robson, gen. ed., *Collected Works* (London and Toronto, Routledge and University of Toronto Press, 1984), Vol. 21, pp. 215–57; and Mill, 'Endowments' (1869), in Robson, gen. ed., *Collected Works* (London and Toronto, Routledge and University of Toronto Press, 1967), Vol. 5, pp. 613–29.

General issues

Part three

Chapter 7

Liberal utilitarianism

Isn't liberalism incompatible with utilitarianism?

A traditional complaint against Mill's form of reasoning is that liberalism cannot be consistently combined with utilitarianism. The problem he fails to recognize, according to a long line of complainers, is that utilitarianism may require that individual rights should be given up for the greater good of the other members of society. If a rich man's private property would yield more aggregate happiness when transferred into the hands of some poor people, for example, or if the whole country could be saved from tyranny by sacrificing the life or liberty of a beautiful woman to some evil aggressor, utilitarianism seems to demand, respectively, the property transfer and the sacrifice. Liberalism's concern to protect certain vital personal interests, as moral rights, is putatively overridden by the demands of general utility maximization.

Supposing that liberal utilitarianism (or, equivalently, utilitarian liberalism) is incoherent, many liberal philosophers have turned to some non-utilitarian form of reasoning to give suitable moral importance to individual rights in relation to competing considerations. Rawls (1971, 1993), for example, in his influential theory of justice, employs an ideal contractarian form of reasoning to give absolute priority to a first principle of equal basic rights over a second two-part principle. He imagines that Mill's doctrine is really a close cousin to his own contract theory, to wit, a 'mixed conception' of justice, in which a liberal principle of equal basic rights is given absolute priority over the utility principle itself (1971, pp. 42–3, n. 23, 122–6, 315–16). That Rawlsian view, elaborated by Hart (1982), is perhaps the dominant reading of Mill's liberalism today.

Indeed, as Ten (1991) has suggested, the 'revisionist utilitarian' doctrines which Gray (1983), Berger (1984), Skorupski (1989) and others have associated with Millian liberalism, seem indistinguishable from what Rawls calls a mixed conception. True, moral considerations internal to utilitarianism itself are said to drive the revisionism. But no good reasons are offered to repel the traditional objection that maximization of collective welfare (or collective self-determination) may demand the sacrifice of individual rights (including rights to self-determination or personal autonomy).[1]

That is not to say that good reasons cannot be offered. In this regard, those who *make* the traditional objection seem to take for granted that they are objecting to an ideal utilitarian conception of the public good. More needs to be said, however, before anyone should accept their assumption. It does not follow that, because some crude or Utopian conception of the public good admits unjustified trammelling of individual rights, a better conception must do so as well.

Another influential objection to Mill's form of reasoning is that utilitarian liberalism is unworkable because we can never hope to acquire the requisite information relating to different persons' happinesses. It is impossible that a reasonable and coherent system of rights could ever be grounded in general utility, so this objection runs, because such a rights-system is inconceivable altogether in our moral world, which is characterized by tragic conflicts among plural and incommensurable values (including positive and negative aspects of liberty itself). This pluralistic complaint applies equally to Rawlsian forms of reasoning, and receives clear expression in Berlin (1969), Taylor (1982) and Gray (1989, 1995), among others.

Gray, for example, argues that liberal utilitarianism faces 'intractable problems' (1989, p. 220). We do not know how to compare different persons' utility gains and losses, he says, as required to calculate general utility. Moreover, if (as Mill assumes) there are different kinds or qualities of utility, we remain in the dark even about how to make *intrapersonal* comparisons of the different kinds. Once we recognize these problems of incommensurability, 'Mill's utilitarianism disintegrates . . . into a sort of muddled and unwitting value-pluralism. It should be evident enough that, from such a value-pluralism, no "one very simple principle" . . . can possibly be derived' (ibid., p. 224).

He duly traces this perspective to Berlin. Berlin, he says, makes the important 'objection' that 'the idea of happiness has in Mill so mutated that its use in any sort of felicific calculus is not a possibility: it has come to designate precisely that irreducible diversity of human goods which Berlin's pluralism identifies' (1995, p. 61). Thus, 'contrary to all of his intentions, Mill's liberalism is not, in the end, an application of utilitarian ethics, for liberal utilitarianism is not ultimately a viable position in moral and political thought' (ibid.).

Liberalism must face the pluralistic music, Gray insists, and content itself with more or less unreasonable sets of conflicting rights, varying across social contexts, any given set a product of a particular cultural history rather than an emanation of universal reason. An ideal liberal conception of the public good, in which a reasonable system of rights is brought into harmony with other social values, is merely another form of rationalistic fiction, as Berlin would have it, and carries the danger that its adherents will embrace some sort of authoritarianism in their deluded 'pursuit of the ideal'. But, again, more needs to be said before anyone should accept the claim that morality is *necessarily* an arena of conflict among plural and incomparable goods. Perhaps further study and Socratic dialogue can generate right answers to what seem on the surface even the most intractable moral dilemmas.

Both the traditional and pluralistic objections to utilitarian liberalism are open to serious doubt. Liberal rule utilitarianism arguably provides a compelling alternative. According to rule utilitarianism, the public good is best pursued indirectly, by complying with an optimal code of rules, rather than directly, as act utilitarianism assumes, by always trying to calculate and perform the particular act that maximizes general utility. Utilitarians will find the most happiness by jointly committing themselves to act in accord with the code: the general happiness will be *higher* than it would be otherwise.

Another point to keep in mind is that, by committing to a code, utilitarians in effect commit themselves to assign worth to certain virtues and dispositions required to devise and comply with the rules. Rule utilitarianism implicitly demands, in other words, that its adherents recognize the great value of a suitable type of personal character. This does not mean that every person must develop that character to perfection, before the code can be implemented at all. But most must recognize the character's worth, and thus develop it at least to some imperfect degree, before an approximation to the ideal code can become predominant in society. If everyone does in fact develop the requisite character to perfection, so that they jointly devise and comply with an ideal utilitarian code, rule utilitarianism becomes indistinguishable from a suitably restricted act utilitarianism. The rules are internalized as dictates of conscience, and every individual acts accordingly. But the underlying reasoning is rule utilitarian in form.

Against the traditional objection

Beginning with the traditional objection, there are good reasons to think that a proper utilitarian conception of the general good involves a *liberal* code of rules, which gives rise to a coherent system of liberal rights and correlative duties. One reason is that people like us are just too selfish always to do what the public good requires in any situation, and it is too costly to change our biased natures overnight. In the meantime, and, in fact, to ever undergo the process of self-improvement that might eradicate our undue self-interest, we need liberty to deliberate and choose our own actions, even if those choices do not always maximize the general welfare. Liberal rights are essential to permit us to deviate from the impossibly stringent demands of unrestricted act utilitarianism, which *obligates* us always to perform whatever particular act maximizes general utility in the circumstances at hand.

A second reason is that liberal rules and rights generate incentives and assurances that are useful for a society of predominantly self-interested people. To maximize production of consumer goods and services, for example, such a society ought to establish certain rules and rights of private property and market contracting that *assure* self-interested producers of the fruits of their own labour and investment decisions, and provide *incentives* to hard work, saving and entrepreneurship. Similarly, to maximize the physical and financial safety of its people, such a society ought to devise certain rules and rights of criminal and civil due process that assure both accusers and accused of a fair trial, and provide incentives to represent the parties diligently, duly collect evidence and so on. By contrast, pure act utilitarianism cannot generate these incentive and assurance effects, which are so collectively valuable for predominantly self-interested persons. If circumstances make it generally advantageous for someone to deviate from the code and violate others' rights, for example, act utilitarianism *per se* must recommend the deviation.[2]

The external signs of all liberal rights and duties might conceivably vanish, of course, if everybody developed the liberal character associated with the implementation of an optimal code. More importantly, many familiar liberal rights might be recognized as suboptimal, and thus vanish from the code of conscience altogether, if everybody educated themselves to become rigidly fair and impartial rather than biased, as they now tend to be, in favour of their own particular interests. If a highly developed person would work hard and invest wisely for the general advantage, with no assurance of anything beyond an equal share of whatever fruits he and his fellows jointly produced, for example, private ownership of productive resources would not need to be recognized by an ideal utilitarian code.

But, whatever the nature of the other rights in an ideal utilitarian society, one right must remain optimal from Mill's perspective, namely, the right to liberty of purely self-regarding conduct. As he makes clear in the *Liberty* (II.26–7, III.6, 11, pp. 247–8, 265, 267), highly developed humans, unlike gods or saints, will need at least that core of liberty to *maintain* (as well as to develop) their admirable capacities, including their capacities to remain rigidly impartial when framing and complying with rules of other-regarding conduct (where harm to others is implicated). It is wrong to think that the need for complete liberty of discussion and personal lifestyle will disappear as progress unfolds (II.31–3, III.18–19, pp. 250–2, 274–5; see, also, Chapter 8 below, second section). Thus, an ideal Millian utilitarian code will continue to distribute and sanction such rights to liberty, even if private property and other familiar liberal rights tied to our particularistic inclinations vanish from the code. Those who develop the characters required to act invariably in accord with the code will develop a due balance between the moral disposition to follow reasonable and impartial rules of other-regarding behaviour, and the Pagan drive to choose as one pleases among purely self-regarding acts that pose no (risk of) harm to others.

Against the pluralistic objection

Turning to the pluralistic objection to liberal utilitarianism, it is doubtless true that we cannot conceive of an ideal morality, if by an ideal morality we mean one in which all bad luck has been eradicated and each and every human virtue flourishes to its fullest extent, never coming into conflict with the others. But it remains an open question whether we can conceive of an ideal utilitarian morality, in which the need to make reasonable compensation for bad luck is recognized and, more generally, a compromise or balance is struck between competing virtues and goods (such as security, subsistence, abundance, equality, liberty and individuality) to maximize the general happiness. In this regard, given that rights to absolute liberty of self-regarding conduct are *indispensable means to*, as well as constituent elements of, an ideal liberal utilitarian morality, it is palpably absurd to associate Mill's doctrine with the danger of authoritarian repression.

As for the rich information about personal welfares required for utilitarianism to work, modern utilitarians have proposed methods of measuring cardinal welfare (i.e., how much welfare a person gains or loses between any options) and of making interpersonal comparisons of welfare (see, e.g., Harsanyi, 1992). Even if those particular methods are not flawless, more argument is required to explain why they are not sufficient for practical purposes, given the alternatives. The naked assertion that such rich information is inconceivable in principle has little if anything to recommend it.

Yet it is worth recalling that Mill, like Bentham, makes no reference to a mechanical procedure for inferring the general happiness from any given set of personal happinesses. Unlike moderns, he apparently conceives of the public good in terms of an ideal liberal code of rules, discernable independently of aggregation procedures even if it can never gain widespread acceptance until most develop the type of personal character requisite to its implementation. At the same time, Mill seems to think that any individual capable of rational persuasion can imagine and affirm this liberal code, and that the individual who works (in any of myriad ways) towards its realization, as an 'ideal end', will find personal happiness 'by the way'. True happiness thereby becomes associated with the promulgation of an ideal code, full compliance with which implies complete liberty of self-regarding affairs. The code is *self-limiting*, in the sense that its rules govern only conduct that poses a risk of harm to others.

How can utilitarianism prescribe *absolute* liberty of self-regarding conduct?

Ten has argued powerfully that *absolute* liberty in self-regarding matters cannot be grounded on utilitarianism as usually defined. As he points out, utilitarians typically must claim that 'the value of liberty . . . is wholly dependent on its contribution to utility. But if that is the case', he asks, 'how can the "right" to liberty be absolute and indefeasible when the consequences of exercising the right will surely vary with changing social circumstances?' (1991, p. 213). His answer is that it cannot be, unless external moral considerations are imported into pure maximizing utilitarianism to guarantee the desired Millian result. In his view, the absolute barrier that Mill erects against all forms of coercion really seems to require a non-utilitarian justification, even if 'utilitarianism' might somehow be redefined or enlarged to subsume the requisite form of reasoning. Thus, 'Mill is a consistent liberal', he says, 'whose view is inconsistent with hedonistic or preference utilitarianism' (ibid., p. 236).

Against Ten, it must be noted immediately that, given a suitable definition of 'harm', the harmful consequences to others of any person's exercise of his right to choose as he likes among self-regarding acts, does *not* vary. As we have already seen, Mill, in the fourth chapter of the *Liberty*, seems to be using the term 'harm' in a fairly straightforward way, as any type of 'perceptible damage' suffered, against one's wishes, to one's body, material possessions, reputation or freedom of action, with the caveat that the perceptible injury must not be wholly a creation of social authority. With that understanding, self-regarding choices never harm others, 'directly, and in the first instance'. The exercise by all of equal rights to absolute liberty of self-regarding choices can never directly cause perceptible damage to anybody against his wishes.

But Ten's objection still has life. He argues that 'Mill's defence of liberty is not utilitarian' because it ignores the dislike, disgust and so-called 'moral' disapproval which others feel as a result of self-regarding conduct: 'A utilitarian cannot disregard any of the effects of my conduct since they are all part of its consequences, and help to determine whether the suppression of my conduct or leaving me free will maximize happiness' (1980, p. 6). Why doesn't the liberal utilitarian count the mere pain and dislike, which the vast majority might well feel at the individual's self-regarding acts? Surely if that is counted, it may outweigh the value of the individual's self-regarding liberty, in which case utilitarianism prescribes interference. What sort of utilitarianism is it that restricts itself to counting harmful consequences, with harm as defined?

But liberal utilitarianism does *not* ignore others' mere dislike of a self-regarding act. Their dislike does count, because it is included in the value of liberty itself. Under Mill's doctrine, society gives others the equal right to complete liberty of self-regarding conduct, including the freedom to select their own friends and to avoid people of whose conduct they disapprove. But your dislike of my self-regarding conduct never justifies suppression of the self-regarding act. That would negate my liberty of self-regarding conduct, and the great good of self-development which depends upon it. Rather than count others' dislikes as a potential justification for suppression, liberal utilitarianism counts them by giving everybody an equal right to self-regarding liberty. Any person is free to act on her mere dislike of others' thoughts and personal lifestyles, and, at least to that extent, to develop her own character, or individuality, as she pleases.

Yet why doesn't liberal utilitarianism consider the possibility that aggregate dislike of the individual's self-regarding conduct might outweigh the value of his liberty, and justify suppression of his conduct? As we have seen, Mill devotes considerable effort to answering this question (III.1, 10–19, IV.8–12, pp. 260–1, 267–75, 280–4). Among other things, liberty in self-regarding matters is essential to the cultivation of individual character, he says, and is not incompatible with similar cultivation by others, because they remain free to think and do as they please, having directly suffered no perceptible damage against their wishes. When all is said and done, his implicit answer is that a person's liberty in self-regarding matters is infinitely more valuable than any satisfaction the rest of us might take at suppression of his conduct. The utility of self-regarding liberty is of a higher kind than the utility of suppression based on mere dislike (no perceptible damages to others against their wishes is implicated), in that any amount (however small) of the higher kind outweighs any quantity (however large) of the lower.

Is this a contestable judgment? It is to people who do not value liberty as much as he values it. But a propensity to disagree with him about the value of liberty must not be confused with an argument against his liberal utilitarianism. By counting others' mere dislike and distress as part of the general utility of complete liberty of self-regarding conduct, and by insisting that the utility of such liberty is of a higher kind than the utility of stamping out what is harmless to others, he shows that rule utilitarianism can consistently recognize equal rights to *absolute* liberty of self-regarding conduct.

As I have argued at length elsewhere (Riley, 1988), Mill's doctrine of liberty and individuality is really a *component* of his complex principle of utility. His doctrine stipulates that the individual has a moral right to choose as he likes in his self-regarding concerns, and that the individual should exercise his right, to promote his permanent interest in self-improvement. Since perceptible damage to others against their wishes is never involved, *each* person's right to liberty can be similarly protected. If each cultivates his individuality, *social* improvement (that is, the intellectual and moral development of each person in society) is maximized. General utility-maximization thereby implies the free development of a plurality of self-regarding lifestyles, one for each individual. Liberal utilitarianism guarantees, by right, a variety of personal ways of living, without any resort to the metaphysical trappings of value pluralism.

Don't 'natural penalties' defeat Mill's self–other distinction?

But the distinction between purely self-regarding and other spheres of life breaks down, some continue to complain, because Mill himself admits that self-regarding conduct can cause harm in the form of 'natural penalties' (IV.5, 11, pp. 278, 282). Hamburger, for example, claims that the distinction is merely a rhetorical ploy, used by the fake champion of liberty to disguise his true ambition, namely, to destroy prevailing moral ideas and beliefs and replace them with a repressive new utilitarian religion. To that end, the opinions of 'superior' intellectuals like himself would be used as subtle tools of coercion, to force the 'inferior' commercial and Christian majority to refashion even the self-regarding aspects of their lives, including their habits of drinking, gambling, prostitution, idleness and so on. Far from countenancing self-regarding liberty for such people, Hamburger insists, he really aimed to shame and humiliate them to give up their 'selfish' and 'miserable' lifestyles, by means of the natural penalties inflicted by a disapproving 'liberal' vanguard:

> [A]s a consequence, Mill's well-known distinction between conduct harmful to others and self-regarding conduct, which was supposed to demarcate a realm of liberty, is shown not to be viable. It was supposed to distinguish between what was subject to penalties and what was immune from penalties; but, as it turned out, conduct on both sides of the distinction suffered penalties . . . He argued eloquently and openly against the pressures and moral coercion of public opinion as it affected self-regarding conduct, giving the overwhelming impression that he was opposed to all such pressure, while, in fact, he regarded the pressure of opinion coming from superior natures

with individuality, which was intended to be coercive, as quite legitimate.

(1995, pp. 42, 51–2)

By implication, we miss the point if we take seriously his talk of rights to complete liberty of self-regarding conduct. In fact, he was prepared to employ coercion to stamp out self-regarding conduct and dispositions of which he disapproved.

Hamburger seems far too eager to attribute illiberal ambitions and strategies to Mill, which contradict the text. Moreover, his remarkable thesis is fatally flawed. In the first place, the well-known self–other distinction is not between conduct subject to penalties and conduct immune to them. Mill 'openly' admits that natural penalties may attach to self-regarding conduct. The distinction is a different one, between conduct that is directly harmful to others and conduct that is harmless to them.

Second, self-regarding conduct does not directly harm *others*. The natural penalties, which are inseparable from it, fall on the *agent*. True, my liberty to avoid what displeases me, and to advise others to avoid it, deprives you of my company and support. But that is a direct consequence of your own action, not of any prior design on my part to inflict perceptible hurt on you against your will. We both may regret the loss of friendship and other mutual benefits caused by our disagreement over choice of personal lifestyle. But, even if such deprivations are perceptible injuries, neither of us suffers them *against our wishes*. You wish to pursue one personal lifestyle, whereas I wish to pursue another incompatible with the first. Neither of us is harmed, in the sense of suffering perceptible damage against our wishes, unless one of us is forced to live as the other wants him to live.

Third, there is not the slightest textual evidence for the claim that Mill was ready to prescribe coercion against purely self-regarding conduct that he may have found contemptible. He disdains even the idea of a 'morally superior' self-regarding choice, contrary to what Hamburger suggests. Self-regarding matters are strictly beyond morality, he makes clear, and so are not subject to deliberate social punishment, whether by law or by organized efforts to humiliate in public. Every competent adult (not merely some 'superior' class of intellectuals) ought to enjoy absolute liberty to choose among self-regarding acts. That includes the liberty to walk away from engagements with others in jointly self-regarding matters.

Fourth, and related, persuasion, advice, counsel, encouragement, attempts to inform and the like, are not the same thing as coercion. Such measures are compatible with complete liberty of self-regarding conduct. By contrast, coercion involves at least a threat of harm to the victim, in the sense of perceptible damage against his wishes.

Fifth, Mill is evidently willing to let any 'class struggle' over ideas and personal lifestyles be settled under conditions of complete liberty of discussion and experimentation by all. The intellectual minority should certainly have 'freedom to point out the way' to the majority, in his view. But he explicitly rejects the sort of 'heroic' authoritarianism advocated by Carlyle, whereby some 'strong man of genius' (such as Cromwell or Frederick the Great) forces the masses to 'do his bidding' (III.13, p. 269). Open discussion, Socratic dialogue, free experiments of living and mass education are held out as the means to a liberal utilitarian society. The coercive machinations of some 'superior' class are not in the picture.

It does not seem to occur to Hamburger that the doctrine of the *Liberty* permits society to evolve in a direction away from that *recommended* by Mill. If people increasingly turn to sex, drugs and rock and roll music in their personal lifestyles, for example, sober and straight intellectuals may well tend to face natural penalties for their 'superior' self-regarding choices. Indeed, the possibility of social 'decline' toward 'barbarisms' of this sort, usually provokes conservatives and even some liberals to castigate Mill as naive, for proposing a doctrine that is far too permissive.

At the same time, it must be said that Millian liberalism (unlike some modern liberalisms) is not neutral between competing conceptions of personal good. It is biased in favour of an ideal liberal kind of personal character, the development of which by all members of society is associated with the maximization of general happiness. But the claim that the individual should be *compelled* to develop such a character, through the use of coercion in matters of purely self-regarding concern, is no part of Mill's doctrine.

Isn't there a danger of isolated and disturbed individuals?

It might seem that liberal utilitarianism carries a grave danger of isolation and anomie among the members of society. Doesn't his right to absolute liberty in self-regarding matters imply that the individual is permitted to live as he pleases within his purely personal sphere, unencumbered by moral duties to other people aside from those which he may voluntarily choose to incur? Isn't it likely, therefore, that Mill's liberal dream is really a nightmare, in which self-obsessed people devote all of their time to their families and businesses but ignore wider social issues of justice and charity? If the individual cannot insulate himself within his self-regarding sphere, on the other hand, how can we say that he has absolute liberty of self-regarding conduct? If he is obligated to perform certain other-regarding acts, does this not imply that his right to liberty is not absolute?

But the doctrine is not plagued by insurmountable difficulties here. Two considerations are relevant. First, a right to choose as one pleases among self-regarding acts does not imply any right to choose as one pleases between self-regarding acts and harmful other-regarding conduct. Absolute liberty within the self-regarding realm is compatible with constraints on one's freedom to move between the realms as one likes. Nobody has a moral right to choose as he pleases among acts or inactions, some of which pose a risk of perceptible injury to other people against their wishes.

Second, it is implausible to think that the individual *can* (let alone should) freely choose the choice situations in which he finds himself. Nobody has perfect control over whether, or when, he will have to consider making choices harmful to other people. Neptune, a qualified lifeguard, may be innocently reading a book in the privacy of his seaside cottage, for example, when he happens to look through his window to see Venus about to drown. Aware of her distress, he infers immediately that a strong swimmer could rescue her with little risk of harm to himself. Like it or not, he now must choose whether or not to act to prevent harm to her. Given his qualifications, his failure to do anything might reasonably be thought to constitute a violation of her moral right to be helped in the circumstances. In any case, his purely self-regarding act of reading has been transformed, as a result of events beyond his control, into an *inaction* that may contribute to another's loss of life against her wishes. If he continues to do nothing but read after becoming conscious of her need, he effectively *intends* that she will suffer harm, and thereby engages in harmful other-regarding conduct. This sort of inaction might be permissible in some circumstances, e.g., perhaps Nep has recently become paralysed in an auto accident. But it is never a matter of Nep's moral right to choose as he likes. Rather, society properly has jurisdiction, and ought to establish reasonable rules to govern such situations.

There is no necessary conflict between a right to absolute liberty of self-regarding conduct and a duty to assist another in dire need. As the example illustrates, what was once self-regarding conduct has vanished for reasons beyond the control of the agent, to be replaced by other-regarding conduct. It is certainly true that Nep did not *choose* this to happen. But the idea that we can always freely choose the kinds of choices we face, independently of other factors (which we might for convenience subsume under the term 'luck'), is not worth taking seriously. The role of luck in this sense raises fascinating questions. How often will the individual be transported outside the self-regarding realm by factors not within his control? When is he obligated to act to prevent harm to others?

To take another example, a relatively wealthy person is contemplating his existence behind the walls of his remote castle, when he receives a letter from his impoverished neighbours requesting his financial aid. Even if he ignores the request, factors beyond his control have presented him with a choice whether or not to help others. If he fails to help, he cannot pretend that he is merely choosing as he pleases within his self-regarding realm. He intends to leave unremedied the risk of perceptible damage suffered by others.

More generally, other-regarding choices will make their appearance within any person's life, whether or not he chooses them to appear. He may be forced to defend himself from the violent acts of others, for example, if not directly, then indirectly, by participating in the political mechanism for enacting legal rights and duties of other-regarding conduct. Others may also approach him for help, or for advice concerning their projects, which, as a member of their society, he will have reasonable customary obligations to provide. The idea that the individual can or should somehow exist as an isolated being, an atom voluntarily choosing whether, and to what extent, to participate in the society of his fellows, is no part of Mill's liberalism.

Absolute liberty of self-regarding conduct can coexist in harmony with obedience to reasonable rules of other-regarding behaviour. When faced with choices involving harm to others, the individual ought to satisfy his moral obligations under the rules, and is properly subject to coercion for that purpose. He ought to satisfy his obligations of justice correlative to others' rights (including their rights to be rescued from grave dangers when little risk is posed to the rescuer), as well as his obligations of charity, which do not correlate to others' rights. These obligations to others may result in a relatively large number of interruptions in the self-regarding activities of some people, as occasions arise more frequently for them to rescue or assist their fellows. But, at least in the present state of education, reasonable rules will not require anything approaching the extreme levels of self-sacrifice associated with unrestrained act utilitarianism.[3] *A fortiori*, such measures as Harris' (1975) 'survival lottery', designed to maximize harm-prevention by forcing randomly selected organ donors to sacrifice their equal rights so that a greater number of otherwise doomed patients may live with transplanted organs, can be dismissed as suboptimal in terms of liberal utilitarian rules.[4]

Suggestions for further reading

The most prominent defenders of rule utilitarianism are Brandt and Harsanyi. See, e.g., Richard B. Brandt, *Morality, Utilitarianism, and Rights* (Cambridge, Cambridge University Press, 1992); John C. Harsanyi, 'Morality and the Theory of Rational Behavior' (1977), in A.K. Sen and B. Williams, eds, *Utilitarianism and Beyond* (Cambridge, Cambridge University Press, 1982), pp. 39–62; Harsanyi, 'Does Reason Tell Us What Moral Code to Follow and, Indeed, to Follow Any Moral Code At All?' *Ethics* 96 (1985): 42–55; Harsanyi, 'On Preferences, Promises and the Coordination Problem', *Ethics* 96 (1985): 68–73; and Harsanyi, 'Game and Decision Theoretic Models in Ethics', in R.J. Aumann and S. Hart, eds, *Handbook of Game Theory* (Amsterdam, North-Holland, 1992), Vol. I, pp. 669–707.

For interesting discussions pertaining to any attempt to ground moral rights on some system of social rules, see L.W. Sumner, *The Moral Foundation of Rights* (Oxford, Clarendon Press, 1987); and Joel Feinberg, *Freedom and Fulfillment* (Princeton, Princeton University Press, 1993), Chapters 8–10.

For further discussion of the structure of the liberal rule utilitarianism that I attribute to Mill, see J. Riley, *Mill's Radical Liberalism: An Essay in Retrieval* (London, Routledge, forthcoming), Chapters 5–6; and Riley, *Maximizing Security: A Utilitarian Theory of Liberal Rights* (forthcoming).

For influential statements of the view that liberal utilitarianism is problematic, see H.L.A. Hart, 'Natural Rights: Bentham and John Stuart Mill,' in his *Essays on Bentham* (Oxford, Oxford University Press, 1982), pp. 79–104; C.L. Ten, *Mill on Liberty* (Oxford, Clarendon Press, 1980); C.L. Ten, 'Mill's Defence of Liberty', in J. Gray and G.W. Smith, eds, *J.S. Mill: On Liberty in Focus* (London, Routledge, 1991), pp. 212–38; and John Gray, *Liberalisms: Essays in Political Philosophy* (London, Routledge, 1989), Chapter 10.

Hamburger's argument that Mill's self–other distinction is a rhetorical ploy may be found in Joseph Hamburger, 'Individuality and Moral Reform: The Rhetoric of Liberty and the Reality of Restraint in Mill's *On Liberty*', *The Political Science Reviewer* 24 (1995): 7–70.

Chapter 8

Liberty, individuality and custom

Doesn't Mill's idea of individuality presuppose a radically unsituated individual?

It is often said that liberalism in general, and Mill's doctrine of liberty in particular, posits an incredible personal character ideal, which is incompatible with every civil society's culture and moral traditions. Gray, for example, claims that 'by individuality Mill means a form of self-realization in which the powers of autonomous thought and choice that mark the human species are exercised [to fulfil] the needs peculiar to each person's nature' (1989, p. 224). Self-realization in this sense is achieved by means of

> experiments of living ... embodied in plans of life ... conceived and implemented by individuals who have detached themselves critically from the social conventions which surround them and who, once so detached, are able to discover the unique needs of their natures.
>
> (ibid.)

167

The growth of knowledge fuelled by those experiments of living is apparently central to Mill's account of human progress or development. 'For Mill', says Gray, 'progress is an inherent tendency of the human mind, with historical development being controlled ultimately by innovation in the realm of ideas. What is most noteworthy is that the growth of knowledge is theorized as an autonomous tendency of the mind' (ibid., p. 227), manifested in the conception and implementation of experiments of living by critically detached individuals.

Gray rightly claims that there are fatal objections to this way of thinking about individuality and progress. The conception of individuality is incredible because it requires the individual to be 'radically unsituated', that is, 'unencumbered' by any social conventions when engaging in discussion or conducting experiments of living. Self-development in that sense is simply not feasible, given that the individual cannot transcend altogether the social context in which he finds himself. Moreover, the approach misleads us into condemning as devoid of individuality all traditional forms of living: 'The man who accepts the way of life in which he was born . . . and who has no interest in trying out alternatives to it, cannot for Mill exhibit individuality, however stylish his personality may be' (ibid., pp. 224–5).

Similarly, the 'idea of an experiment of living is a rationalistic fiction' because it assumes that each individual has 'a quiddity, or unique nature, that is his to realize', independently of cultural circumstances (ibid., pp. 225–6). Custom is then falsely seen as hostile to self-realization when in fact 'personal individuality and human flourishing [depend] on a cultural tradition' (ibid., p. 226). By implication, tradition is not the *enemy* of liberty and progress. Instead, 'social conventions [are] a precondition not only of peace, but also of liberty', because they play an 'indispensable role . . . in enabling diverse individuals and ways of living to coexist without constant recourse to legal coercion. A society without strong conventions would unavoidably be chaotic, resembling . . . a Hobbesian state of nature' (ibid.). Thus, 'convention and tradition are to be regarded as conditions of progress and not (as Mill ignorantly supposes) obstacles to it' (ibid.). Indeed,

if there is such a thing as an experiment of living, it is collective and not individual, it is conducted by social groups held
together by common traditions and practices and it is tried, not
over a single lifetime, but across the generations.

(ibid.)

But Mill surely does not think of individuality and progress in
the way attributed to him by Gray. By individuality, he apparently
means the habitual love of liberty; in other words, the settled disposition to make choices according to one's own judgment and
inclinations. It is a descriptive term, in that there can be an ideal liberal
(or 'noble') kind of individuality as well as illiberal ('miserable')
kinds, depending on the nature of the choices the relevant agent is
firmly disposed to make. As we have seen, Mill recommends that the
individual should develop a noble Periclean kind of character, and, to
that end, insists on a right to complete liberty of purely self-regarding
conduct. Outside the purely self-regarding sphere, however, individual
liberty is not necessarily permissible, and is never granted as a matter
of moral right. Rather, society has the right to employ coercion to
prevent harm to others, and should employ it expediently, even though
the individual thereby loses the means of self-improvement which
'gratifying his inclinations to the injury of others' would make possible
(III.9, p. 266). A person with noble individuality understands this, and
voluntarily conforms to the rules of other-regarding conduct which
the majority (or its representatives) establishes as reasonable in the
given context.

The Millian idea of individuality (noble or otherwise) does
not presuppose a radically unsituated self. Since his judgments and
inclinations are themselves situated in some institutional setting, any
person's *liberty* – the choices he freely makes, without interference by
others, in accord with his own judgment and inclinations – as well as
his *individuality* – his disposition to choose thus – are both inseparable from his cultural beliefs and practices. But the fact of situatedness
does not imply that personal character and desires are mechanically
determined by existing social conventions. Otherwise, custom would
inevitably establish an homogeneous society of distressingly similar
individuals, who imitated each other's way of life in all particulars.

Given that we observe the contrary, we are entitled to infer that a person encumbered by popular norms and beliefs is nevertheless capable of deciding to choose differently than the majority of his fellows. No great ingenuity is required to see that the situated individual can do this, provided he can remember and/or imagine beliefs and practices other than those which currently happen to prevail among the majority. He need not be critically detached in the absurd sense that his self-image transcends his society entirely, including its traditions and conceivable futures. How could any reasonable person altogether ignore his society's accepted rules of correct inference, for example, let alone simply abandon its rules of language?

If memory and imagination are not arbitrarily banished from human nature, the idea of an experiment of living is straightforward, independently of all metaphysical talk about quiddities or unique personal natures. Such an experiment is in effect any uncommon choice or practice, that is, any way of living believed by most people to be peculiar or eccentric. By definition, such experiments must be carried out by the individual or by a voluntary group of persons comprising a minority of society.

Against quiddities

It is worth emphasis that quiddities – unique *noumena* whose properties are not contingent on social circumstances – are precisely the sort of merely intuitive entities which Mill seeks to eradicate from his lean *phenomenalist* epistemology (see Riley, 1988, pp. 133–63). So far as I am aware, he never makes the assertion often attributed to him that each of us has some such unique essence awaiting discovery. Rather, he asserts the contrary, in his *Political Economy*: 'Of all vulgar modes of escaping from the consideration of the effect of social and moral influences on the human mind, the most vulgar is that of attributing the diversities of conduct and character to *inherent* natural differences' (1871, p. 319, emphasis added). Indeed, the idea that plural and incommensurable quiddities inhere in different persons or groups seems to rest more easily within a value-pluralistic moral universe, of the sort posited by Gray and Berlin, than within liberal utilitarianism.

As opposed to being possessed of quiddities, Mill suggests that individuals are sufficiently similar by nature that they might ideally come to display unity in their judgments and opinions. Even if such rational unity were attained, however, their personal desires, dispositions and characters may continue to differ in important respects, provided their circumstances (including their endowed capacities) remain heterogeneous. In general, he emphasizes that 'the circumstances which surround different classes and individuals . . . shape their characters' (III.18, p. 274). Diverse characters are apparently caused by diverse environments, not by unique individual essences. Thus, he dismisses the romantic notion that a 'superior excellence' inheres in some individuals, classes or nations. When any such distinction exists, it 'exists as the effect, not the cause' of individuality (ibid.).[1]

His claim that individuals are unequal with respect to their endowed capacities (including their given powers of will) should not be conflated with the claim that each person has a unique essence awaiting discovery. All adults to whom the liberty doctrine applies apparently possess intellectual and moral capacities *to some degree*, although generally to unequal degrees. Individuals do not differ in kind on this score (see, e.g., Mill, 1833). All are fallible and subject to weakness of will.

An unequal distribution of choice-making capacities across individuals does not imply that different persons have distinct essences, or that they must have plural and incommensurable basic values. Despite their unequal powers of judgment, reasoning and willing, for example, all individuals may share a similar nature, insofar as each is motivated in decipherable ways by some basic notion of happiness.

Gray has recently reiterated that Mill wanted to combine two distinct empirical claims, namely, that what makes man happiest is the exercise of his capacities of autonomous thought and action, and that his exercise of those powers will lead each person to the discovery of his unique and peculiar quiddity: 'Mill's theory of individuality, then, combines the claim that man is his own maker with the claim that, for each man, a nature exists which awaits discovery' (1991, p. 207). The first claim may be empirical, although we must be careful about what Mill is claiming. He does not claim that all persons now actually *do* take pleasure in making their own choices. Most are observed to imitate others blindly, he thinks. Nor does he claim that people *ought* to assign priority to autonomous choice-making if it conflicts with reasonable rule-abidingness and security in other-regarding matters. His claim is that people will be most happy if they develop a certain liberal character, in which autonomy or individuality has come to mean choosing as one pleases in self-regarding matters (for no other reason than it pleases one), and also choosing as required by reasonable general rules in other-regarding matters (because choosing thus is most pleasing to a person of highly developed character).

As for the second claim attributed to Mill by Gray, I have already suggested that Mill never makes it. Moreover, it is difficult to see how quiddities could ever be inferred from empirical observation. What empirical evidence could support such an hypothesis? If two persons had identical choice-making capacities and always occupied the same circumstances, then perhaps we could test it. But such stringent conditions are never met, even in the case of identical twins reared in the same family. Even Kant admits that knowledge of noumena is inaccessible to human beings, in which case we can never really know whether each of us is comprised of some unique substance that distinguishes us from everyone else. The question is irrelevant for practical purposes.

No reliance on ideal observers

Whether or not they are blessed with quiddities, fallible individuals arguably *need* rights to discuss ideas and experiment with distinctive personal environments freely, to improve their imperfect intellectual and emotional capacities. Prior to such discussion and experimentation, we may be expected to hold various more or less ignorant opinions of happiness, and to come into conflict accordingly.

Intellectual and moral development is not, for Mill, some autonomous tendency of the human mind (whether individual or collective). He does not rely on unsituated ideal observers to produce warranted opinions, personal lifestyle choices or reasonable rules of other-regarding conduct in any social context. Rather, he says that:

> [T]he source of everything respectable in man either as an intellectual or as a moral being [is] that his errors are corrigible. He is capable of rectifying his mistakes by discussion and experience ... Wrong opinions and practices gradually yield to fact and argument: but facts and arguments, to produce any effect on the mind, must be brought before it. Very few facts are able to tell their own story.
>
> (II.7, p. 231)

Complete liberty of discussion among situated and fallible people replaces the fictitious observer who is 'sufficiently capacious and impartial' to distil truth from conflicting opinions. Similarly, complete liberty of self-regarding conduct replaces the fiction of an ideal mechanism that automatically selects socially optimal rules and customs from conflicting practices.

The motor that drives this halting and imperfect process of improvement is the individual's disposition to choose in accord with his own judgment and wants. Of course, this individuality is situated within and constrained to some extent by a given society's existing customs and beliefs, including its rules of correct inference. But human fallibility implies that no actual society's rules of correct reasoning and judgment are perfect. Thus, there is inevitably room for the individual to discover novel and surprising causal regularities among phenomena (including mental phenomena). In that sense, the idea of 'truth' is open-ended, despite any particular society's attempts to fix its meaning in terms of a set of procedures. No rules and customs can entirely replace the individual's power to discover better alternatives to those very rules and customs. As Mill emphasizes, 'no routine or rule of thumb can possibly make provision' for the 'ever-varying circumstances' in which our mental capacities have occasion to be exercised (1832, p. 338). Individuality remains indispensable for bringing about generally expedient reforms in response to ever-varying circumstances. Thus, every civil society seeking progress should protect by right the individual's liberty to discuss and act upon his opinions without harm to other people.

Isn't the need for liberty inversely related to social progress?

Gray goes on to claim that Mill's argument from human fallibility is ultimately self-defeating:

> If human nature is progressively knowable, and moral knowledge cumulative, the sphere of liberty will wane as human knowledge waxes ... That progressive enlightenment about the conditions and content of the good life may weaken toleration of forms of life which enlightenment has discredited, is an irony that haunts all those liberalisms which ground the worth of liberty in the fact of human fallibility.
>
> (1986, p. 245)

But is that claim valid?

Assume for the sake of argument that all members of society have progressed as far as human capacities can allow. Does it follow that liberty is no longer desirable? It may seem so because any person of noble character could serve as an infallible dictator, whose enlightened judgments and commands could be recorded and passed down to everybody else (including subsequent generations) as the only beliefs and actions which are tolerable in the best possible human society. Liberty to deviate would carry a chance of social regress. Thus, blind obedience by all to certain utilitarian laws and customs would seem to be called for.[2]

But appearances are deceiving. For the need to *maintain* one's advanced understanding and highly developed moral and aesthetic dispositions remains. Mill implies that even the most developed human faculties would atrophy if left idle (III.4, 6, pp. 263, 265). Even the best people may lose their *acquired* wisdom and noble dispositions through lack of mental exercise. Blind obedience gives the mind no exercise, and thus maintains nothing valuable. In short:

> There shall be as much room and as much necessity for genius when mankind shall have found out everything attainable by their faculties, as there is now; it will still remain to distinguish the man who knows from the man who takes upon trust.
>
> (1832, p. 334)

It follows that in an ideal liberal utilitarian society, individuality and its two requisites – liberty and social pluralism – would remain essential to prevent decline.

The permanent value of liberty

Liberty remains essential because humans ultimately have no other criterion of truth, including truth about their own natures (II.6–8, 26, 31–3, III.1, 3–4, pp. 231–2, 247, 250–2, 260–3). By implication, humans can never be absolutely certain that they have attained the best possible society. Infallibility is not really feasible for human beings. Any person's claim of infallibility is merely an attempt to deny liberty to others (II.11, p. 234). In the absence of liberty of discussion and of personal experimentation, no human can properly claim that his beliefs are warranted by the best available evidence. Thus, even in the best possible society, each person must retain a moral right to make whatever self-regarding choices he likes.

It is true that mere 'automatons in human form' could blindly adhere to the best social beliefs and practices, once established. But human beings are not 'pleasure-machines'. Automatons could never by themselves acquire the wisdom of which human nature is capable. Nor can humans automatically preserve their acquired knowledge by virtue of some innate personal excellence that persists independently of their own mental exercise. Even a person of ideal Periclean character, to retain it, needs to exercise, and thereby preserve, his acquired capacity to judge wisely the grounds of his opinions, as well as his acquired strength of will to choose the lifestyle he preferred on the basis of those judgments. Without such mental exercise, he will gradually lose his capacities to enjoy the 'higher' intellectual and moral activities and pleasures, which mark the noble character: 'it really is of importance, not only what men do, but also what manner of men they are that do it' (III.4, p. 263).

The permanent value of social pluralism

Social pluralism, as the other requisite of individuality, must also remain a feature of liberal utilitarian society. Critics sometimes suggest that if any ideal utilitarian society were ever realized, then the participants in that ideal social way of life would necessarily be choosing to live every detail of their personal lives in the same way. But that implication simply does not follow. Mill is committed only to the much weaker claim that every participant would choose to conform to rules of justice that distribute and protect the same basic rights for all, including equal rights to liberty with respect to purely self-regarding concerns; that every member would also choose to conform to rules of charity and goodwill that enjoin each person to give help to others when he can reasonably afford to do so; and that, within these limits of justice and charity, every member would also choose to accept fair competitive processes, conducted without force or fraud, to allocate economic goods and services, broadly defined. Even if all are possessed of the same noble character, many personal choices, both self-regarding and other-regarding, may differ. Different personal circumstances may continue to generate different personal judgments and inclinations. Social pluralism need not vanish unless two additional assumptions are introduced arbitrarily, namely, that such highly developed individuals must unanimously want an entirely homogeneous society; and that, having agreed thus, these individuals are omnipotent, having the power to eradicate all natural and artificial differences among individuals. The second assumption may be safely ignored. Moreover, the first is clearly rejected by Mill. Thus, there is nothing incoherent about the idea of a socially optimal way of life that itself admits complete freedom for the individual and voluntary group to experiment with a plurality of self-regarding lifestyles.

Why doesn't the individual have a right to parade his bad manners and indecent behaviour in public?

If the individual has a right to complete liberty of self-regarding conduct, it may be asked, doesn't that imply a right to behave indecently and cause offence in public? Granted that he may be situated in a particular social context, doesn't he still have the right to defy the polite conventions of the majority, since these rules seem to have nothing to do with the prevention of harm to others? And, assuming he has such a right, isn't it reasonable to fear that these social conventions would tend to erode under Millian liberalism? Indeed, by ushering in this social decline, wouldn't the liberty doctrine indirectly cause a form of severe harm to the public at large?

If three adults engage in consensual sex in a public place to the astonishment of onlookers, for example, or if one person publishes the intimate details of his love affair without the consent of his friend, why is the shock of the onlookers, or the offence taken by the friend, anything other than mere dislike or emotional distress? What is the *perceptible damage* suffered by any of these people? Given that none can be identified, shouldn't the great good of individuality be safeguarded, despite the fact that its pursuit in these ways causes shock and outrage to others?

Similar questions arise when an individual desecrates the flag in front of a group of army veterans, or rudely tells his wife in front of the neighbours to go fuck a donkey, or parades as a member of the Klu Klux Klan down the main street of a city where blacks are residents, or hands his dying Jewish mother a local newspaper ad in which he expresses his joy at her impending death and announces his plan to bury her ashes in an urn engraved with Hitler's image. All of these acts, and countless more like them, may cause intense dislike to other people. But why are they not self-regarding acts on the Millian notion of harm?

Many who consider themselves liberal have decided to jump off the Millian ship at this point. Perhaps the most influential strategy is to admit that these cases cannot be adequately covered by a harm-prevention principle (however 'harm' to others is conceived), and to add a supplementary principle, according to which society has legitimate authority to employ coercion to prevent the individual from causing offence or shock to others in public. Hart, for example, argues that an admittedly fine distinction can and should be drawn between 'shock or offence to feelings caused by some public display', and distress caused by 'the bare knowledge that others are acting in ways you think wrong' or by 'the belief that others are doing what you do not want them to do' (1963, pp. 46–7). The consequences of an act done in public are thereby distinguished from the consequences of the same act done in private. In particular, person A's mere dislike of B's action in public has a different quality, it appears, than A's mere dislike of B's act in the privacy of, say, his own home. The first sort of dislike may justify coercion, whereas the second sort does not.

But Hart does not clarify why the source or the locale of a person's mere dislike should have this significance. Rather, he jumps quickly to the conclusion that utilitarianism can justify a right to not suffer distress in public, even if a right to not suffer distress from the same conduct in private must be denied for the value of individual liberty to receive any social recognition. As it stands, this seems to give society unlimited jurisdiction over all individual behaviour in public. Remarkably, Hart appears undisturbed by this alarming extension of the legitimate field of coercion by law or stigma. He says only that the individual who is prohibited from engaging in offensive conduct in public, is left 'at liberty to do the same thing in private, if he can' (ibid., p. 48). Why being left free to do the thing in private, 'if he can', provides a reason for prohibiting the thing in public merely because others dislike it, remains mysterious.

The various ways in which Hart's approach has been elaborated in the literature are worth further study (see, e.g., Feinberg, 1984–8, Vols 1–2). But it is more important for our purposes to consider whether the argument of the *Liberty* really requires such modification. Recall that Mill says 'it is unnecessary to dwell' on public violations of good manners, 'as they are only connected indirectly with our subject' (V.7, p. 296). These cases fall outside the ambit of the principle of self-regarding liberty, he seems to be saying, because harm really is suffered by the victims of others' bad manners or shocking behaviour in public. There is something about public performance that can transform what is otherwise a purely self-regarding act into an act that poses a risk of perceptible damage to others against their wishes. What requires clarification from a Millian perspective is how bad manners and indecent conduct in public can be seen to involve harm thus understood, 'directly, and in the first instance'.

In this regard, Mill clearly views as harmful to others the individual's failure to satisfy certain recognized obligations distributed and enforced by established social rules of justice and goodwill (including 'good manners'), which regulate interactions (including interactions in 'public') among the members of society to their mutual benefit. Disappointment of legitimate expectations emanating from these laws and conventions is a type of perceptible injury suffered against one's wishes, even if the expectations are not protected by recognized rights. According to the liberty doctrine, however, such rules should not create obligations to refrain from causing other people to feel mere dislike or distress. Rather, obligations must be designed solely to prohibit acts which cause perceptible injury to others against their wishes.

Consistently with this, he complains that existing customs of politeness do inhibit the individual from expressing his mere dislike of others' behaviour. One person ought to be far more free than is customary to tell others that he thinks them foolish or despicable in their self-regarding affairs, for example, and to warn them that their company will no longer be welcome unless they smarten up:

> It would be well, indeed, if this good office were much more freely rendered than the common notions of politeness at present permit, and if one person could honestly point out to another that he thinks him in fault, without being considered unmannerly or presuming.
>
> (IV.5, p. 278)

In any case, the key point is that certain reasonable rules of polite behaviour and courtesy toward others are justified to prevent harmful other-regarding conduct. The argument of the *Liberty* goes through, therefore, provided we can identify the relevant forms of harm.

Prevention of disease

Some reasonable rules of polite behaviour can perhaps be seen as social precautions against the risk of disease. Public displays of urination, defecation, vomiting and even sneezing may be regulated to minimize the risk of perceptible damage to the health of others, as might consumption of the various waste materials. 'Public display' seems here to mean 'acting so as to cause a health risk', as determined by social authority (including the sewerage and health authorities).

Worth pondering is that the line between permissible and impermissible behaviour does not seem to correspond to any conventional distinction between private and public. It may be permissible to defecate in remote woods or in a public lavatory but not in a city street, for example, or in the toilet of a private home but not on the floor. Similarly, a ban against cannibalism or other mistreatment of corpses can be justified for health reasons, however 'private' the acts in question are conventionally thought to be.

Time, place and manner restrictions

Other reasonable rules of decent behaviour toward others seem to be time, place and manner restrictions to prevent nuisances, as argued by Feinberg and Ten. Sexual intercourse between consenting adults may be prohibited in busy public parks or office buildings, for example, because it can be freely practised in less crowded settings, such as homes, hotels and country fields, where it does not inconvenience others by interfering with their activities. The majority has legitimate authority to allocate scarce public space between *competing* uses (each of which necessarily interferes with the others), and ought to enforce effectively such restrictions as it thinks are fair. Given that most think sexual intercourse is not a high priority use of the public space, people who ignore such a restriction *do* pose a threat of perceptible damage to others against their wishes. Crowds of onlookers or imitators may block the free flow of traffic, for example, costing others time and money as they are forced to wait.

It is not that the alternative uses of the public space would cause no such inconvenience to others (including those who want to engage in public sex). *Any* permitted use will render some competing uses impermissible, and thus cause perceptible damage to people who wish to pursue those competing uses freely. But the uses permitted are reasonably judged to be less generally inconvenient than public shows of sexual intercourse.

Many other activities which are liable to draw crowds, including parades, demonstrations, marches and other forms of public expression, are properly subject to suitable time, place and manner restrictions. Also, the liberty principle does not imply that society has to adopt a laissez-faire policy toward those who make it their business to solicit demonstrations or protests which are designed to insult other individuals or groups, or those who sell 'hate literature' and the like for a profit. Analogous things may be said about the producers and sellers of 'pornographic literature', designed to degrade women or other groups. As Mill suggests repeatedly, generally expedient regulation of the producers and sellers of these forms of public expression is compatible with perfect liberty of the consumer to view them, in times, places or manners deliberately established by society to shield other adults from undue inconvenience and to protect children, and others unable to manage their own affairs, from bad influences.

'Special' restrictions, analogous to the special prohibitions against consumption of alcohol which he recommends for individuals with a history of violent drunken behaviour toward others (V.6, p. 295), may also legitimately be established for individuals or groups (including Nazis and the Klan) with a history of violence toward others of a particular religion, ethnic background, gender or race. Nazis and the Klan have wantonly killed and tortured minorities in the past. Anyone who affiliates himself with such odious organizations, by wearing their uniforms and brandishing their symbols, reveals (intentionally or otherwise) a sympathy for that history. As such, special bans against Nazi marches in communities with Jewish residents may be entirely appropriate, for example, to remove a credible threat that the marchers and their sympathisers will inflict physical injury, property damage and the like, on the residents.[3]

Indeed, special restrictions against the public display and dissemination for profit of hate literature, pornography and the like by such groups might also be justified on similar grounds.

Protection of reputation

Still other rules of polite behaviour can be viewed as precautions against the risk of perceptible damage to the *reputations* of others. Someone's reputation may be damaged by another's misrepresentation to third parties of his personal character or his intimate affairs. By spreading malicious gossip about his personal affairs, against his wishes, for example, the other can harm his standing in the community. Idle rumours may be worked to provoke broad, though unwarranted, resentment against him, and all that that implies. To prevent this sort of harm to reputation, customs against malicious gossiping and the like are legitimate rules of other-regarding conduct.

Mill himself provides an illustration, in which someone publishes personal correspondence not intended by the author for publication. In a letter to Elizabeth Cleghorn Gaskell, probably written during July 1859, he says that the discretion of an editor properly does not extend to such publication:

> The case being simply that in the exercise of the discretion of an Editor you neglected the usual and indispensable duties which custom (founded on reason) has imposed of omitting [sic] all that might be offensive to the feelings of individuals . . . Miss [Charlotte] Bronte [*sic*] was entitled to express any foolish expression that might occur to her [about Mill's wife Harriet] in a private letter – It is the Editor who publishes what may give just offence who is alone to blame.
>
> (1859b, pp. 629–30)

Gaskell herself, in her comments on Mill's letter, refers to the customary obligation 'of omitting what would be offensive to the feelings and perhaps injurious to the moral reputation of individuals' (Haldane, 1930, pp. 269–71). Legitimate offence is linked here to perceptible damage to moral reputation, where the latter is inseparable from existing social conventions of polite behaviour towards others.

Harm to another's reputation can also occur in other ways, perhaps more subtle. Thus, when a husband rudely tells his wife in front of the neighbours to go fuck a donkey, he forces her to endure a public misrepresentation of her character to others, which tends to damage her reputation in the community. By showing her so little courtesy and respect in comparison to what a wife may legitimately expect under existing customs, he raises doubts in the minds of others about her character (not to mention his own) if she continues to live openly with him, unless he makes a similarly public apology. Repeated instances of this sort of thing may force her to consider a separation, in order to preserve her reputation and self-respect. Otherwise, she may be ostracized along with him against her wishes, by neighbours who wish to preserve common standards of public decency.

Rules to prevent loss of reputation may extend far inside what is conventionally considered private space. When a son threatens to bury his Jewish mother's ashes in an urn engraved with Hitler's image, for example, it does not matter whether he advertises the plan in the local newspaper or whispers it confidentially in her ear. In either case, he threatens perceptible damage to her reputation against her wishes. Even if it is unwitnessed by anyone else, his whispered threat may properly be prohibited by rules of polite behaviour. Perhaps the rules cannot be expediently enforced by law or opinion in cases of whispered as opposed to open threats, so that enforcement is left to the relevant person's conscience, admittedly non-operative in the case at hand. But that does not alter the fact a Millian liberal can legitimately assess the son's action as immoral, by arguing that his mother (and anyone else in her circumstances) ought to have a right to be protected from this (risk of) harm to her reputation. But then a liberal utilitarian code can legally prohibit the son's burial plan, unless he can provide witnessed documentation attesting to her consent. Such precautions arguably help to promote general security of legitimate expectations.

The danger of social decline

These cases should also remind us that public discussion or expression is not truly self-regarding conduct, as Mill admits, although he thinks it should 'almost' always be treated as such because the risk of harm it poses is 'almost' always outweighed by the likely benefits of self-development associated with it (I.12, pp. 22–26). Even two people engaging in a fair and voluntary public debate over some issue do pose a risk of directly misleading others against their wishes about certain facts, warranted conclusions and so on.

At the same time, it is doubtless true that there is a risk of social decline (as opposed to direct harm to other individuals) in a society that virtually never interferes with the content (as opposed to the time, place and manner) of public expression. Reconsider the example of the rude husband telling his wife to fuck off in front of the neighbours. If she relishes this form of public 'expression' and returns the same in kind to him, they pose no risk of harm to each other, since their ugly 'conversation' is mutually consensual. Given that children are not present, any risk of direct harm to others (to others' reputations, for example, or to their understanding of issues related to the 'discussion', including their ideas about the nature of marriage) seems minimal, so that censorship cannot, under liberal utilitarianism, be generally expedient. Such a rude and tasteless couple might suffer 'natural penalties', as neighbours freely choose to avoid the company of both. Yet, if sufficient numbers engage in this crude sort of public behaviour, such that existing rules and expectations begin to erode, general civility and goodwill are in decline. Society is regressing toward a state of barbarism, in other words, where individuals are as impolite and intimidating to each other as they please.

The question arises here yet again whether Mill may have been overly optimistic in his judgment that it is rarely generally expedient to regulate the content (if not manner) of public expression.[4] Some might claim that his judgment ought to be reconsidered in the context of societies like ours, involving public media, such as television and the World Wide Web, which he could not have anticipated. But I suspect that he would stick to his guns, and reassert that the danger of social decline is unavoidable, even in a society that duly respects individual liberty. Certainly, on his view, social decline cannot be prevented by *suppressing* self-regarding liberty or cognate liberties such as freedom of expression.

No need for modification

Good manners and like rules of decent other-regarding conduct are justified under Mill's doctrine, to prevent various forms of perceptible injury to others against their wishes. The majority has every right to employ such forms of coercion as are considered generally expedient to prevent the relevant risks of disease, undue waste of time or money, loss of reputation and so on, which would otherwise be suffered unwillingly by others. Society may sometimes decide to leave enforcement of the rules to the internal sanctions of conscience, or to rely on stigma rather than legal penalties. But it has legitimate jurisdiction, and the liberty principle does not apply.

At the same time, it is rarely generally expedient to regulate by law or stigma the content and perhaps even manner (as opposed to time and place) of public discussion and expression. Even violent and pornographic materials should rarely be suppressed, for example, since, with suitable caveats relating to those with a history of violence toward other people, consumers of these materials can and do use them without harming others. Virtually perfect freedom to engage in a public debate over some dirty book or to watch a live sex show at a public theatre is, however, quite compatible with expedient time, place and manner restrictions, as well as expedient regulation of the for-profit producers and sellers of the relevant goods and services.

In short, there is no need to modify Millian liberalism in the direction proposed by Hart and others (let alone in the directions proposed by conservatives). Indeed, from Mill's perspective, Hart's approach essentially begs the question. For that approach does not bother to identify the forms of perceptible damage which are suffered unwillingly by the victims of offensive or indecent behaviour in public. The prevention of harm to others in that sense is a *necessary* Millian condition of legitimate social coercion. It is that condition, in other words, which sets a *limit* to social regulation of individual acts, in public as much as in private.

Suggestions for further reading

For arguments that liberalism fails to appreciate adequately the normative significance of the fact that the individual is situated in a particular community, see Michael Sandel, ed., *Liberalism and Its Critics*, 2nd edn (Cambridge, Cambridge University Press, 1995).

For Gray's attack on what he takes to be Mill's view of individuality, see John Gray, *Liberalisms: Essays in Political Philosophy* (London, Routledge, 1989), Chapter 10; and Gray, 'Mill's Conception of Happiness and the Theory of Individuality', in J. Gray and G.W. Smith, eds, *J.S. Mill: On Liberty in Focus* (London, Routledge, 1991), pp. 190–211. Gray's claim that any defence of liberty from human fallibility is self-defeating may also be found therein.

For a liberal view that rational self-determination or autonomy is compatible with the affirmation of reasonable moral rules and obligations, see Gerald Dworkin, *The Theory and Practice of Autonomy* (Cambridge, Cambridge University Press, 1988).

Hart's suggestion that Millian liberalism requires a separate principle recognizing society's legitimate authority to employ coercion to prohibit public offence, was offered in the context of his well-known debate with Lord Devlin over the 1957 Wolfenden Report. The debate revolved around the issue of whether homosexual behaviour between consenting adults in private should be outlawed. More generally, Hart argued that society ought not to use the law to enforce ideas of morality in private settings, whereas Devlin argued the reverse, suggesting that society could properly prohibit any conduct which aroused the intense disgust of the average man in the street. In 1967, the Report's recommendation to drop legal restrictions on homosexual conduct in private was implemented, in the Sexual Offences Act. Meanwhile, in the US, essentially moribund state laws against sodomy and other sexual practices are still on the books. In a 1986 decision (*Bowers* v. *Hardwick*), the US Supreme Court declined to nullify the laws as unconstitutional, preferring to leave it up to the state legislatures to repeal them. For further insights into the Hart-Devlin debate, see H.L.A. Hart, *Law, Liberty, and Morality* (Oxford, Oxford University Press, 1963); Patrick Devlin, *The Enforcement of Morals* (Oxford, Oxford University Press, 1965); C.L. Ten, *Mill on Liberty* (Oxford, Clarendon Press, 1980), pp. 86–108; Joel Feinberg, *The Moral Limits to the Criminal Law*, 4 vols (Oxford, Oxford University Press, 1984–8), Vol. 4, esp. Chapter 30; and Michael Martin, *The Legal Philosophy of H.L.A. Hart* (Philadelphia, Temple University Press, 1987), pp. 239–71.

For Feinberg's elaboration of Hart's suggestion that a liberal principle of public offence is needed, see Feinberg, *The Moral Limits to the Criminal Law*, Vol. 2. Despite its interest, Feinberg's approach is a far cry from the liberalism of Mill's 'text-book', a point taken up more generally in Chapter 9 of this GuideBook. Indeed, Mill's original argument is in danger of being obliterated by Feinberg's type of liberal revisionism. For example, some have claimed recently, apparently under Feinberg's influence, that a Millian liberal can consistently support an outright ban on all violent pornography for one reason or another. No careful reader of the *Liberty* can agree with such a remarkable claim, unless the pornographic materials themselves involve children, retarded people, unwilling adults or animals. For the claims in question and discussion surrounding them, see David Dyzenhaus, 'John Stuart Mill and the Harm of Pornography', *Ethics*

102 (1992): 534–51; Robert Skipper, 'Mill and Pornography', *Ethics* 103 (1993): 726–30; Richard Vernon, 'John Stuart Mill and Pornography: Beyond the Harm Principle', *Ethics* 106 (1996): 621–32; and Danny Scoccia, 'Can Liberals Support a Ban on Violent Pornography?', *Ethics* 106 (1996): 776–99. This debate is discussed further in J. Riley, *Mill's Radical Liberalism: An Essay in Retrieval* (London, Routledge, forthcoming), Chapter 9.

The doctrine of
Liberty in practice

How can anyone seriously think that Mill's doctrine is workable?

A familiar complaint, pressed initially by religious and moral idealists such as Green and Bosanquet, and resonant in the literature ever since, is that Mill's liberty principle provides little, if any, practical guidance. Various related reasons have been offered in support of the charge. The principle is misleading in practice, some have said, because it relies on an arbitrary distinction between self and other, which even Mill himself abandons in his 'specimens of application'. Or it is vacuous because all acts can be interpreted to harm others, in which case there are no purely self-regarding acts. Or it is inapplicable because it is inseparable from complex utilitarian mechanics that no one can really carry out. Or it is simplistic because, on any sensible idea of harm, it must be supplemented by other principles (such as a principle of public offence) to explain adequately our moral intuitions about justified

coercion. These and other reasons have been put forward to create the impression that any attempt to actually implement the doctrine of *Liberty* would result in chaos.

But, as even Plamenatz (hardly a defender of liberal utilitarianism) suspected, any such sweeping objection to the practicality of the liberty principle is unpersuasive. There may not be any acts which are always and everywhere defined as self-regarding in kind, he seems to suggest, because the same act may have consequences which are harmless to others in some circumstances, yet harmful to them in other circumstances. Getting drunk at home with the cat can be purely self-regarding, for example, whereas getting drunk on duty as a police officer poses a risk of perceptible injury to others against their wishes, since the officer may fail to perform his duties. 'But this in no way invalidates Mill's criterion', he points out, anticipating a central argument of Ten's, 'nor does it make it less easy to apply than any other' (1965, p. 130).

The fact that an act's entry into the self-regarding realm is contingent on the consequences of the act may make the realm seem ambiguous, yet 'Mill has as much right to be vague as any other moralist in a matter in which greater precision is not possible' (ibid.). Moreover, 'the objection that Mill's criterion leaves almost no liberty to the individual . . . is not well founded' (ibid.). There are many acts which harm other people 'not at all, or so little as to be not worth regarding', he insists:

> [W]e all know they are many, and that people love to interfere with what does not concern them. We may argue, then, that Mill's criterion is not strictly consistent with his utilitarian principles, but we cannot say that it is impossible to apply it or unimportant to do so.
>
> (ibid.)

Plamenatz seems quite right about this, even if his strictures against the possibility of liberal utilitarianism are unfounded, and even if he exaggerates the imprecision that attaches to any definition of the self-regarding sphere.

On the latter point, the fact that the class of purely self-regarding acts can only be defined *after* we infer the likely consequences of particular acts, does not make its definition ambiguous. True, we must abandon the notion that we can simply turn to our conventional language for general terms (such as 'getting drunk') that will enable us to see the boundaries of the self-regarding realm in some sort of pristine clarity, *prior* to our experience of their consequences in concrete situations. But who, other than perhaps a mad idealist seeking after Plato's timeless concepts, would think to complain about this? Those who seek such precision as is possible to humans, must discover the particular consequences of particular acts, through experience and discussion, and properly build those consequences into more qualified (and thereby more precise) definitions of acts (getting drunk while home alone with the cat, getting drunk while serving as a police officer, and so on).

Mill treats as a warranted induction from 'ordinary experience' the proposition that there are acts which are self-regarding or private in the sense that they do not harm other people, by directly causing them perceptible damage against their wishes; and he also argues that individual rights to choose among those acts as one pleases are justified by a liberal version of utilitarianism, in which the immense value of individuality or self-development is recognized. This simple proposition, that the individual has a moral right to complete liberty of self-regarding conduct, is not, however, the sole element of utilitarian liberalism. It is properly viewed as stating a necessary but not sufficient condition for justified coercion.

Given that society has legitimate authority to employ coercion against other-regarding acts to prevent harm to others, questions remain about whether that coercive authority can be expediently exercised in the case at hand, and, if so, in what form (i.e., law or stigma). The answers to those questions, he makes clear, depend on further utilitarian calculations, which he seems content to leave to informed majority opinion in any given social context, about rules of reasonable other-regarding behaviour. But, clearly, it may sometimes be generally expedient for society to forego coercion and adopt a policy of laissez-faire. Thus, necessary and sufficient conditions for utilitarian coercion are that the act to be prohibited must harm others in the relevant sense, and that the social benefits of interfering with the act (including the harms prevented) outweigh the costs of interference (including the harms created by it, as well as the resources consumed in drafting and implementing the relevant rules). In short, it must be generally expedient to establish and enforce social rules to govern when (if ever) the harmful other-regarding act may be performed, and under what conditions (if any) the perceptible injuries which it causes to others against their wishes will be permitted.

Nobody has demonstrated that Mill is wrong about any of this. I have argued as well, when interpreting his text, that he does not abandon his self–other distinction in his practical illustrations of his liberty principle (see above, Chapter 6). But what of the influential charge, levelled by such eminent philosophers as Hart (1963), Ten (1980) and Feinberg (1984–8), that Mill's doctrine, inaptly renamed the harm principle (i.e., the principle that liberty ought to be interfered with to prevent harm to others), is simplistic, even if it can be saved in some form, and requires to be supplemented by other principles?[1]

Not simplistic but radical

It is incumbent on those who object that Mill's doctrine is naive or crude to explain clearly why their negative conclusion is inescapable, given *his* idea of harm (rather than some revisionist notion of their own). Part of the problem with the objection is that it seems to be tied up with a fatally flawed revisionist reading of the doctrine. In general, the revisionists apparently labour under the misimpression that his purpose is to give us a complete picture of where the individual ought to be free from coercion by law or stigma. The answer to that question for Mill must be: wherever coercion is *not* generally expedient. But we know that he thinks coercion is not always expedient even within the *other-regarding realm*, the sole realm where it can be legitimately employed for the prevention of harm to others.

A liberal utilitarian society may choose to distribute and enforce many sorts of legal or customary rights other than a right to complete liberty of self-regarding conduct, including property rights, voting rights, rights to due process and so on. In that case, the social rules of other-regarding conduct identify and protect some (subsets or pockets of) other-regarding acts, among which the right-holder can choose without fear of coercion.

In addition, society may prudently choose not to regulate by law or custom many acts conducted without force or fraud, including those in a reasonably competitive market, after judging that the social benefits of laissez-faire outweigh the harms which successful competitors cause to others. Thus, some people will properly enjoy some freedom to choose as they wish, *outside* the self-regarding realm.

But Mill's aim in his essay is not to delineate for us everywhere the individual ought to be free from coercion. He is not trying to give a complete statement of the necessary and sufficient conditions for justified coercion. Rather, his aim is to focus our attention on the self-regarding realm where the individual ought to have a right to absolute liberty. That an act is self-regarding, in the sense that it directly causes no perceptible damage to other people against their wishes, is said to be sufficient – *but not necessary* – to render coercion illegitimate. The individual has a moral right to choose among self-regarding acts as he pleases. Coercion is never justified against him. Thus, an irreducible core of liberty ought to be recognized and protected by every civil society, he insists, to promote the cultivation of individuality.

Even if it can be separated from the flawed revisionist reading of Mill's purpose, the charge of oversimplification generally seems to be conflated with a different charge, namely, the liberty principle is radical and 'extreme'.[2] It is one thing to say that harm-prevention cannot be the only good reason for interfering with liberty of action, quite another to say that the failure to take seriously other reasons is an extreme (as opposed to mild) departure from our moral convictions about the issue. The latter assertion immediately invites the question: which theory of morality is (at least implicitly) being offered as an alternative to Mill's liberal utilitarianism?[3]

In this regard, Mill is distinctive because he departs so clearly and radically from established social rules, and from majoritarian convictions which are largely shaped by them, in modern industrial societies like our own. Purely self-regarding acts include all manner of sexual acts between consenting adults outside marriage, for example, assuming suitable precautions are taken to prevent perceptible damage to third parties (including parties called into being by the act itself) against their wishes. Such precautions include birth control measures, measures to prevent the spread of disease, and finding a place and time not likely to seriously inconvenience, and thereby offend, others in the pursuit of their projects. With analogous caveats, many other acts which are viewed by many as provocative are self-regarding. These include: a person's expression of his atheistic beliefs; his consumption of opium, heroin, cocaine and any other drug of choice; his gambling activities; his reading pornography and any other smut he likes; and so on. According to the liberty principle, the individual has a moral right to do these things as he pleases, short of harm to others. Needless to add, such a right is far from being recognized in modern societies, where it is likely to be seen by most as a serious danger to established religion and morality, if not to the very survival of the community.

Moreover, Mill is surely not guilty of oversimplification in his defence of absolute liberty of self-regarding conduct. He is careful to set out the 'obvious limitations' to his principle in practice. His masterful discussion of the matter in the fifth chapter of his essay is concise and to the point, giving rise to auxiliary insights or precepts relating to application of the liberty maxim.

Auxiliary precepts

Based on our earlier discussions, in Chapters 6 and 8 of this guide, the main precepts might be stated as follows:

- The absolute liberty of the individual to consume products and services harmless to others must be carefully distinguished from a policy of laissez-faire in production and exchange.
- An individual's liberty can be legitimately circumscribed to facilitate the prevention of crimes, or accidents, not only in cases where uncertainty inherent in the situation itself makes it impossible to know beforehand that he intends to engage in self-regarding conduct, as opposed to conduct harmful to others or unintentionally injurious to self, but also in cases where special personal circumstances transform into harmful other-regarding conduct what in most people is self-regarding conduct.
- The liberty of the individual can properly be limited if his otherwise self-regarding action is performed in public, in violation of reasonable rules of goodwill and polite behaviour toward others.

- Although general expediency dictates a presumption in favour of treating solicitation of self-regarding acts as if it too were self-regarding, that presumption can be defeated when special classes of producers and sellers make it their occupation to publicly advertise and encourage self-regarding acts (gambling, for example, or fornication) of which the majority disapproves.
- Taxation of self-regarding conduct can be legitimate for the purpose of raising essential state revenues, though never merely to prohibit or discourage the conduct in question.
- Although, as a general rule, general expediency dictates that society ought to enforce contracts negotiated by people in their jointly self-regarding affairs, there are exceptions, for example, voluntary slavery contracts, where non-enforcement is justified to preserve liberty and individuality.
- Beyond the moral right of the parties to release each other by unanimous consent, general expediency sometimes dictates that society should permit one party to be released from his legal obligations to another, against the wishes of the other, under a contract negotiated by them in their jointly self-regarding concerns, with the caveat that complete liberty is improper in these situations since breaking a contract is not a self-regarding act.
- The liberty principle does not give any individual or group a moral right to exercise power as pleased over other people, including husbands over wives, political officials over citizens or parents over children.
- Independently of the liberty principle, though for similar reasons, general expediency dictates that society ought to encourage individuals and groups to perform voluntarily many acts beneficial to other people, rather than rely on government provision of the benefits.

These practical precepts clarify how the liberty principle may be most expediently applied, without in any way contradicting the simple statement of it. Expedient application of the liberty maxim is essential to expedient application of its logical complement, the social authority maxim, and vice versa.

In the remainder of this chapter, some further remarks are offered, to combat the view that Mill's doctrine is simplistic, or otherwise fatally flawed, for practical purposes.

Isn't it unreasonable to demand a complete ban on paternalism?

An obvious implication of the liberty principle is that paternalism is unjustified, where paternalism refers to any interference with the individual's liberty of self-regarding action. The only possible purpose of such interference is to prevent the agent from directly causing himself perceptible injury, or to make him do something that he does not want to do for his own good. His self-regarding act is harmless to others. Strictly speaking, it is also *harmless to himself*. The individual *wishes* to cause injury to himself, or to act in ways others dislike. But *harm* is perceptible injury suffered against one's wishes. Paternalism in Mill's sense is a form of coercion, allegedly for the individual's own good. It involves meddling with his freedom to choose among his self-regarding acts as he pleases, because others allegedly know better than he does what is best for him in his personal affairs.

Mill's absolute ban on paternalism in this sense is often presented in a confusing way, because different meanings are placed on the term in the literature.[4] Hart suggests that any departure from economic laissez-faire is paternalistic, for example:

> [P]aternalism – the protection of people against themselves – is a perfectly coherent policy. Indeed, it seems very strange in mid-twentieth century to insist upon this, for the wane of laissez-faire since Mill's day is one of the commonplaces of social history, and instances of paternalism now abound in our law, criminal and civil.
>
> (1963, pp. 31–2)

But government intervention in the market for the purpose of preventing harm to others, or providing positive benefits to them, is thereby conflated with intervention against a self-regarding act solely for the agent's own good. There is a crucial difference between prohibiting an informed person from consuming a drug that is harmless to other people, for example, and preventing him from producing pollutants that pose a risk to others' health, or preventing him from misleading others into buying dangerous products or bogus 'medicines'. Similarly, there is a crucial difference between meddling with his self-regarding consumption, and forcing him to obey regulations and pay taxes so that government might provide public benefits and services which are more expediently provided through voluntary associations.

Mill, of course, favoured a general policy of laissez-faire (though with important exceptions), and he discouraged inexpedient expansions of government power. But his principle of absolute liberty of self-regarding conduct must not be conflated with those measures. Moreover, Hart compounds the problem by suggesting that so-called paternalistic government regulations are often clearly desirable (ibid., pp. 32–4). Indeed, 'Mill carried his protests against paternalism to lengths that may now appear to us fantastic' (ibid., p. 32).

Feinberg's treatment of paternalism is also perplexing from a Millian perspective. He recognizes that talk of paternalism is pointless if there is no self-regarding realm of conduct harmless to others: 'all "paternalistic" restrictions, in that case, could be defended as necessary to protect persons other than those restricted, and hence would not be (wholly) paternalistic' (1984–8, Vol. 3, p. 22). From his perspective, such a realm is apparently comprised of acts that do not wrongfully set back others' interests or cause them offence, in other words, violate their moral rights. He also recognizes that the individual cannot be said to harm himself by his intentional acts, if damage willingly incurred is not harm (ibid., pp. 10–11). Rather than condemn all interference with intentional self-regarding conduct, however, he breathes new life into paternalism by redefining harm to mean 'simple setback to interest', willingly incurred or otherwise (ibid., p. 11). But that redefinition contradicts not only the broad idea of harm which I have attributed to Mill, but also the original revisionist idea, which Feinberg himself employs when referring to the prevention of harm to others. Both of those ideas exclude damage or setback willingly incurred. Feinberg's dubious strategy allows the paternalist to claim legitimately that he is concerned to prevent *harm* to self, even if the putative victim wishes to act as he does and does not agree that his interests, as perceived by himself rather than by other people, are likely to suffer any setback.

Moreover, despite his avowed anti-paternalism, Feinberg, like Hart, seems attracted at times to what, for a Millian, can only be seen as paternalism. Part of the explanation for this might be that he ties paternalism to benevolent motivations (ibid., pp. 17–18). Non-benevolent meddling with someone's conduct solely for his own good is apparently seen as non-paternalistic, having an 'alternative rationale' in pure moralism – the view that the conduct is inherently immoral, regardless of its consequences.

At the same time, Feinberg seems to think that interference with conduct that directly causes no perceptible damage to others against their wishes can at times be justified in terms of prevention of harm or offence to them. He leaves the impression, for example, that laws prohibiting the consumption of drugs like opium, heroin and mari-juana may be justified, if too many people engage in such self-regarding conduct (ibid., pp. 17–23).

Soft (anti-) paternalism

Mill's absolute ban on paternalism *can be* compatible with what is often called 'soft' or 'weak' paternalism. That milder sort of pater-nalism, which, as Feinberg (ibid., pp. 14–15) remarks, is perhaps better viewed as anti-paternalism, is meant to assure others that the indi-vidual has common knowledge of the likely consequences of his proposed act, sufficient to permit the act to be classified as a choice that could be made by a minimally rational agent.

Evidently, alternative criteria of rational choice will give rise to alternative versions of the approach. Indeed, if suitably thick criteria are imposed, the approach might merely serve as a guise for true ('hard' or 'strong') paternalism. But thin criteria are apparently what Mill has in mind, whereby the individual is aware of common beliefs about the consequences of acts, which any competent person is expected to want to know before acting. Such knowledge might be highly speculative, however, and will surely not obviate myriad mistakes on the part of the decision-maker.

In any case, once assured that he possesses such information, others must not interfere with the individual's self-regarding choices. Does the person intend to incur the risk of self-injury which most believe is associated with crossing a particular dangerous bridge, for example, or with consuming a particular poisonous substance? By temporarily seizing him to warn him of the danger, or by posting warning signs or labels without his consent, others may assure themselves of his intentions, without really interfering with his liberty. Again, liberty means acting as one wishes. But one does not wish to fall into the river, perhaps, or to be made ill by the poison. If not, there is no interference with his *liberty* in these cases. Moreover, by preventing unintentional self-injury, the relevant interference does prevent *harm* to self. Indeed, far from meddling with his freedom to choose as he pleases, those who interfere with him prevent perceptible damage to another against his wishes.[5]

At the same time, of course, if a person is not minimally rational, true paternalism is justified because the liberty principle does not apply. We can never be confident that a child, or an insane adult or a savage barbarian, understands the likely consequences of his behaviour. Thus, others must take responsibility for that individual's good, with a view to developing his intellectual and emotional capacities, if possible. Coercion is justified in these cases, because the agent is not informed by minimal standards of rationality in what he wishes to do.

Must reasonable liberals be for hard paternalism?

Despite these caveats, Mill's anti-paternalism remains dubious to some. Most of the arguments offered in defence of paternalistic coercion of minimally rational adults are of little interest from a Millian perspective. The attempt to justify paternalism by distinguishing between earlier and later selves of the individual, for example, such that coercion of the former prevents harm to the latter, is problematic.[6]

Also problematic are attempts to justify paternalism by referring to the prevention of various indirect 'public harms', as when compulsory seat-belt or motorcycle helmet legislation is defended by referring to the consequent reduction in medical and health costs of accident victims, which must ultimately be borne by the taxpayer and/or consumers of insurance. Feinberg seems to find that sort of argument for coercion rather appealing, although, as he makes clear, he assigns even more weight to the prevention of others' emotional distress ('psychic costs') consequent on the relevant accidents (1984–8, Vol. 3, pp. 134–42). In any case, self-financing private-sector insurance schemes could in principle be designed so that different classes of consumers would pay different premiums according to the risks which they, respectively, choose to bear.

If others are made uncomfortable by the plight of uninsured or underinsured accident victims, especially when that plight is the result of bad luck rather than the victim's deliberate conduct, philanthropy is always an option. Moreover, in a wealthy modern industrial society, general utility may well recommend a universal public health care programme, financed by taxpayers, with legal rights to adequate care for all, including those who choose to not wear seat-belts or helmets. Just because the majority enacts generous public health care measures, however, it does not follow that paternalistic legislation (as opposed to education, advice and the like) is justified to keep down the costs of care.

But one argument for paternalism has provoked considerable interest, because Mill himself is said to have implicitly accepted it. Specifically, given that minimally rational persons can choose to become slaves, it seems to follow that his call for non-enforcement of voluntary slavery contracts constitutes an exception to his anti-paternalism. Feinberg echoes received opinion when he asserts that 'his solution' to the problem of voluntary slavery 'is paternalistic in spirit' (ibid., p. 72). Feinberg also suggests that liberals must in principle tolerate slavery contracts, if the parties really enter into the agreement on a voluntary basis (ibid., pp. 71–9). Interference with such contracts can only be justified, it seems, by casting doubt on the voluntariness of the agreement, or by what amounts to paternalism from a Millian perspective (ibid., pp. 79–81).

But, as I have already argued in Chapter 6, and as Ten (1980, pp. 118–19) also suggests, Mill's approach to slavery does not seem to contradict his anti-paternalism. The key point is that, if voluntary slavery is recognized, society creates genuine uncertainty, which cannot be resolved, about whether the slave is being held against his wishes, and thus harmed, by the slavemaster in the future. No society that decides to prohibit *involuntary* slavery can recognize the voluntary sort, because recognition of the latter destroys all possibility of distinguishing the former. Given that involuntary slavery is a form of perceptible damage suffered against one's wishes, society has legitimate authority to refuse to enforce slavery contracts, to prevent the risk of harm to others. Moreover, since the potential harm is of an extremely serious kind, general expediency dictates that society should make use of that authority.[7]

It follows that any society guided by Mill's liberty principle has legitimate authority to refuse to enforce slavery contracts. A decision to become a slave is a decision to resign (among much else) one's right to liberty of self-regarding conduct. But that decision is not itself self-regarding. Nobody ought to be perfectly free to resign his right, or to negotiate with others to resign their rights, for some consideration, such as a lump-sum payment to third parties. Rather, any such choice is, in a Millian context, a challenge to legitimate social authority.

This analysis would be misplaced if the right to liberty could only be viewed as a subterfuge that permits others to coerce the right-holder on the basis of their mere dislike or distress at what he does. But the right to liberty is meant to protect the right-holder from such coercion. True, the voluntary slave wishes to forego permanently the benefit which the right protects, namely, his freedom to choose among self-regarding acts as he pleases. But he can waive his right without calling on society to enforce the waiver, just as he can resume exercising the right in the future if society refuses to recognize his voluntary resignation of it.

Another complication for Mill's anti-paternalism arises, perhaps, if grave self-injury, including death, is a *certain* consequence of one's self-regarding act, or of one's contractual agreement with another (including a doctor). Despite Von Humboldt's suggestion that liberty must extend to these extremes, Mill seems inclined to interfere with a person's freedom to commit suicide by venturing onto a condemned bridge (V.5, p. 294), for example, even if, elsewhere, in 'Utility of Religion', he suggests that those who have found happiness during a long life 'would have had enough of existence, and would gladly lie down and take their eternal rest' (1874, p. 427). Moreover, by analogy with voluntary slavery contracts, he might well argue against enforcement of voluntary euthanasia contracts, where one party resigns his life and liberty to another party. Those contracts too are permanently irrevocable, and destroy all possibility of self-development in the future.

To justify interference with suicide and grave self-mutilation, as well as non-enforcement of euthanasia agreements, he could argue that a minimally rational adult would never voluntarily conduct himself thus: to behave in such a way, the person must either be coerced by others, or be too young, deluded or depressed to understand the consequences of his behaviour. But, perhaps, as Feinberg suggests, the premises of that argument are too strong (1984–8, Vol. 3, pp. 344–74). If competent adults can choose death over life, however, an ambiguity arises because the form of argument used to justify interference with voluntary slavery is not available in the context of voluntary suicide and euthanasia. There is nobody corresponding to the slave who subsequently changes his mind and is thereby harmed if the contract is enforced. Thus, since there is no such risk of harm to others, it seems that a moral right to liberty of suicide and euthanasia is justified, and that (presuming all parties are competent) enforcement of assisted-suicide contracts will always be generally expedient.

Perhaps a Millian can accept this sort of liberty without departing too much from Mill's own apparent reluctance in the matter, by arguing that a minimally rational adult would make such tragic choices only if he had no other options, for example, he is terminally ill with no hope of recovery. In that case, the point of the liberty principle is defeated for such persons, who are, by hypothesis, incapable of self-improvement.

Despite this ambiguity, it seems fair to claim that Mill's anti-paternalism is coherent and defensible, however extreme it may seem to those who, like Hart and Feinberg, do not subscribe to his doctrine of absolute liberty of self-regarding conduct.

Doesn't the liberty principle give crude answers to such hard cases as abortion and the Parfit baby problem?

Abortion is a difficult social issue.[8] Feinberg suggests that freedom of abortion (the pro-choice view) may be justified, at least in the early stages of pregnancy, because nobody is harmed, in the revisionist sense, by the death of a foetus prior to its becoming a *person*, with interests and rights of its own. 'A prepersonal fetus . . . presumably has no actual interests', he says, 'from which it follows that no actual harm can be done to it while it is in that state' (1984–8, Vol. 1, p. 96). True, the foetus will have interests and rights once it evolves into a person. But the act of abortion defeats that process of evolution, so that no setback of any actual person's interests ever takes place:

> Death to a fetus before it has any actual interests . . . is no harm to it. The aborted fetal preperson has no actual interests that can be harmed, and since it dies before any 'potential interests' can become actual, no harm can be done to these either.
>
> (ibid.)

Feinberg recognizes that his argument will hardly impress anyone who claims that personhood begins with conception, although he finds the latter view 'extremely implausible' (ibid.). Yet what makes abortion such a difficult issue for many, it seems, is the obvious bias underlying any such boundary between persons and prepersons. After all, the line is drawn by people who are judges in their own cause, with no voice accorded to prepersons.

Even so, the difficulties of abortion have nothing to do with Mill's liberty principle. Abortion might be classed as a self-regarding act by those who argue that it causes no direct perceptible damage to other *actual* persons or sentient beings.[9] But the argument is a red herring. Even if it is not yet a person with rights, or a sentient being with wishes of its own, a foetus is likely to become such. Thus, the destruction of a foetus is validly inferred, from 'ordinary experience', to involve a *risk* of perceptible damage to another person against his wishes, where the risk refers to the probability that the foetus would develop into an independent human being. Thus, the act of destroying a foetus is a harmful other-regarding act, even if the foetus is not yet a sentient being with a will of its own. As such, abortion is beyond the ambit of the liberty principle.

Society clearly has legitimate authority to regulate abortion. Even if general expediency recommends in favour of laissez-faire (pro-choice) as a general rule, that policy must be distinguished sharply from any moral right to absolute liberty of abortion. One reason is that a general absence of legal or customary sanctions against abortion, does not imply that a pregnant woman ought to choose as she pleases in the matter. Rather, she ought to follow the dictates of conscience, in other words, make a choice which she could in good faith recommend as best for anyone else (including the hypothetical person whom the foetus could become) to make in circumstances like hers. In a context where many qualified people are willing to adopt children, the implication may be that she should decide to abort only in quite unusual circumstances, including rape, incest and a risk of serious damage to her own health posed by bringing her pregnancy to term.

A second reason against conflating the liberty principle with a general policy of laissez-faire here is that the latter (unlike the former) allows for exceptions. Legal prohibition of abortion may well be generally expedient in some situations, including where pregnant children seek abortions without the knowledge or consent of their parents, for example, or where women seek procedures during the third trimester, none of the excuses mentioned earlier being applicable.

At the same time, sellers of abortion services may properly be required by law to post suitable warnings of the risk of surgery, provide advice and educational materials relating to the feasible options, and ensure that any decision to abort is made without force or fraud, after due deliberation.

Parfit's baby problem

Just as the issue of a morally defensible abortion policy is beyond the scope of the liberty principle, the so-called 'Parfit baby problem' creates no difficulties for the principle.[10] The problem arises in situations like the following. A woman deliberately gets pregnant, despite her doctor's warning that her child will certainly suffer from a permanent handicap sufficiently severe to render his life miserable, for example, his arms and legs will be withered as a result of some diseased condition of her own. The damage to the child is not so serious, however, as to render non-existence preferable to his wretched life.

Such a case is 'puzzling', Feinberg insists, because the mother's act of giving birth does not harm anyone else, by putting the other's interest 'in a worse condition than it would have been' had she not acted (ibid., Vol. 4, p. 26). In particular, despite the reprehensible behaviour of his parents, the defective baby is not harmed in the revisionist sense, because (by assumption) he would be even worse off if he had never been conceived. The implication that such parents should be free to engage in this sort of behaviour is so counterintuitive, Feinberg admits, that he is willing to abandon his otherwise 'bold liberal' convictions, to admit some coercion based on pure moralism (ibid., pp. 324, 326–8).

But this type of case is not problematic for Mill's doctrine. The act of causing the existence of another person is *never* a purely self-regarding act, even if the sexual intercourse is between consenting adults, and even if the parents are assumed to know beforehand that their child will *not* be born with a severe and permanent handicap. Any person (however normal or healthy) faces myriad risks of perceptible damage against his wishes during his lifetime. The act of causing his existence is thus of a kind that poses risks of harm to others, and is properly within society's jurisdiction.[11]

Nobody has a moral right to produce children as he or she pleases. Rather, society has legitimate authority to regulate such acts of production. Moreover, general expediency dictates that society should exercise coercion against those who, by proposing to bring others into the world without a reasonable chance of a satisfying life, threaten to cause grave harm to them. As we have already discussed in Chapter 6, Mill makes clear that couples ought to be prevented from giving birth to children who will not have 'at least the ordinary chances of a desirable existence' (V.15, p. 304). In countries 'either overpeopled, or threatened with being so', moreover, interference with even the most caring and well-off couples seeking to produce children 'beyond a very small number', may also be justified, to prevent harm to labourers, whose competitive wages tend to be driven below a customary subsistence level by overpopulation (ibid.).

To force people to satisfy their moral obligations in this matter, marriage may be legally prohibited between parties who cannot 'show that they have the means of supporting a family' (ibid.). Compulsory birth control legislation might also be expedient in some contexts. Even harsh legal measures might be appropriate to protect unlucky children and punish their irresponsible parents, including placement of the children in foster homes, fines and compulsory work programmes for the parents in aid of child support, and so on.

Perhaps some assume even today that society has no business meddling with the freedom of couples to expand their families as they see fit. But the assumption is 'misplaced' from the perspective of Mill's liberty principle:

> It still remains unrecognized, that to bring a child into existence without a fair prospect of being able, not only to provide food for its body, but instruction and training for its mind, is a *moral crime*, both against the unfortunate offspring and against society; and that if the parent does not fulfil this obligation, the State ought to see it fulfilled, at the charge, as far as possible, of the parent.
>
> (V.12, p. 302, emphasis added)

Would implementation of the doctrine result in a social revolution?

It seems that J.T. Mackenzie may have been on to something back in 1880, when he insisted that Mill's doctrine reaches into all corners of life as we know it in modern commercial societies, and contains the seeds of 'a social revolution' (as reprinted in Pyle, 1994, pp. 397–8). Among many other things, its implementation would put a stop to the employment of any form of coercion against harmless wrongdoing and all that.

From a Millian perspective, so-called 'harmless wrongdoing' is an incoherent phrase. There is no such thing, notwithstanding Feinberg's impressive classification of putative acts of this sort (1984–8, Vol. 4, p. 19, Diagram 28–1). Purely self-regarding acts, harmless to other people, are properly beyond morality. If there is no perceptible damage to others against their wishes, there can be no immoral act, or wrongdoing. Rather, there is a moral right to absolute liberty of self-regarding conduct. Any form of coercion against self-regarding acts is illegitimate, and constitutes unjustified paternalism. Such paternalism can be hidden by redescribing others' mere dislike of self-regarding conduct as some type of 'impersonal' evil that lurks in the social atmosphere, independently of any perceptible damage to them. But, underneath the patina of murky terminology, it remains unjustified paternalism.[12]

Mill's simple and radical liberal message vanishes under a cloud of redefinitions and distinctions in Feinberg's approach, where it is replaced by a complex, and ultimately ambiguous, message that departs cautiously, if at all, from the current convictions of American legal culture. After distinguishing two senses of harmless wrongdoing (corresponding to his two senses of harm), Feinberg argues that liberals must consider coercion to prevent what he calls 'non-grievance evils', that is, allegedly regrettable consequences of acts and omissions which are not 'grounds for personal grievances' because nobody's rights are violated. Non-grievance evils are of two types: 'welfare-connected', which are indirectly related to personal interests yet either do not involve any setback of such interests (as in the Parfit baby example), or do not involve any wrongful setback because it was willingly courted; and 'impersonal' or 'free-floating' evils, which are unrelated to anybody's interests.

The first type of evil generally does involve perceptible damage to others, although such damage is not harm in the Millian sense if the others consent to it. The second type is never harm in the Millian sense, and includes at least four subspecies: an inherently 'sinful' or 'immoral' quality that attaches to some acts; cultural change or erosion; consented-to exploitation, as in some forms of blackmail, where immoral gains for some are consented to by their victims; and degradation of character and taste.[13]

Feinberg assigns little if any weight to these various non-grievance evils within his liberalism, with the notable exception of the sort exemplified by the Parfit baby case, discussed earlier. Millian liberalism is not bothered by the baby case, which is properly within society's jurisdiction. Moreover, it also assigns an infinitesimal weight to the remaining non-grievance evils in comparison to the value of liberty to do as one pleases. Acts said to generate free-floating evils or consensual welfare-connected evils are really self-regarding acts from a Millian perspective. Indeed, the terms 'free-floating evil' and 'welfare-connected' setbacks of interests willingly accepted, are merely guises for the mere dislike or distress felt by others at such acts.

People who want to preserve traditional cultural norms, for example, redescribe their mere dislike of the individual's critical opinions, or of his uncommon self-regarding lifestyle, as a justified concern on their part to prevent evil social change or to prohibit inherently immoral acts. Similarly, people who do not like to see the individual played for a sucker, or to see him consent to self-injury, redescribe their dislike as a legitimate concern to promote his own good, or to prevent unjust exploitation of him by third parties. And those who want to elevate the character and tone of social life also regard their mere disgust at the person's beliefs or private lifestyle as a legitimate basis for prohibiting that of which they disapprove. But, in all these cases, nobody can identify any perceptible damage directly caused to others against their wishes by the self-regarding conduct.

The situation is very different, of course, if these non-grievance evils are in effect the icing on the cake of harm to others in the Millian sense. If a perfectionist argues for coercion to elevate the characters of minimally rational adults if and only if such coercion is already justified in order to prevent perceptible damage to other people against their wishes, for example, then, as Feinberg admits, perfectionism 'becomes a mere redundancy, or epiphenomenon' (1984–8, Vol. 4, p. 287). Harm-prevention is the reason for coercion in this situation, even if the promotion of a virtuous character is superadded to it.

Thus, Mill might argue that rigid rules of other-regarding conduct ought to be enforced not only to prevent perceptible injuries to others against their wishes, but also to encourage people to develop the dispositions comprising an ideal liberal character. That argument does not presume that coercion itself can produce the requisite dispositions, nor that coercion would be justified if harm to others was not involved. Rather, by preventing the individual from harming others, or punishing him when he does so, legal and social sanctions may encourage him to develop the dispositions required to refrain voluntarily from violating the recognized rights of others, or otherwise ignoring their reasonable requests for help. Needless to add, interference with any person's purely self-regarding conduct remains illegitimate. Each individual ought to learn for himself which self-regarding acts bring him the most personal happiness, and which cause him the most pain.

Suggestions for further reading

Refer also to the suggestions for further reading in Chapter 6 above.

On paternalism, see C.L. Ten, *Mill on Liberty* (Oxford, Clarendon Press, 1980), pp. 109–23; Joel Feinberg, *The Moral Limits to the Criminal Law*, 4 vols (Oxford, Oxford University Press, 1984–8), Vol. 3; and Rolf Sartorius, ed., *Individual Conduct and Social Norms* (Belmont, Wadsworth, 1975).

On such life and death issues as wrongful conception, abortion and euthanasia, see Feinberg, *The Moral Limits to the Criminal Law*, Vol. 1, pp. 95–104; Vol. 3, Chapter 27; and Vol. 4, pp. 27–33, 325–8; Feinberg, *Freedom and Fulfillment* (Princeton, Princeton University Press, 1993), Chapters 1–2, 8–12; and Ronald Dworkin, *Life's Dominion: An Argument About Abortion, Euthanasia, and Individual Freedom* (New York, Vintage Books, 1994). For Parfit's original discussion of the baby problem, see Derek Parfit, 'On Doing the Best for Our Children', in M.D. Bayles, ed., *Ethics and Population* (Cambridge, Mass., Schenkman, 1976).

Feinberg's discussion of 'harmless wrongdoing' may be found in Feinberg, *The Moral Limits to the Criminal Law*, Vol. 4.

Notes

1   Mill and the *Liberty*

1   Bain says that '[John] was, quite as much as Grote, a Greece-intoxicated man' (1882a, p. 94). The same was true of James Mill. See, also, Clarke (1962), pp. 105, 115, 134–49, 168–86.

2   Indeed, Grote writes in 1866 that

> of all persons we have known, Mr. James Mill was the one who stood least remote from the lofty Platonic ideal of Dialectic . . . (the giving and receiving of reasons), competent alike to examine others, or to be examined by them on philosophy.
>
> (quoted in Clarke, 1962, p. 21)

3   At the same time, Mill admits that 'various persons who saw me in my childhood . . . thought me greatly and disagreeably self-conceited; probably because I was disputatious'. He apparently acquired a 'bad habit' of contradicting adults, 'having been encouraged in an unusual degree to talk on matters beyond my age, and with grown persons, while I never had

NOTES

inculcated in me the usual respect for them'. 'Yet with all this I had no notion of any superiority in myself; and well was it for me that I had not' (1873, p. 37).

4   Also unpersuasive is any suggestion that Mill was so influenced by his father that he conflated liberty with voluntary conformity to social rules of reasonable conduct, such as the rules imposed on him in the context of his early training programme. In *On Liberty*, 'liberty' does *not* mean self-government or self-discipline in accord with certain impartial dictates of reason. It means acting spontaneously, as one pleases or desires, independently of social rules of reasonable behaviour. Liberty in that sense must be kept distinct from familiar ideas of rational or moral 'autonomy'. The latter term is not found in Mill's essay.

5   Mill makes a similar point in connection with Roebuck's character (1872, pp. 153–7).

6   For illuminating discussions of Bentham's philosophy, see Hart (1982), Harrison (1985), Rosen (1983, 1992, 1996) and Kelly (1990).

7   Mill claims that his use of the *Review* as a vehicle for this purpose 'to a certain extent, succeeded' (1873, p. 221). But his attempt to use the journal for a second purpose, 'to stir up the educated Radicals ... and induce them to make themselves' into 'a powerful party capable of taking the government of the country', 'was from the first chimerical' (ibid., pp. 221–3).

8   The minister of the congregation (South Place Chapel) was W.J. Fox, in whose journal the *Monthly Repository* Mill published most of his essays during 1831–5. Unhappy in his marriage, Fox fell in love with the unmarried Eliza Flower, who was Harriet's dearest friend. A public scandal ensued in 1834, during which the majority of his congregation refused to accept his offer of resignation. He began to live openly with Eliza and continued to serve as a minister until 1852, subsequently going into Parliament. She was apparently a distinguished composer but died young in 1846. Browning adored her (she seems to have been the inspiration for *Pauline*) and Mill describes her as 'a person of genius' (1873, p. 195). For related discussion, see Mineka (1944), pp. 188–96.

9   Mill himself was annoyed by rumours of impropriety in their relationship, and he did not hesitate to distance himself even from old friends such as the Austins or Grotes if he associated them with such gossip. Thus, he became estranged from the Grotes about 1837, for example, after Harriet Grote apparently made some catty

remarks. (Although intelligent and gregarious, Harriet Grote could also be meddlesome and overbearing, it seems, since she alienated Molesworth and Roebuck for similar reasons.) Mill was also disappointed at the time (as he later admitted, unreasonably so) by George's performance as a leader of the embryo Radical party in Parliament, and George disapproved of Mill's modified radicalism as exhibited in his conduct of the *Review*. But the two men seem to have resumed their friendship by 1845, and Mill reconciled with Harriet Grote shortly after the death of his own Harriet. Indeed, Mill became sufficiently close to her that he tried to comfort her when George had a protracted affair with Susan Durant during 1862–8. See Clarke (1962), pp. 55–102.

10   For different reasons, Clarke speculates that Harriet Grote is to Grote as Aspasia is to Pericles (1962, p. 124).

11   On this point, see Himmelfarb (1974), pp. 36–56.

12   It should be noted that Hart, Feinberg and even Ten depart in important ways from what they consider the simplistic liberalism of Mill.

13   Some interpretations of Mill's argument are so preposterous that the charge of deliberate misrepresentation is difficult to avoid. Nevertheless, as he says himself, it is often impossible to distinguish such unfair discussion from honest mistakes (II.44, pp. 258–9).

14   It must be remembered that most professors in Britain, if not the US were also ministers when Mill was writing, and that the liberal struggle to separate higher education from undue religious influence was regarded by conservatives as yet more evidence of the erosion of traditional moral values and the decline of civilization. Mill called Oxford and Cambridge 'impostor-universities' in 1834, and the inroads into the curriculum subsequently made by his *Logic*, *Political Economy* and other writings were bitterly resisted by many. For Grote's fights to make lay appointments even to the faculty at University College (founded in London about 1828, as perhaps the first institution of higher education which aimed to keep free of church control), see Clarke (1962), Chapter 7.

15   Rees (1956) provides a synopsis of much of the commentary appearing during Mill's lifetime, which he depicts as largely hostile. Pyle (1994) collects selected reviews which were published in journals during 1859–83. Most are fairly described as hostile.

16   The exchange between Morley and Stephen is reminiscent of the well-known debate between Hart (1963) and Devlin (1965), which raised similar issues.

17   Eisenach (1995) suggests other disciples. But if people such as Fitzjames Stephen are to be included as 'disciples', it is pointless to speak of enemies. Even friends like Bain and Grote, devotees of James Mill, could not wholeheartedly accept John's novel radical creed but restricted their admiration to many smaller points.

This is not to deny that Mill's essay on liberty exerted an influence on religious intellectuals such as Mark Pattison, by encouraging free discussion of received church doctrines and stimulating interest in ecclesiastical history. But, of course, Newman, Pusey and other leaders of the Oxford movement (in which Pattison was involved) had long been arguing to similar effect (see, e.g., Mill, 1842). More generally, while the new religious and moral idealism defended by Green, Bradley, Bosanquet and many others may have been somewhat more liberal than would have been the case without Mill's influence, it is a serious mistake to see such idealism as similar to, or continuous with, his novel utilitarian liberalism. For further discussion, see Riley (forthcoming b), Chapter 3.

18   Some of the flaws in the arguments of Himmelfarb and Cowling have been discussed by Rees (1985, pp. 106–15, 125–36) and Ten (1980, pp. 144–73), among others. I say something about Hamburger's arguments below, in Chapter 7.

2   Introductiory (Chapter I, paras 1–16)

1   This view of liberty is emphasized in the Federalist papers written during 1787–8 by James Madison, Alexander Hamilton and John Jay to encourage the people of the State of New York to ratify the US Constitution.

2   Under the amendment formula of the US Constitution, moreover, the people can legally alter the list of basic rights with which government must not interfere. Supermajorities have supreme authority to amend or even abrogate such constitutional rights as free speech or free exercise of religion. Those popular decisions, should they occur, would in principle be binding on the courts. Thus, there are no legal (as opposed to moral) limits on popular consensus, even though limits are placed on simple majorities and their elected representatives.

3   On this point, see also Hamburger (1965), p. 103, n. 62, and p. 262, n. 47. More generally, the failure of Mill and other 'philosophical radicals' during the 1830s to form a new political party in England was due at least in part to popular apathy, which they tended to blame

on middle-class preoccupation with business and commerce. Hamburger depicts the radical political movement as 'doctrinaire', a vain grasp for power by uncompromising intellectuals with preconceived notions of the general good which were far removed from what was actually wanted by the majority at the time. A more sympathetic observer might say that the majority was not yet sufficiently educated to appreciate radical liberal reforms far in advance of their time.

4   I have in mind such documents as the Virginia Statute for Religious Freedom (drafted by Jefferson in 1777, enacted 1786), Madison's 'Memorial and Remonstrance Against Religious Assessments' (written in 1785 to help enact Jefferson's Statute for Religious Freedom), and the First Amendment to the US Constitution. For relevant discussion, see Buckley (1977) and Peterson and Vaughan (1988).

3   Of the liberty of thought and discussion (Chapter II, paras 1–44)

1   Mill's picture of Aurelius seems to have had an impact on Matthew Arnold and Walter Pater, among others. See the suggestions for further reading in Chapter 4.

2   Mill says later in the text that Christ himself preached an admirable, if incomplete, morality (II.37–8, pp. 254–7). But Christian doctrine has evolved into something quite different, its content apparently for the most part a reflection of prevailing social customs. In a predominantly commercial culture, Christian doctrine so-called becomes tied up with norms of work, saving and wealth in ways discussed by Marx and Weber, among others.

3   Various writers in the Victorian era claimed that early Christian teachings had been corrupted by the subsequent development of the Roman Catholic church and/or Protestant sects. A version of the claim is associated with Newman, Pusey and the so-called 'Oxford Movement', for example. See Mill (1842) and Nockles (1994). Analogous themes are sounded during the Renaissance. Thus, for example, Machiavelli, Guicciardini, Paruta and Sarpi emphasize that the emergence of a highly-centralized Roman church, controlled by a papacy with imperialist pretensions, represented a corruption of the true spiritual church, as well as a constant threat to the republics of Florence and Venice. For relevant discussion, see Bouwsma (1968).

4   Mill says that Christ was 'probably the greatest moral reformer, and martyr to that mission, who ever existed upon earth', a man of 'pre-eminent genius' who

> supposed himself to be – not God, for he never made the smallest pretension to that character and would probably have thought such a pretension as blasphemous as it seemed to the men who condemned him – but a man charged with a special, express and unique commission from God to lead mankind to truth and virtue.
>
> (1874, p. 488)

Moreover,

> religion cannot be said to have made a bad choice in pitching on this man as the ideal representative and guide of humanity; nor, even now, would it be easy, even for an unbeliever, to find a better translation of the rule of virtue from the abstract into the concrete, than to endeavour so to live that Christ would approve our life.
>
> (ibid.; cf. ibid., pp. 421–2)

A utilitarian 'Religion of Humanity' would, therefore, certainly make room for Christ's maxims of conduct. More generally, see Mill (1874), for his discussion of the Religion of Humanity and his rational 'scepticism' or agnosticism about the existence and attributes of a divine Creator.

5   This sort of isolation among self-interested individuals is usually attributed to political liberalism itself, rather than to Christian morality.

6   Mill's assertions about Christian passivity may require some modification now, if not then. Consider, for example, the modern doctrine of 'passive resistance' which Christian leaders such as Martin Luther King found in Gandhi's work and elaborated during the struggle against racial segregation in the United States. Or consider the insistence of many Christians that all have a constitutional duty to protect the lives of the unborn and the terminally ill, often with the understanding that the relevant parties can never waive their correlative rights.

7   Mill's insistence that a complete morality must find room for both Christian and Pagan elements, is echoed by various Victorian and Renaissance writers, who admire Periclean Athens and/or the Roman

Republic as well as Christ's teachings. He returns to this theme in the next chapter.

4 Of individuality, as one of the elements of well-being (Chapter III, paras 1–19)

1 Although he singles out Von Humboldt, Mill might also have mentioned various other German philosophers who were just as committed to a 'many-sided' character-ideal, in which some sort of harmonious fusion of different human capacities and powers is attained. Goethe says, for example: 'Man ... can only accomplish the unique, the wholly unexpected, if all his qualities unite within him and work together as one. This was the happy lot of the ancients, especially the Greeks in their golden age' (1994, pp. 100–1).

2 The idea of a 'clerisy' can be construed to mean something like a system of universities, perhaps subsidized by the taxpayer, whose faculties control appointments and enjoy job tenure during good behaviour.

5 Of the limits to the authority of society over the individual (Chapter IV, paras 1–21)

1 Mill certainly does not advocate indifference to self-regarding vices, as Hart emphasizes (1963, pp. 76-7). But natural penalties are not the same thing as deliberate moral blame or punishment. Social stigma, the intentional display in public of disapproval, does not legitimately extend to self-regarding conduct because such conduct is harmless to others.

2 For Hume's distinction between natural and artificial virtues and vices, see Hume (1978), pp. 294-8, 474-5, 477-621; and Hume (1975), pp. 169-284, 303-11.

3 Recall his related claim that thoughts and opinions are not properly termed immoral (II.11, p. 234).

4 This situation, where the individual has an incentive to defect from an agreement under which everyone (including himself) would be better off, is a classic example of what is sometimes called the 'Prisoners' Dilemma' in the theory of games.

6 Applications (Chapter V, paras 1-23)

1　For his view of the generally expedient functions of government, see Mill (1871), pp. 797-971.

2　Recall that if a commodity only has uses which involve harm to other people, society can legitimately prohibit its production altogether.

3　'In whatever way we define or understand the idea of a right', Mill insists in his *Representative Government*, 'no person can have a right (except in the purely legal sense) to power over others: every such power, which he is allowed to possess, is morally, in the fullest force of the term, a trust' (1861a, p. 488). The power of the franchise, for example, is a moral trust, as is the power of attorney or the authority granted to parents over children. See also Mill's distinction between two 'intrinsically very different' dispositions, namely, 'the desire to exercise power over others' and the 'disinclination to have power exercised over [oneself]' (ibid., p. 420).

4　Mill (1869b) elaborates on this argument.

5　For further discussion of the design of an optimal democratic constitution, see Mill's *Representative Government* (1861a).

6　A possible reason is that the distribution of benefits is unequal, and that the third party dislikes his share of the benefits as too small relative to the shares of others. Even though he suffers no absolute setback, his unequal share might be defined as perceptible damage to him. If so, the action (though it confers advantages on him) would be harmful to him, and thus subject to social control. Even if the idea of harm is stretched in this fashion, however, the argument in favour of laissez-faire, pursued later in this section of the text, is not affected.

7　This is one place (among many others) where Mill evidently rejects traditional act-utilitarian reasoning. See also his letter of 10 January 1862 to Grote, in Mill (1862).

8　For further discussion pertinent to this point, see Taylor (1982, 1987).

7 Liberal utilitarianism

1　Ten is apparently attracted to the non-standard versions of 'utilitarianism' ascribed to Mill by revisionist scholars, but he prefers to treat such interpretations as 'non-utilitarian' (1991, pp. 236–7). His caution is certainly understandable.

2　True, certain social conventions (e.g., of promising) may exist, which enable self-interested citizens to predict and rely on one another's behaviour. Act utilitarianism may well take account of such conventions, when making its prescriptions of which acts to perform. But it cannot itself recommend such conventions, let alone tell us which may be optimal.

3 For a helpful discussion of various issues surrounding justified coercion against failures to prevent harm to others, see Feinberg (1984–8), Vol. 1, pp. 126–86. Feinberg's notion of harm, as setback of an interest which ought to be considered a right, is, however, distinct from Mill's idea.

4 Ten, in contrast, suggests that Mill rejects 'an unrestricted policy of maximizing harm-prevention' because his 'utilitarianism is tempered by the recognition of some *independent* principle of distribution' (1980, pp. 64–5, emphasis added).

8 Liberty, individuality and custom

1 Given his defence of 'moral causationism' (determinism) as opposed to the free will doctrine, Mill's view that circumstances (including our given power of will) determine individual character is hardly surprising. More generally, he follows Hume in holding that the doctrine of universal causation is compatible with our practical feeling of moral freedom, i.e., our feeling that we do have some power to alter our circumstances, if we wish. See Mill (1843), pp. 836–43; and (1865), pp. 437–69.

2 In a similar vein, Plato surmised that in an ideal city, where all were highly developed philosophers, nobody would wish to be bothered with political administration, preferring instead to rely on the wise judgments and commands of others.

3 Feinberg arrives at a similar conclusion. Yet he argues that harm to others is not involved, in his revisionist sense of harm, thereby suggesting that this type of case cannot be handled by Mill's doctrine. See Feinberg (1984–8), Vol. 2, pp. 86–96, 162–4.

4 Indeed, Mill seems to suggest that society should rarely use coercion even against the *manner* of a public debate (II.44, pp. 258–9). But his remarks may not have been intended to apply to potentially more boisterous forms of public expression, such as parades, demonstrations and the like. At the same time, there seems little doubt that he would support restrictions on the manner in which, say, sexually explicit materials are sold to the public, e.g., suitable packaging of 'dirty magazines' to prevent exposure to children.

9 The doctrine of *Liberty* in practice

1   I say 'inaptly renamed' because the harm principle is not viewed by these scholars as a *necessary* condition for justified coercion – it is merely one reason among others. Moreover, it is certainly not a *sufficient* condition for justified coercion, nor does Mill ever pretend otherwise.

2   Feinberg (1984–8) defines as 'extreme liberalism', for example, the doctrine that prevention of harm to others is the sole reason for legal coercion. Mill's liberalism is thereby classed as extreme, unless his definition of harm is carefully distinguished from Feinberg's.

3   Feinberg is deliberately obscure about his own theory of morality (1984–8), Vol. 1, pp. 6–7, 14–19, 25–6.

4   For some of the diverse meanings, see Feinberg (1984–8), Vol. 3, pp. 3–26.

5   For further discussion of soft or weak (anti-)paternalism, see Ten (1980), pp. 109–17; and Feinberg (1984–8), Vol. 3, pp. 12–16, 98–343. In defending such an approach as part of his liberal doctrine, Feinberg refers to criteria of voluntary choice as opposed to minimally rational choice. I do not adopt that terminology, so as to allow for the possibility that voluntary choice may fall short of standards of minimal rationality. Otherwise, if we say that some individuals (children, for example, or the insane) engage in non-voluntary behaviour, then we literally cannot even speak of coercing them, because they have no wishes with which to interfere. But coercion is essential to the meaning of paternalism in Mill's sense.

6   For a devastating critique, see Ten (1980), pp. 119–23.

7   Ten argues that 'if there is a "slavery" contract, renewable at frequent intervals, and imposing limits to what may be required of a slave without his existing consent, this should be enforceable' (1980, p. 119). Perhaps so. But such a personal services contract is surely not a slavery contract, whose essential feature is that it is revocable only at the discretion of the slavemaster (who does not have to sell the slave to anyone else – including the slave himself – unless he wishes).

8   For a liberal defence of the existing state of American constitutional law on abortion, rooted in the Supreme Court's *Roe* v. *Wade* decision in 1973, see Dworkin (1994).

9   The Millian idea of harm is not necessarily restricted to perceptible damage suffered by other *persons* against their wishes. It can, and probably should, be extended to include harm to other sentient

creatures with (imputed) wills of their own. That extension would narrow somewhat the self-regarding realm of absolute liberty. Even so, laissez-faire remains an option. General expediency may sometimes militate against social enforcement of rules of other-regarding conduct, including rules designed to prevent perceptible injury to many animals against their wishes.

10 The baby problem, developed by Derek Parfit, is discussed by Feinberg (1984–8), Vol. 1, pp. 95–104; Vol. 4, pp. 26–33, 325–8.

11 Any individual faces risk of harm in Mill's sense during his lifetime. It is irrelevant that options even more harmful than his actual life may be conceivable, such as non-existence, for example, or some possible life of deplorable misery.

12 For a revisionist liberal rejection of this Millian equation of pure moralism with paternalism, see Feinberg (1984–8), Vol. 4, pp. 7–8.

13 For detailed discussion of these various 'non-grievance evils', see Feinberg (1984–8), Vol. 4, pp. 39–317.

Bibliography

Mill's works

All references are to J.M. Robson, gen. ed., *The Collected Works of J.S. Mill* (henceforth *CW*), 33 vols (Toronto and London: University of Toronto Press and Routledge, 1963–91).

Mill, J.S. (1832) 'On Genius', *CW*, Vol. I, pp. 327–39.
—— (1833) 'Thoughts on Poetry and Its Varieties', *CW*, Vol. I, pp. 356–64.
—— (1840a) 'Coleridge', *CW*, Vol. X, pp. 117–63.
—— (1840b) 'De Tocqueville on Democracy in America, Part II', *CW*, Vol. XVIII, pp. 153–204.
—— (1842) 'Puseyism', *CW*, Vol. XXIV, pp. 811–22.
—— (1843) *A System of Logic*, *CW*, Vols. II–III.
—— (1846) 'Grote's History of Greece, Vols. I, II', *CW*, Vol. XI, pp. 271–305.
—— (1849) 'Grote's Greece, Vols. V and VI', *CW*, Vol. XXV, pp. 1128–34.
—— (1853) 'Grote's History of Greece, Vols. IX, X, XI', *CW*, Vol. XI, pp. 307–37.

—— (1859a) 'A Few Words on Non-Intervention', *CW*, Vol. XXI, pp. 109–24.

—— (1859b) Letter of (perhaps) July to E.C. Gaskell, *CW*, Vol. XV, pp. 629–30.

—— (1859c) *On Liberty*, *CW*, Vol. XVIII, pp. 213–310.

—— (1861a) *Considerations on Representative Government*, *CW*, Vol. XIX, pp. 371–577.

—— (1861b) 'Utilitarianism', *CW*, Vol. X, pp. 203–59.

—— (1862) Letter of 10 January to G. Grote, *CW*, Vol. XV, pp. 761–4.

—— (1865) *An Examination of Sir William Hamilton's Philosophy*, *CW*, Vol. IX.

—— (1867) 'Inaugural Address at St Andrews', *CW*, Vol. XXI, pp. 215–57.

—— (1869a) 'Endowments', *CW*, Vol. V, pp. 613–29.

—— (1869b) *The Subjection of Women*, *CW*, Vol. XXI, pp. 259–340.

—— (1870) 'Treaty Obligations', *CW*, Vol. XXI, pp. 341–8.

—— (1871) *Principles of Political Economy* (1848), 7th edn, *CW*, Vols. II–III.

—— (1873) *Autobiography*, *CW*, Vol. I, pp. 1–290.

—— (1874) *Three Essays on Religion*, ed. H. Taylor, *CW*, Vol. X, pp. 369–489.

—— (1879) 'Chapters on Socialism', *CW*, Vol. V, pp. 703–53.

The seventh edition of the *Political Economy*, together with the 'Chapters on Socialism', is also reprinted in J. Riley, ed., *John Stuart Mill: Principles of Political Economy and Chapters on Socialism* (Oxford: Oxford University Press, 1994).

Other works

Adair, D., ed. (1945) 'James Madison's Autobiography', *William and Mary Quarterly*, 3rd Series, 2: 191–209.

Alexander, E. (1965) *Matthew Arnold and John Stuart Mill* (New York, Columbia University Press).

Arnold, M. (1968) 'Marcus Aurelius' (1863), in his *Essays in Criticism: First Series* (1865), ed. Sister T.M. Hoctor (Chicago and London, University of Chicago Press), pp. 204–24.

Arrington, L.J. and Bitton, D. (1992) *The Mormon Experience: A History of the Latter-Day Saints*, 2nd edn (Champaign, University of Illinois Press).

Bain, A. (1882a) *James Mill: A Biography* (London, Longmans, Green).

—— (1882b) *John Stuart Mill: A Criticism, with Personal Recollections* (London, Longmans, Green).

Berger, F. (1984) *Happiness, Justice and Freedom: The Moral and Political Philosophy of John Stuart Mill* (Berkeley, University of California Press).

Berlin, I. (1969) *Four Essays on Liberty* (Oxford, Oxford University Press).

—— (1981) 'The Originality of Machiavelli' (1972), in his *Against the Current*, ed. H. Hardy (Oxford, Oxford University Press), pp. 25–79.

—— (1991) 'The Pursuit of the Ideal' (1988), in his *The Crooked Timber of Humanity*, ed. H. Hardy (New York, Knopf), pp. 1–19.

Blocker, J.S. (1989) *American Temperance Movements: Cycles of Reform* (Boston, Twayne).

Bosanquet, B. (1923) *The Philosophical Theory of the State* (1899), 4th edn (London, Macmillan).

Bouwsma, W.J. (1968) *Venice and the Defense of Republican Liberty* (Berkeley, University of California Press).

Brandt, R.B. (1992) *Morality, Utilitarianism, and Rights* (Cambridge, Cambridge University Press).

Buckley, T.E. (1977) *Church and State in Revolutionary Virginia, 1776–1787* (Charlottesville, University Press of Virginia).

Burrow, J.W. (1988) *Whigs and Liberals: Continuity and Change in English Political Thought* (Oxford, Clarendon).

Carlyle, T. (1841) *On Heroes, Hero-Worship, and the Heroic in History* (London: Fraser).

Chapman, J.K. (1954) 'The Mid-Nineteenth-Century Temperance Movement in New Brunswick and Maine', *Canadian Historical Review* 35: 43–60.

Clarke, M.L. (1962) *George Grote: A Biography* (London, Athlone Press).

Clarkson, F. (1996) *Eternal Hostility: The Struggle Between Theocracy and Democracy* (New York, Common Courage Press).

Clor, H.M. (1996) *Public Morality and Liberal Society: Essays on Decency, Law, and Pornography* (Notre Dame, University of Notre Dame Press).

Coleridge, S.T. (1818) *The Friend*, 3 Vols (London, Rest Fenner).

—— (1839) *On the Constitution of Church and State, and Lay Sermons*, ed. H.N. Coleridge (London, Pickering).

Cowling, M. (1990) *Mill and Liberalism* (1963), 2nd edn (Cambridge, Cambridge University Press).

DeLaura, D.J. (1969) *Hebrew and Hellene in Victorian England: Newman, Arnold, Pater* (Austin, University of Texas Press).

Devlin, P. (1965) *The Enforcement of Morals* (Oxford, Oxford University Press).

Dingle, A.E. (1980) *The Campaign for Prohibition in Victorian England: The United Kingdom Alliance, 1872–95* (New Brunswick, NJ, Rutgers University Press).

Dow, N. (1898) *The Reminiscences of Neal Dow, Recollections of Eighty Years* (Portland, Maine, The Evening Express Publishing Co.).

Driggs, K.D. (1988) 'The Mormon Church–State Confrontation in Nineteenth-Century America', *Journal of Church and State* 30: 273–89.

—— (1990) 'After the Manifesto: Modern Polygamy and Fundamentalist Mormons', *Journal of Church and State* 32: 367–89.

Dworkin, G. (1988) *The Theory and Practice of Autonomy* (Cambridge, Cambridge University Press).

Dworkin, R. (1977) *Taking Rights Seriously* (London: Duckworth).

—— (1985) 'Do We Have a Right to Pornography?', in his *A Matter of Principle* (Cambridge, Mass., Harvard University Press), pp. 335–72.

—— (1994) *Life's Dominion: An Argument About Abortion, Euthanasia, and Individual Freedom* (New York, Vintage Books).

Dyzenhaus, D. (1992) 'John Stuart Mill and the Harm of Pornography', *Ethics* 102: 534–51.

Eisenach, E. (1995) 'Mill's Reform Liberalism as Tradition and Culture', *The Political Science Reviewer* 24: 71–146.

Feinberg, J. (1984–8) *The Moral Limits to the Criminal Law*, 4 Vols. (Oxford, Oxford University Press).

—— (1993) *Freedom and Fulfillment* (Princeton, Princeton University Press).

Freeden, M. (1978) *The New Liberalism: An Ideology of Social Reform* (Oxford, Oxford University Press).

Goethe, J.W. von (1994) 'Winckelmann and His Age' (1805), in J. Geary, ed., with E. von Nardoff and E.H. von Nardoff, trans., *Goethe: The Collected Works* (Princeton, Princeton University Press), Vol. 3, pp. 99–121.

Gray, J. (1983) *Mill on Liberty: A Defence* (London, Routledge).

—— (1984) *Hayek on Liberty* (London, Routledge).

—— (1986) *Liberalism* (Minneapolis, University of Minnesota Press).

—— (1989) *Liberalisms: Essays in Political Philosophy* (London, Routledge).

—— (1991) 'Mill's Conception of Happiness and the Theory of Individuality', in J. Gray and G.W. Smith, eds, *J.S. Mill: On Liberty in Focus* (London, Routledge), pp. 190–211.

—— (1993) *Post-Liberalism: Studies in Political Thought* (London, Routledge).

—— (1995) *Berlin* (London, Fontana).

—— and Smith, G.W., eds (1991) *J.S. Mill: On Liberty in Focus* (London, Routledge).

Green, T.H. (1986a) 'Lecture on "Liberal Legislation and Freedom of Contract"' (1881), in P. Harris and J. Morrow, eds *T.H. Green: Lectures on the Principles of Political Obligation and Other Writings* (Cambridge, Cambridge University Press), pp. 194–212.

—— (1986b) 'On the Different Senses of "Freedom" as Applied to Will and to the Moral Progress of Man' (1885), in P. Harris and J. Morrow, eds, *T.H. Green. Lectures on the Principles of Political Obligation and Other Writings*, (Cambridge, Cambridge University Press), pp. 228–49.

Grote, G. (1846–56) *A History of Greece: From the Earliest Period to the Close of the Generation Contemporary with Alexander the Great*, 12 Vols (London, John Murray).

Haldane, E. (1930) *Mrs. Gaskell and Her Friends* (London, Macmillan).

Hamburger, J. (1965) *Intellectuals in Politics: John Stuart Mill and the Philosophic Radicals* (New Haven, Yale University Press).

—— (1991a) *How Liberal Was John Stuart Mill?* (Austin, University of Texas Press).

—— (1991b) 'Religion and *On Liberty*', in M. Laine, ed., *A Cultivated Mind: Essays on J.S. Mill Presented to John M. Robson* (Toronto, University of Toronto Press), pp. 139–81.

—— (1995) 'Individuality and Moral Reform: The Rhetoric of Liberty and the Reality of Restraint in Mill's *On Liberty*', *The Political Science Reviewer* 24: 7–70.

—— and Hamburger, L. (1985) *Troubled Lives: John and Sarah Austin* (Toronto, University of Toronto Press).

Harris, J. (1975) 'The Survival Lottery' *Philosophy* 50: 81–7.

Harrison, B. (1971) *Drink and the Victorians: The Temperance Question in England 1815–72* (Pittsburgh, University of Pittsburgh Press).

Harrison, R. (1985) *Bentham* (London, Routledge).

Harsanyi, J.C. (1982) 'Morality and the Theory of Rational Behavior', in A. Sen and B. Williams, eds, *Utilitarianism and Beyond* (Cambridge, Cambridge University Press), pp. 39–62.

—— (1985a) 'Does Reason Tell Us What Moral Code to Follow and, Indeed, to Follow Any Moral Code At All?' *Ethics* 96: 42–55.

—— (1985b) 'On Preferences, Promises and the Coordination Problem', *Ethics* 96: 68–73.

—— (1992) 'Game and Decision Theoretic Models in Ethics', in R.J. Aumann and S. Hart, eds, *Handbook of Game Theory* (Amsterdam, North-Holland), Vol. I, pp. 669–707.

Hart, H.L.A. (1963) *Law, Liberty, and Morality* (Oxford, Oxford University Press).

—— (1982) 'Natural Rights: Bentham and John Stuart Mill', in his *Essays on Bentham* (Oxford, Oxford University Press), pp. 79–104.

Hayek, F. (1951) *John Stuart Mill and Harriet Taylor* (London, Routledge and Kegan Paul).

Henry, M.M. (1995) *Prisoner of History: Aspasia of Miletus and her Biographical Tradition* (Oxford, Oxford University Press).

Himmelfarb, G. (1974) *On Liberty and Liberalism: The Case of J.S. Mill* (New York, Knopf).

—— (1994) 'Liberty: "One Very Simple Principle?"' in her *On Looking Into the Abyss: Untimely Thoughts on Culture and Society* (New York, Knopf), pp. 74–106.

—— (1995) *The De-Moralization of Society: From Victorian Virtues to Modern Values* (New York, Knopf).

Hinchliff, P. (1987) *Benjamin Jowett and the Christian Religion* (Oxford, Clarendon Press).

Honderich, T. (1982) '"On Liberty" and Morality Dependent Harms', *Political Studies* 30: 504–14.

Humboldt, K.W. von (1969) *The Limits of State Action* (1851, in German), ed. J.W. Burrow (London, Cambridge University Press).

Hume, D. (1975) *Enquiries Concerning Human Understanding and Concerning the Principles of Morals* (1777), ed. L.A. Selby-Bigge with revisions by P.H. Nidditch, 3rd edn (Oxford, Clarendon Press).

—— (1978) *A Treatise of Human Nature* (1739), ed. L.A. Selby-Bigge with revisions by P.H. Nidditch, 2nd edn (Oxford, Clarendon Press).

Jefferson, T. (1982) *Notes on the State of Virginia* (1785), ed. W. Peden (New York: Norton).

Jensen, R.L. and Thorp, M.R., eds (1990) *Mormons in Early Victorian Britain* (Salt Lake City, University of Utah Press).

Kagan, D. (1991) *Pericles of Athens and the Birth of Democracy* (New York, Free Press).

Kaplan, F. (1983) *Thomas Carlyle: A Biography* (Ithaca, Cornell University Press).

Kelly, P.J. (1990) *Utilitarianism and Distributive Justice* (Oxford, Clarendon Press).

Kinzer, B.L., Robson, A.P. and Robson, J.M. (1992) *A Moralist in and Out of Parliament: J.S. Mill at Westminster 1865–68* (Toronto, University of Toronto Press).

Laband, D.N. and Heinbuch, D.H. (1987) *Blue Laws: The History, Economics, and Politics of Sunday Closing Laws* (Amherst, Lexington Books).

Livingston, J.C. (1986) *Matthew Arnold and Christianity* (Columbia, University of South Carolina Press).

Lyman, E.L. (1986) *Political Deliverance: The Mormon Quest for Utah Statehood* (Champaign, University of Illinois Press).

Lyons, D. (1994) *Rights, Welfare, and Mill's Moral Theory* (New York, Oxford University Press).

MacCall, W. (1843) *The Doctrine of Individuality* (London, Green).

—— (1844) *The Individuality of the Individual* (London, Chapman).

—— (1847) *The Elements of Individualism: A Series of Lectures* (London, Chapman).

Madison, J. (1973) 'Memorial and Remonstrance against Religious Assessments' (1785), in R. Rutland *et al.*, eds, *The Papers of James Madison*, (Chicago and London: University of Chicago Press), Vol. 8, pp. 295–306.

Martin, M. (1987) *The Legal Philosophy of H.L.A. Hart* (Philadelphia, Temple University Press).

Mill, James (1979) 'Education' (1818?), in F.A. Cavenagh, ed., *James and John Stuart Mill on Education* (Westport, Conn., Greenwood Press), pp. 1–73.

Mineka, F.M. (1944) *The Dissidence of Dissent: The Monthly Repository 1806–1838* (Chapel Hill, University of North Carolina Press).

Morley, J. (1873) 'Mr. Mill's Doctrine of Liberty', *The Fortnightly Review* 20: 234–56. Reprinted in A. Pyle, ed., *Liberty: Contemporary Responses to John Stuart Mill* (Bristol, Thoemmes Press), pp. 271–97.

Neff, E. (1964) *Carlyle and Mill*, 2nd edn, rev. (New York, Octagon Books).

Nockles, P.H. (1994) *The Oxford Movement in Context: Anglican High Churchmanship, 1760–1857* (Cambridge, Cambridge University Press).

Noel, J.N. (1995) *Canada Dry: Temperance Crusades Before Confederation* (Toronto, University of Toronto Press).

Packe, M. St. J. (1954) *The Life of John Stuart Mill* (London, Secker and Warburg).

Pater, W. (1985) *Marius the Epicurean* (1885), ed. M. Levey (Harmondsworth, Penguin).

Pestalozzi, J.H. (1886) *Enquiries Concerning the Course of Nature in the Moral Development of Human Race* (1787, in German) (Zurich, Hunziker).

Peterson, M.D. and Vaughan, R.C., eds (1988) *The Virginia Statute for Religious Freedom: Its Evolution and Consequences in American History* (Cambridge, Cambridge University Press).

Plamenatz, J. (1965) *The English Utilitarians*, 2nd edn (Oxford, Blackwell).

Pyle, A., ed. (1994) *Liberty: Contemporary Responses to John Stuart Mill* (Bristol, Thoemmes Press).

Radcliff, P., ed. (1969) *Limits of Liberty: Studies of Mill's On Liberty* (Belmont, Wadsworth).

Rawls, J. (1971) *A Theory of Justice* (Cambridge, Mass., Harvard University Press).

—— (1993) *Political Liberalism* (New York, Columbia University Press).

—— (1995) 'Reply to Habermas', *Journal of Philosophy* 92: 132–80.

Rees, J.C. (1956) *Mill and His Early Critics* (Leicester, University of Leicester Press). Reprinted in part in J.C. Rees, *John Stuart Mill's On Liberty*, ed. G.L. Williams (Oxford, Claredon Press, 1985), pp. 78- 105.

—— (1985) *John Stuart Mill's On Liberty*, ed. G.L. Williams (Oxford, Clarendon Press).

Riley, J. (1988) *Liberal Utilitarianism* (Cambridge, Cambridge University Press).

—— (1989) 'Justice Under Capitalism', in J. Chapman and J.R. Pennock, eds, *Markets and Justice: Nomos XXXI* (New York, New York University Press), pp. 122–62.

—— (1989–90) 'Rights to Liberty in Purely Private Matters, Parts I and II', *Economics and Philosophy* 5 and 6: 121–66, 27–64.

—— (1991a) 'Individuality, Custom and Progress', *Utilitas* 3: 217–44.

—— (1991b) '"One Very Simple Principle"', *Utilitas* 3: 1–35.

—— (1994) 'Introduction', in J. Riley, ed., *John Stuart Mill: Principles of Political Economy and Chapters on Socialism* (Oxford, Oxford University Press), pp. vii–xlvii.

—— (1996) 'J.S. Mill's Liberal Utilitarian Assessment of Capitalism Versus Socialism', *Utilitas* 8: 39–71.

—— (1997a) 'Mill on Justice', in D. Boucher and P. Kelly, eds, *Social Justice* (London, Routledge).

—— (1997b) 'Mill's Political Economy: Ricardian Science and Liberal Utilitarian Art', in J. Skorupski, ed., *Cambridge Companion to John Stuart Mill* (Cambridge, Cambridge University Press).

—— (forthcoming a) *Maximizing Security: A Utilitarian Theory of Liberal Rights*.

—— (forthcoming b) *Mill's Radical Liberalism: An Essay in Retrieval* (London, Routledge).

—— (forthcoming c) 'Rule Utilitarianism and Liberal Priorities', in M. Salles and J. Weymark, eds, *Political Liberalism, Utilitarianism, and Justice* (Cambridge, Cambridge University Press).

Robbins, W. (1959) *The Ethical Idealism of Matthew Arnold: A Study of the Nature and Sources of his Moral Ideas* (London, Heinemann).

—— (1966) *The Newman Brothers: An Essay in Comparative Intellectual Biography* (Cambridge, Mass., Harvard University Press).

Robson, J.M. (1966) 'Harriet Taylor and John Stuart Mill: Artist and Scientist', *Queen's Quarterly* 73 (Summer): 167–86.

Rosen, F. (1983) *Jeremy Bentham and Representative Democracy* (Oxford, Clarendon Press).

—— (1992) *Bentham, Byron and Greece: Constitutionalism, Nationalism, and Early Liberal Political Thought* (Oxford, Oxford University Press).

—— (1996) 'Introduction', in J. Bentham, *The Principles of Morals and Legislation*, eds J.H. Burns and H.L.A. Hart (Oxford, Clarendon Press).

Rossi, A.S., ed. (1970) *Essays on Sex Equality: J.S. Mill and Harriet Taylor Mill* (Chicago, University of Chicago Press).

Ryan, A. (1987) *John Stuart Mill*, 2nd edn (London, Macmillan).

Sandel, M., ed. (1995) *Liberalism and Its Critics*, 2nd edn (Cambridge, Cambridge University Press).

Sartorius, R., ed. (1975) *Individual Conduct and Social Norms* (Belmont, Wadsworth).

Scanlon, T. (1972) 'A Theory of Freedom of Expression', *Philosophy and Public Affairs* 1: 204–26.

—— (1979) 'Freedom of Expression and Categories of Expression', *University of Pittsburgh Law Review* 40: 519–50.

Scoccia, D. (1996) 'Can Liberals Support a Ban on Violent Pornography?', *Ethics* 106: 776–99.

Sen, A.K. (1970) *Collective Choice and Social Welfare* (San Francisco, Holden-Day), pp. 78–88.

—— (1985) *Commodities and Capabilities* (Amsterdam, North-Holland).

—— and Williams, B., eds (1982) *Utilitarianism and Beyond* (Cambridge, Cambridge University Press).

Shiman, L.L. (1988) *Crusade Against Drink in Victorian England* (New York, St Martin's Press).

Silber, K. (1973) *Pestalozzi: The Man and his Work* (New York, Schocken Books).

Skipper, R. (1993) 'Mill and Pornography', *Ethics* 103: 726–30.

Skorupski, J. (1989) *John Stuart Mill* (London, Routledge).

Spitz, D. (1962) 'Freedom and Individuality: Mill's *Liberty* in Retrospect', in C.J. Friedrich, ed., *Liberty: Nomos IV* (New York, Atherton Press), pp. 176–226.

—— (1965) *The Liberal Idea of Freedom* (Chicago, University of Chicago Press).

—— (1982) *The Real World of Liberalism* (Chicago, University of Chicago Press).

Stadter, P. (1989) *A Commentary on Plutarch's Pericles* (Chapel Hill, University of North Carolina Press).

Stephen, J.F. (1967) *Liberty, Equality, Fraternity* (1873), ed. R.J. White (Cambridge, Cambridge University Press).

Sterling, J. (1848) 'Simonides', in *Essays and Tales*, ed. J.C. Hare, 2 Vols (London, Parker).

Sumner, L.W. (1987) *The Moral Foundation of Rights* (Oxford, Clarendon Press).

Sunstein, C. (1993) *The Partial Constitution* (Cambridge, Mass., Harvard University Press).

Taylor, C. (1982) 'The Diversity of Goods', in A. Sen and B. Williams, eds, *Utilitarianism and Beyond* (Cambridge: Cambridge University Press), pp. 129–44.

Taylor, M. (1982) *Community, Anarchy and Liberty* (Cambridge, Cambridge University Press).

—— (1987) *The Possibility of Cooperation* (Cambridge, Cambridge University Press).

Ten, C.L. (1980) *Mill on Liberty* (Oxford, Clarendon Press).

—— (1991) 'Mill's Defence of Liberty', in J. Gray and G.W. Smith, eds, *J.S. Mill: On Liberty in Focus* (London, Routledge), pp. 212–38.

—— (1995) 'Mill's Place in Liberalism', *The Political Science Reviewer* 24: 179–204.

Turner, F.M. (1981) *The Greek Heritage in Victorian Britain* (New Haven, Yale University Press).

—— (1993) 'The Triumph of Idealism in Victorian Classical Studies', in his *Contesting Cultural Authority: Essays in Victorian Intellectual Life* (Cambridge, Cambridge University Press), pp. 322–61.

Tyrrell, I.R. (1979) *Sobering Up: From Temperance to Prohibition in Ante-Bellum America, 1800–1860* (Westport, Conn., Greenwood Press), pp. 252–89.

Van Wagoner, R.S. (1992) *Mormon Polygamy: A History*, 2nd edn (Salt Lake City, Signature Books).

Vanberg, V. (1986) 'Spontaneous Market Order and Social Rules: A Critical Examination of F.A. Hayek's Theory of Cultural Evolution', *Economics and Philosophy* 2: 75–100.

Varouxakis, G.E. (1995) *J.S.Mill on French Thought, Politics, and National Character*, Ph.D. Thesis in History, University College, London.

Vernon, R. (1996) 'John Stuart Mill and Pornography: Beyond the Harm Principle', *Ethics* 106: 621–32.

Wallas, G. (1951) *The Life of Francis Place, 1771–1854*, 4th edn (London, George Allen and Unwin).

Warren, J. (1852) *Equitable Commerce: A New Development of Principles, as Substitutes for Laws and Governments, for the Harmonious Adjustment and Regulation of the Pecuniary, Intellectual, and Moral Intercourse of Mankind: Proposed as Elements of a New Society* (1846), ed. S.P. Andrews (New York, Fowlers and Wells).

Whitman, W. (1871) *Democratic Vistas*, in J. Kaplan, ed., *Walter Whitman: Complete Poetry and Collected Prose* (New York, The Library of America), pp. 929–94.

Wolff, J. (1997) 'Mill, Indecency and the Liberty Principle', *Utilitas* 9.

Wollheim, R. (1973) 'John Stuart Mill and the Limits of State Action', *Social Research* 40: 1–30.

Index